I0878765

CAERNARFON

THROUGH TIME

Steven Dickens

AMBERLEY

First published 2017

Amberley Publishing
The Hill, Stroud, Gloucestershire, GL5 4EP
www.amberley-books.com

ISBN 978 1 4456 4067 9 (print)
ISBN 978 1 4456 4099 0 (ebook)

British Library Cataloguing in Publication Data.
A catalogue record for this book is available from the British Library.

Origination by Amberley Publishing.
Printed in Great Britain.

Introduction

Caernarfon is a royal town and port in Gwynedd, with a population of approximately 9,615. It overlooks Ynys Mon (Anglesey) and the Menai Strait. Its close neighbour is the city of Bangor, which is 13.8 kilometres (8.6 miles) to the north-east. Parc Cenedlaethol Eryri (Snowdonia National Park), Beddgelert and the Aberglaslyn Pass are included in this book, as is the Welsh Highland Railway and other historic railways, which are an integral part of the economic infrastructure of North Wales. The town of Caernarfon, of course, comprises a major portion of the book, and is treated in similar fashion to the city of Bangor in its companion volume *Bangor & Around Through Time*. The theme continues, with views of the A4085 out of Caernarfon and the A5 and A4086 heading out of Bangor, and giving us some comparative views around the peak of Yr Wyddfa (Snowdon).

The area has a rich history, with the Ordovices, a Celtic tribe, occupying the region at the time of the Roman invasion of Wales. The fort at Segontium dates to AD 79, although there is evidence of the earlier occupation of Caernarfon and the region at the hill forts of Twthill and Dinas Dinlle. After the Romans withdrew from the region, Caernarfon became a part of the Kingdom of Gwynedd. The Normans constructed a motte-and-bailey castle at Caernarfon when they invaded the north of Wales in the eleventh century. However, Wales was to remain independent until 1283 and the arrival of Edward I, who began to construct Caernarfon Castle in 1284. At the same time he established the county of Caernarfonshire by the Statute of Rhuddlan and made Caernarfon a borough and market town in the same year.

Caernarfon rapidly established itself as the seat of English government in North Wales. By the time of the Tudor accession to the throne, the previous animosity between Wales and England had diminished somewhat. Today Caernarfon is a major tourist centre and the seat of Gwynedd County Council. Its attractions include the harbour and marina, which draw large numbers of yachts and pleasure craft to the town in the summer months. Caernarfon's population can boast the largest percentage of Welsh-speaking citizens anywhere in Wales, and it has a unique status – that of a Royal Borough, which was granted by Queen Elizabeth II in 1963 and amended to the title of Royal Town in 1974. The castle and town walls are part of a World Heritage Site known as the 'Castles and Town Walls of King Edward in Gwynedd'. Therefore, many of the photographs presented in this book relate to this important era in Caernarfon's history.

Caernarfon, like many other towns and villages in Gwynedd, prospered with the development of the Welsh slate trade, and the opening of many quarries noted throughout the region, from the huge Penrhyn Quarry at Bethesda to those along the Nantlle Valley – at Llanberis and Blaneau Ffestiniog, for example. New ports for the distribution of slate, nationally and for export, were developed, notably at Caernarfon, Bangor and Porthmadog. Caernarfon's Slate Quay was constructed as a direct result of this expansion of the slate quarrying industry. The development of the railways further increased production and export, with the remains of railway tracks still visible on the quayside today. These historic rail routes across the rugged Snowdonia mountains owe their very existence to the development of this industry, although tourism is their main means of survival today. Therefore, many of the photographs shown in this book relate to the Slate Quay, its associated railways and the shipping which created a vital link between Caernarfon and the outside world. One does not have to go further than Castle Square (Y Maes) in order to identify Caernarfon's most notable icon. David Lloyd George was the town's MP, leader of the Liberal Party and Britain's prime minister from 1916–22. He is honoured by a statue, which recalls his ability as a supreme statesman at the post-war Paris Peace Conference of 1919, and life in his home village of Llanystumdwy. The statue overlooks Y Maes and Queen Eleanor's Gate of Caernarfon Castle.

Most photographs have been loaned for copying, some of which have been copied themselves, so it has not always been possible to locate the original source. When, through ignorance, no acknowledgement is noted, it is sincerely hoped that this apology will be accepted. Caernarfon has changed and developed immensely over the last century, changes which have been recorded in this book. However, by presenting the beauty and heritage of the Snowdonia National Park, it is anticipated that some of the timeless and unchanging nature of the region has been captured for the readers' enjoyment. Finally, in relation to language, I have tried to keep Welsh/English translation in the text to a reasonable level, so that it does not become too confusing. Welsh, or English, translations have been written in brackets where deemed appropriate or necessary. Discretion has been used where needed regarding translations relating to the length of text and word counts. This means that it has not been possible to include all translations throughout the text.

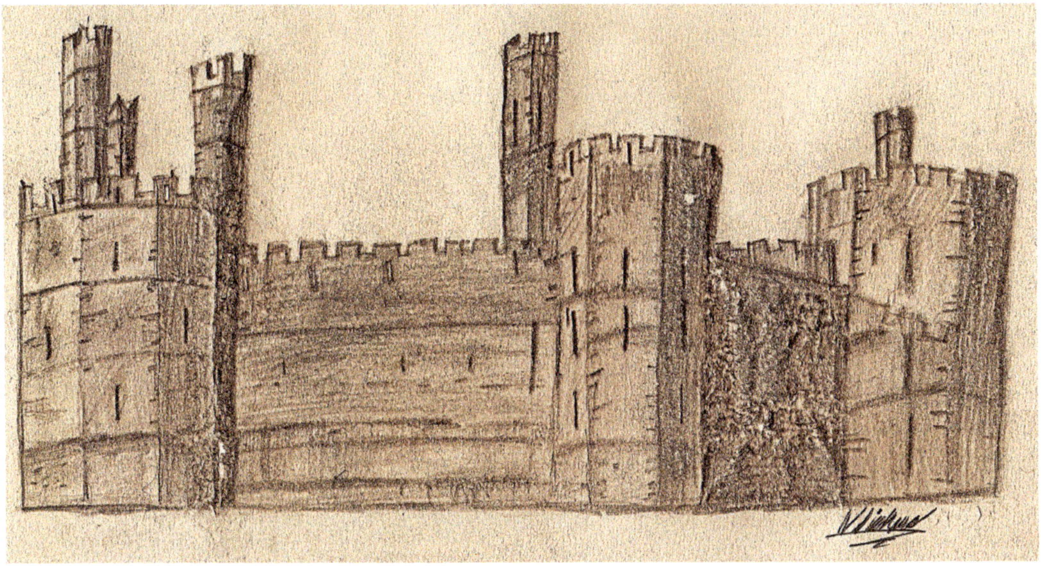

Caernarfon Castle from the Afon Seiont (Nirel Dickens)

This view, from the Afon Seiont and the Slate Quay, of Caernarfon Castle, shows the imposing fortifications constructed during the reign of Edward I. The castle is immediately recognisable to most of the residents of Britain. Building began in 1284, and the fact that these battlements have remained virtually intact is a testament to the skill and construction techniques of thirteenth-century craftsmen. The castle and medieval walled settlement provide a unique experience for the visitor to this royal town.

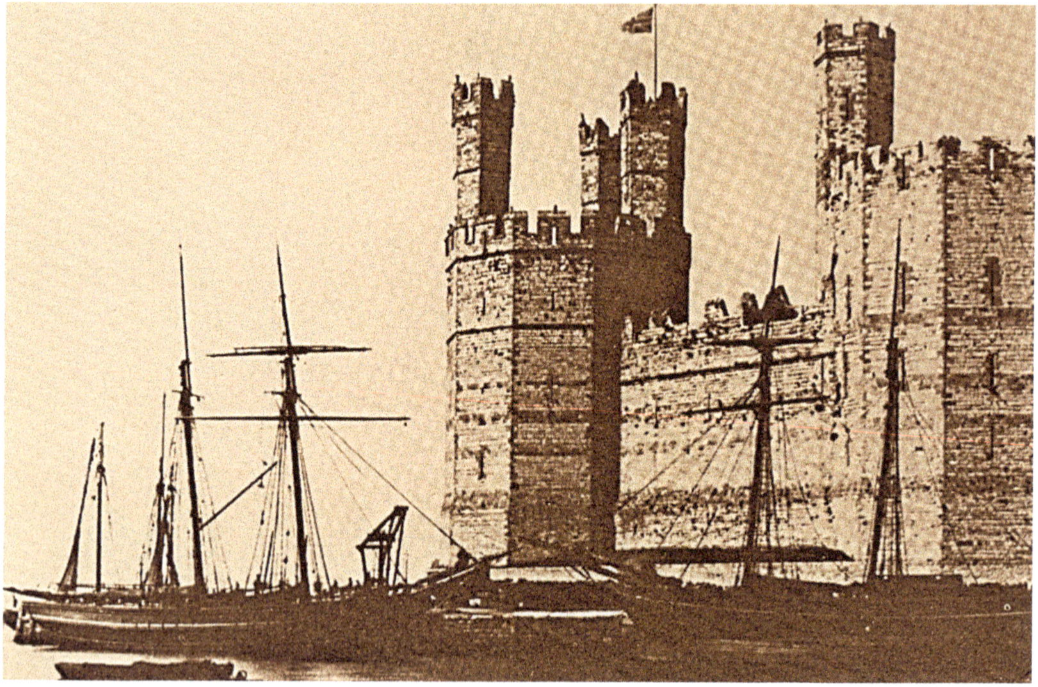

Caernarfon Castle from the Afon Seiont, *c.* 1880

Caernarfon is considered by many to be the most famous castle in Wales and one of the most identifiable in the British Isles. The main towers are designed and constructed in an uncommon polygon style. They were built at a period in time when tower design was in transition from square towers to round towers. Corners on a tower were considered to be a natural weakness in a castle's defences. Caernarfon's curtain wall, with nine towers and two gatehouses, survive today.

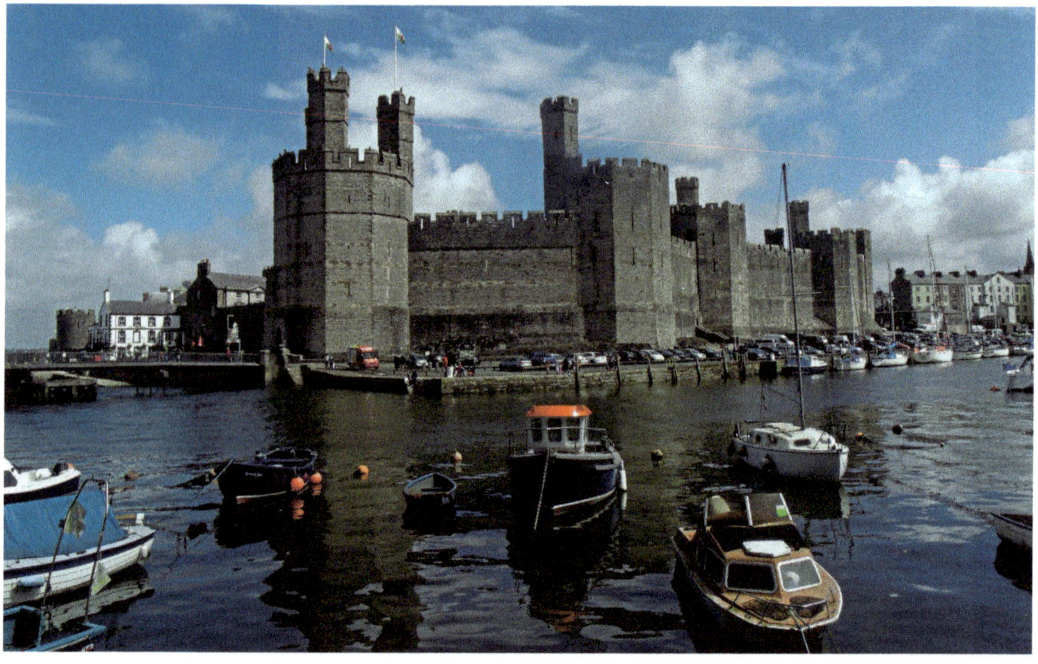

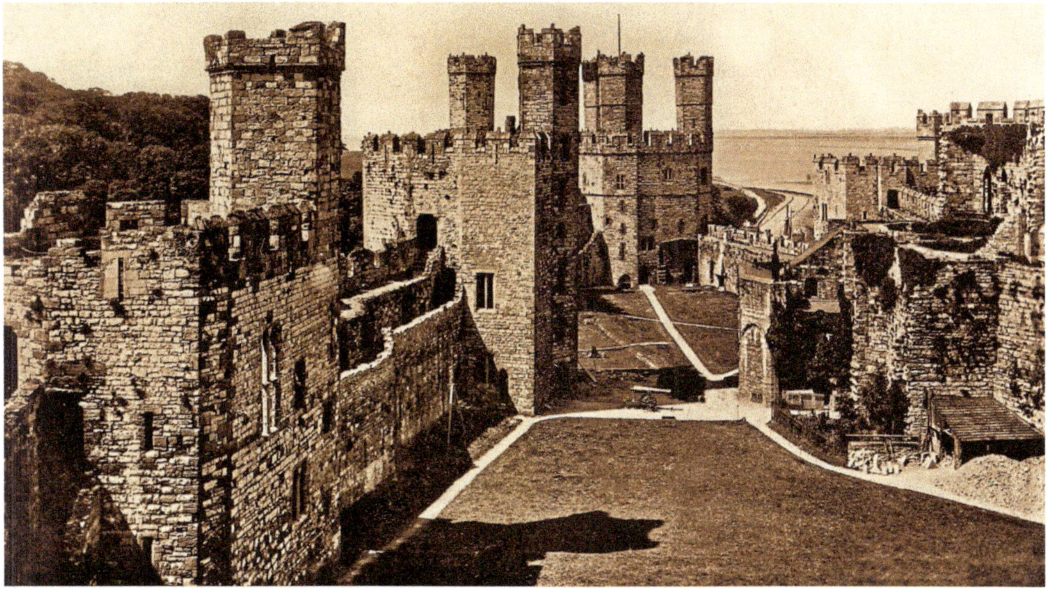

Caernarfon Castle Interior, Looking Towards the Eagle Tower, *c.* 1900

While the castle was still being constructed it was captured by the Welsh leader, Madog ap Llywelyn, in 1294. It was retaken in 1295, leading to the defences being further reinforced and extended in order to discourage any further attempts to attack. This was successfully achieved, with sieges being withstood in 1403 and 1404 by Owain Glyndwr. The castle's architect, James of St George, possibly modelled the castle on the walls of Constantinople, being aware of the town's legendary associations.

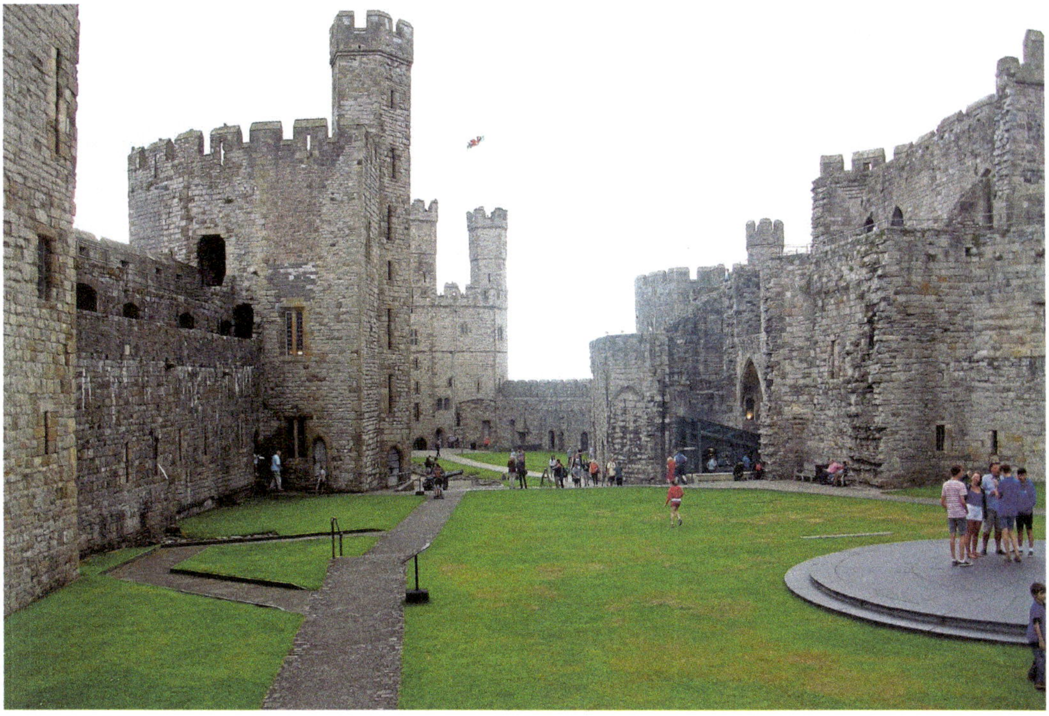

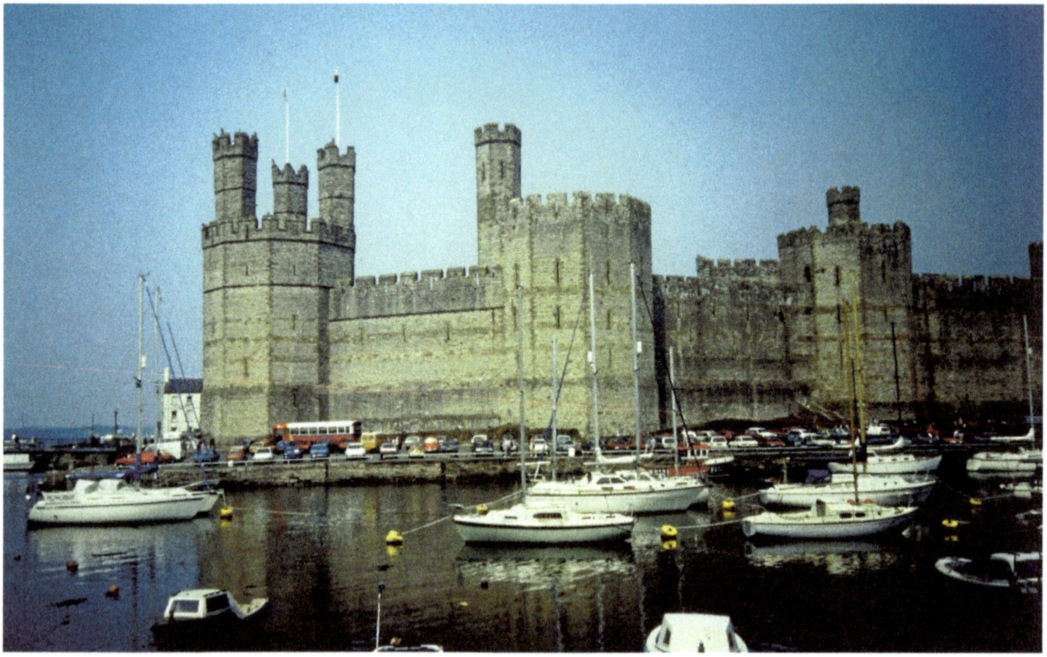

Caernarfon Castle and Slate Quay from the Afon Seiont, 1989

The castle was built by Edward I after he had subdued Wales. Construction began in 1283–1330 on the site of a smaller Norman castle and continued for around forty years. However, the castle was never fully completed. Many of the internal walls were not constructed as the castle was built and designed as a statement of intent to the people of Wales. Edward I's dominance over the country at this time and the architectural ideals of the perfect castle are predominant at Caernarfon.

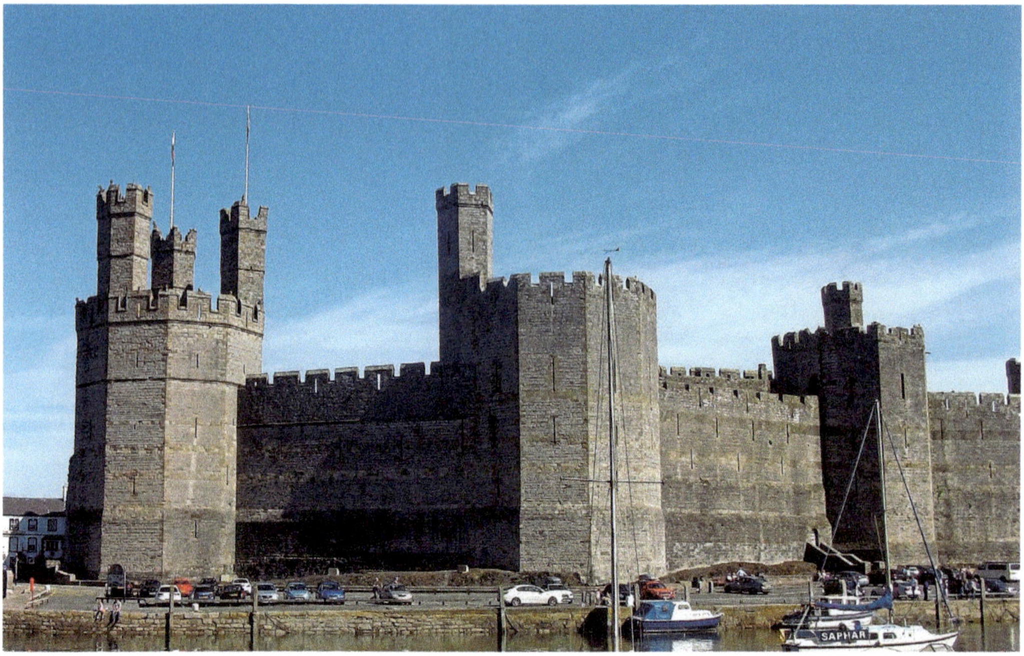

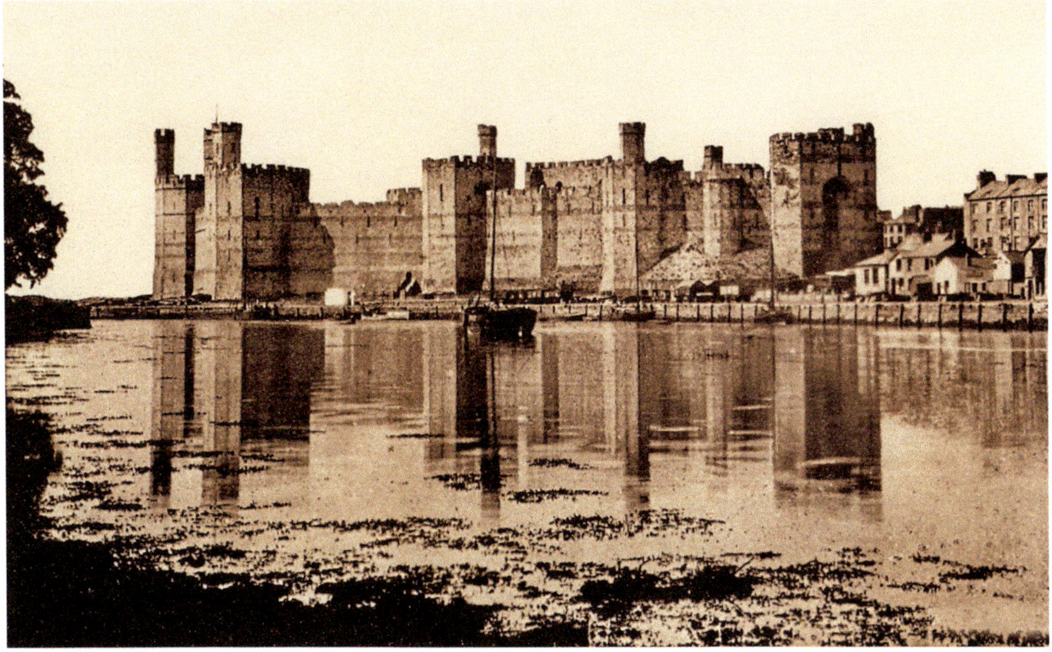

Caernarfon Castle and Slate Quay from the Afon Seiont, *c.* 1920

The above view shows the castle from the old Slate Quay. Today the Slate Quay is mainly a car park. The only remaining clue to the quay's industrial past is the old railway track embedded in the surface of the quayside. The ships that once moored along here to transport Welsh slate all over the world have now been replaced by yachts and pleasure craft. Tourism and the attractions of Caernarfon Castle, including the museum of the Royal Welch Fusiliers, have now supplanted slate and engineering as the town's main employers.

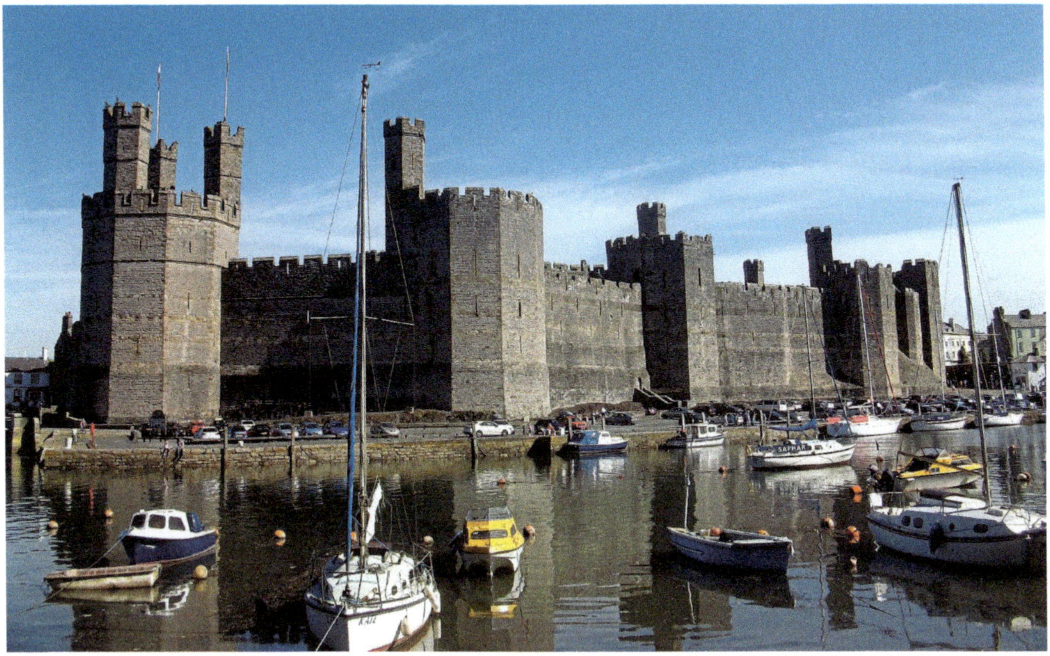

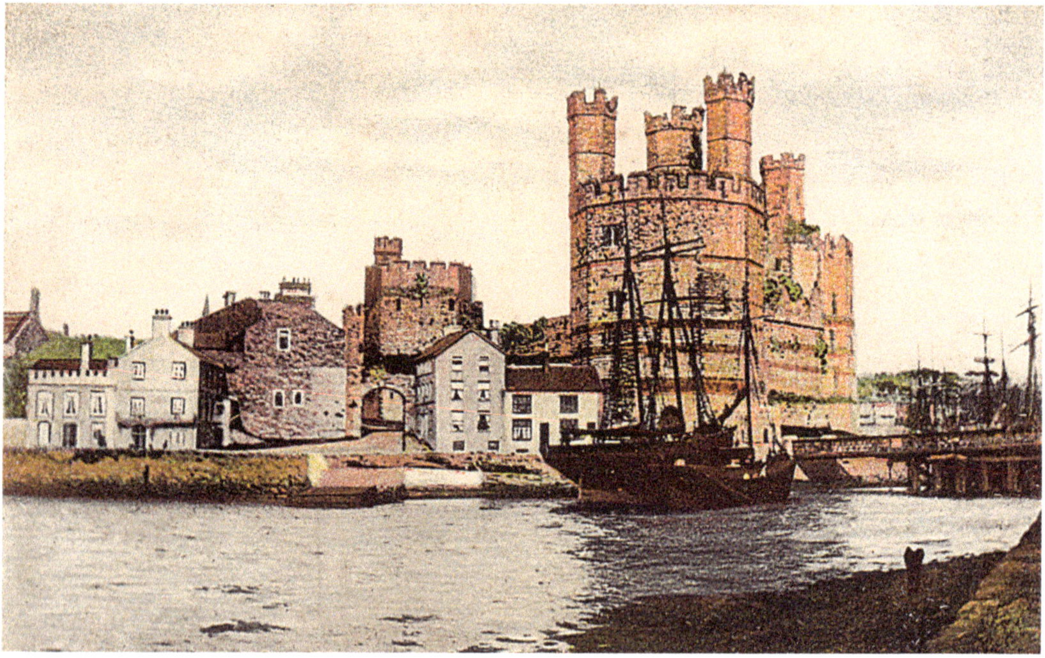

Caernarfon Castle and Pont Yr Aber, *c.* 1900

The Pont Yr Aber footbridge is a pedestrian bridge across the Afon Seiont between the Watergate entrance to Caernarfon Castle and the Aber foreshore. It is beyond this point that the Afon Seiont enters the Menai Strait. The current swing bridge was built in 1970 and it replaced an earlier bridge that dated back to 1900. In 2015 there were plans to close the footbridge, leaving residents facing a diversion of nearly 2 miles. The bridge allows residents to access the town centre and park.

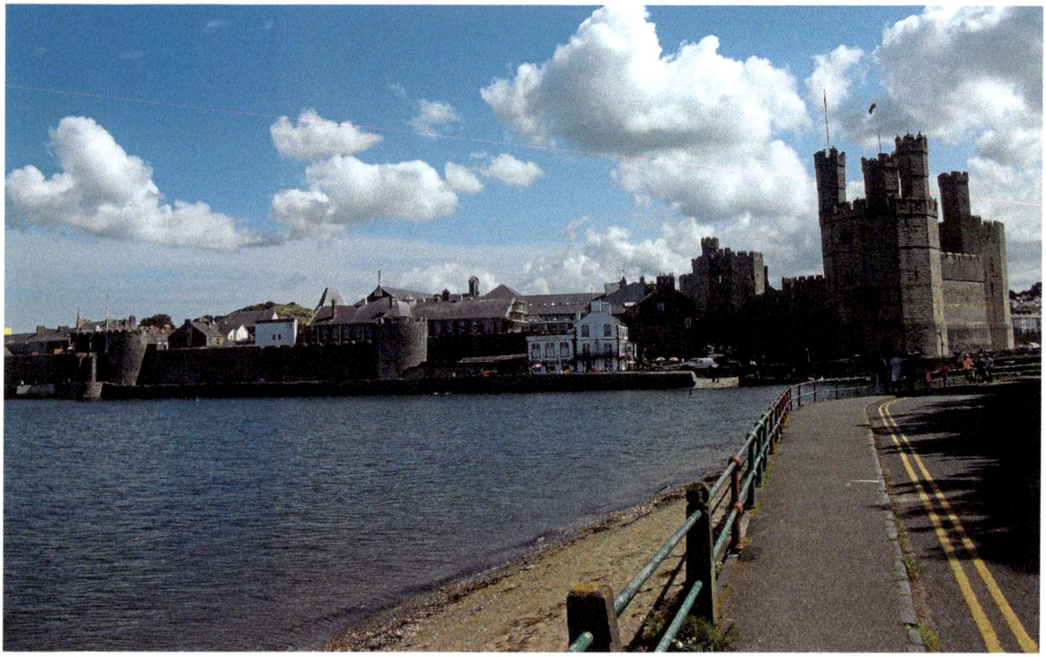

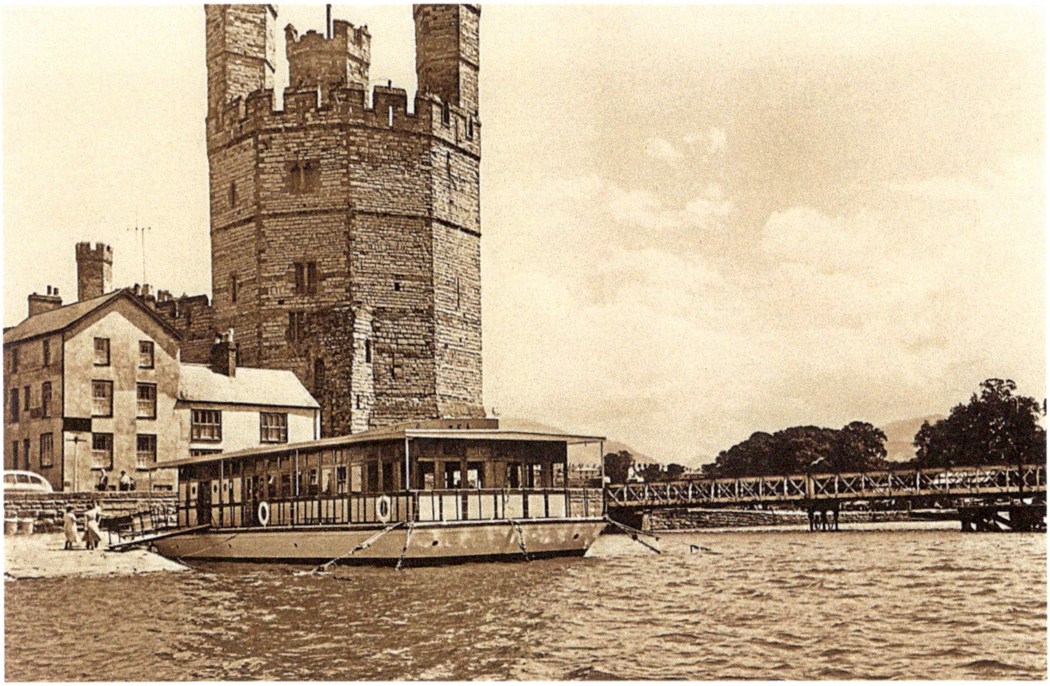

Floating Restaurant, Eagle Tower and Pont Yr Aber, Caernarfon, *c.* 1950
The boat was built in 1946 by a local firm of boatbuilders and was moored each summer by the town's castle. An equivalent replacement to meet modern standards would cost somewhere in the region of £500,000 today. The boat was decommissioned in 2011 as it began to deteriorate. It was a great loss to the town, having been a feature of Caernarfon for over sixty years. It was one of two similar vessels operating as a restaurant in Britain.

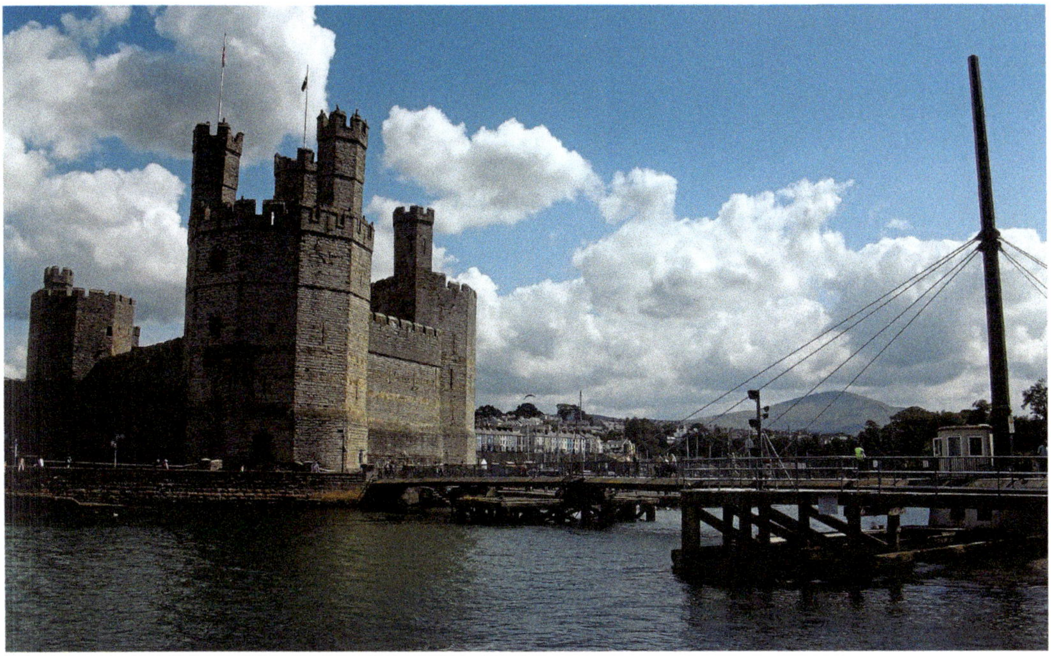

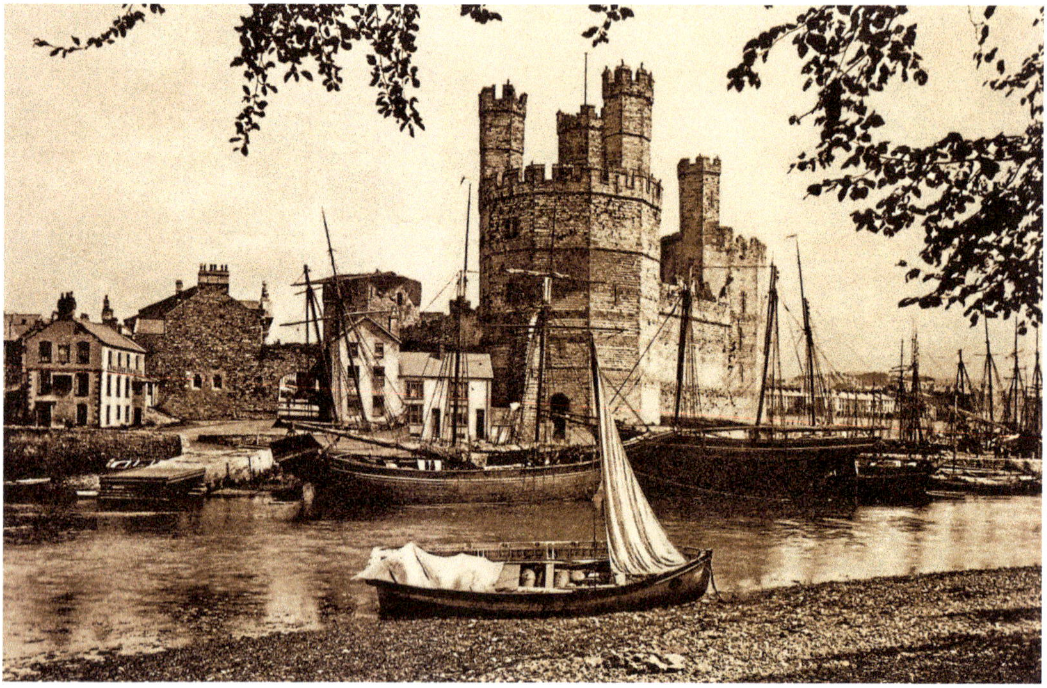

Caernarfon Castle and Slate Quay, *c.* 1880

The warehouse facilities in which the minerals and ores were stored before they were exported were redeveloped to create the 'Island Site', which are buildings located behind the harbour office. It is likely that the oldest quay was constructed as early as the eighteenth century. The above photograph of around 1880 shows commercial vessels berthed along the busy quayside in readiness for loading with their cargoes of slate and other minerals for export. Today, these same berths are used mainly by private leisure craft.

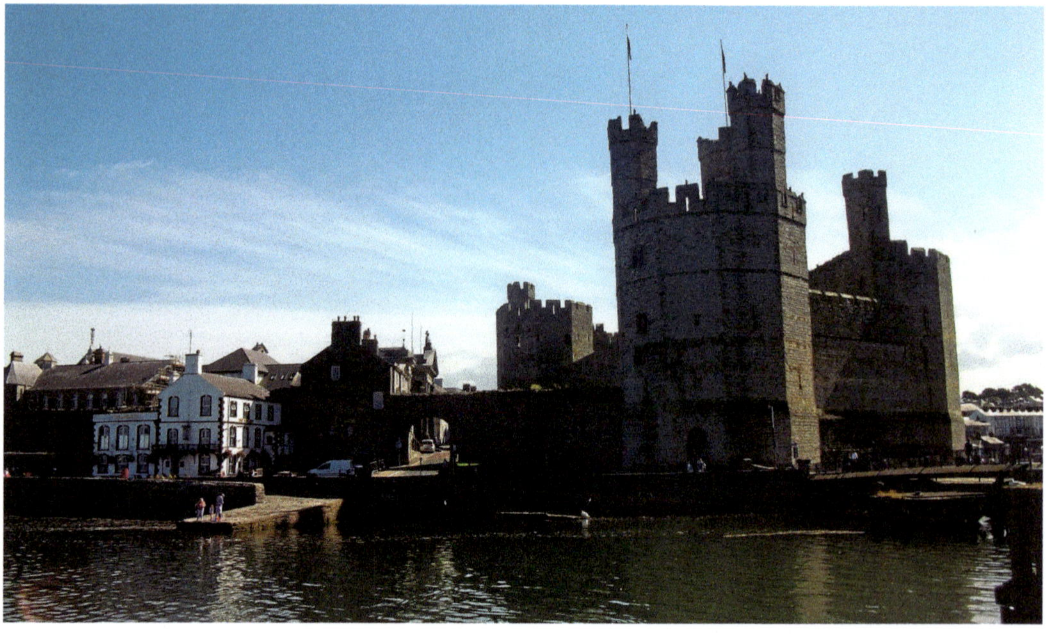

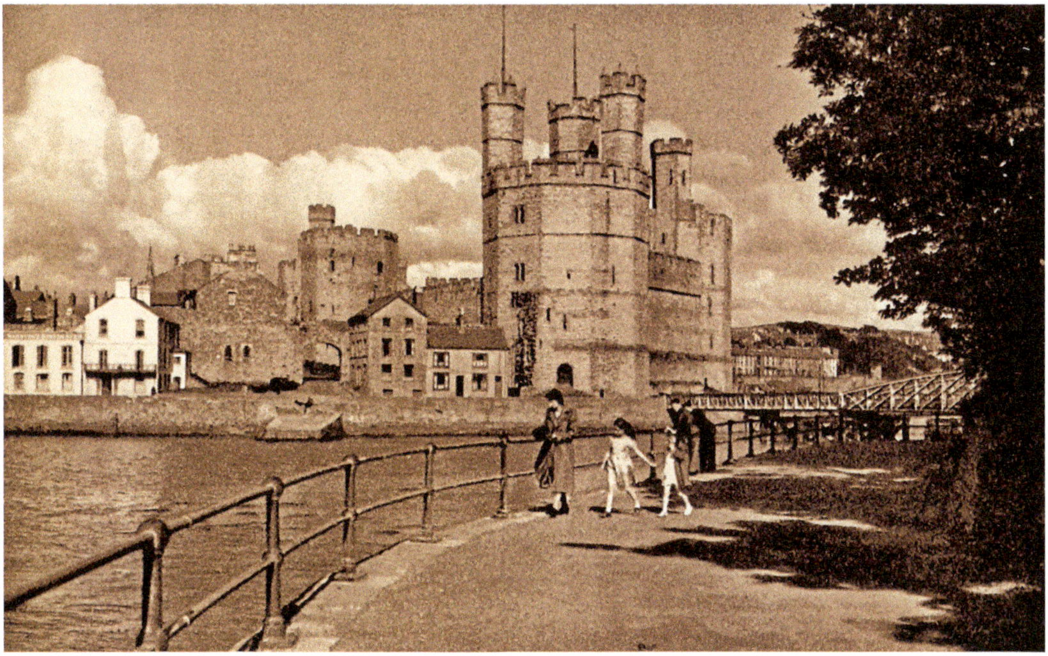

Caernarfon Castle, Pont Yr Aber and the Anglesey Arms Public House, *c.* 1940
The castle has World Heritage status. King Edward I deliberately made its appearance intimidating, as an expression of his power. Polygonal towers were built, with the Eagle Tower the most imposing. It was previously the site of a Norman motte-and-bailey castle and before that a Roman fort stood nearby, ease of access to the sea the reason for the location's popularity. The first English Prince of Wales was born in the castle in 1284. Prince Charles' investiture took place here in 1969.

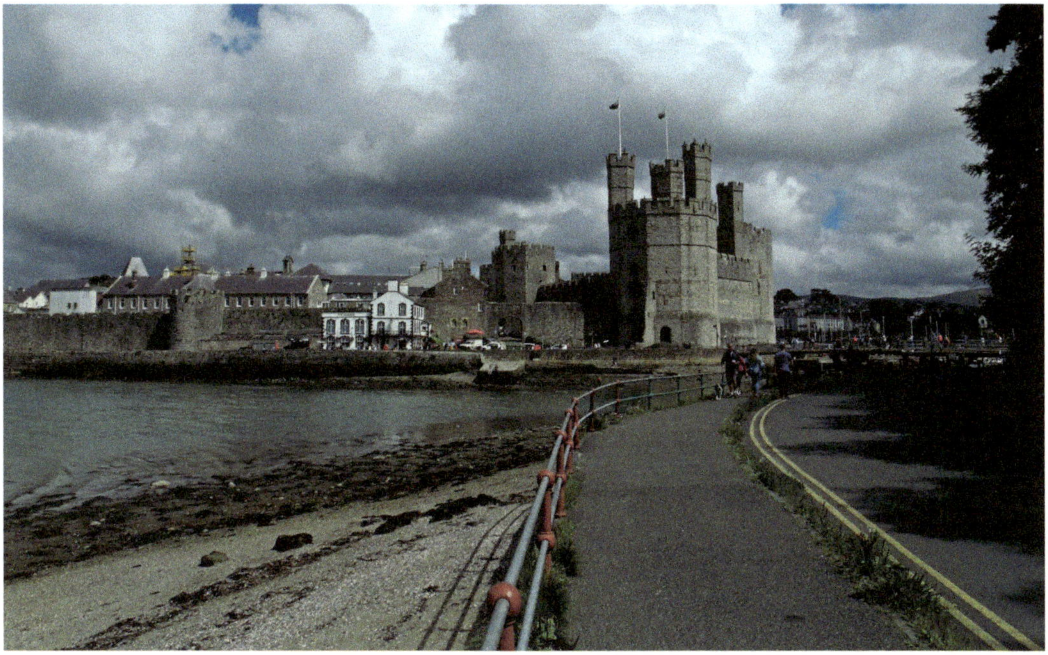

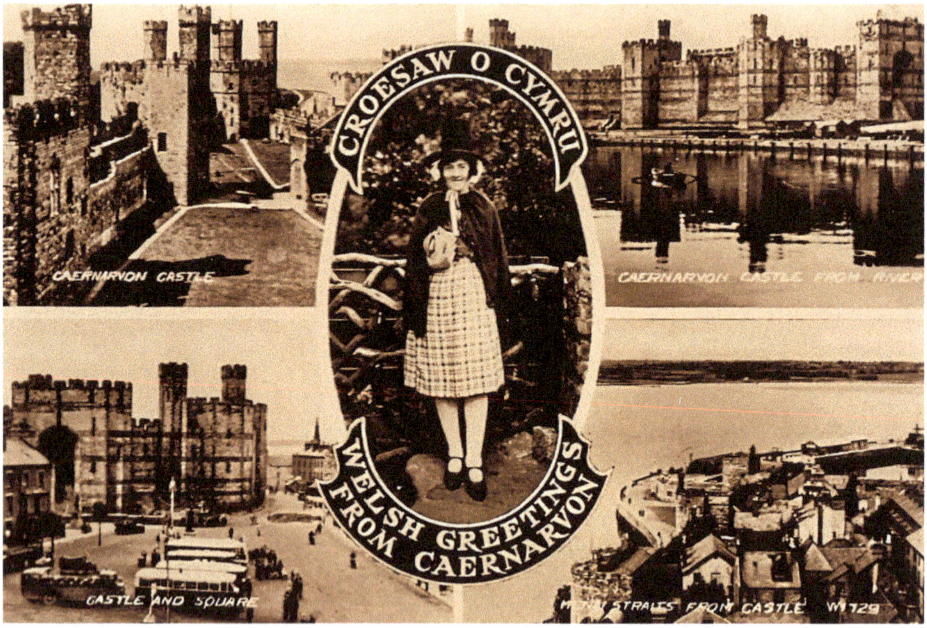

Caernarfon Postcard Multiview, *c.* 1920

Caernarfon is a royal town and port located on the eastern shore of the Menai Strait, opposite Ynys Mon (the isle of Anglesey). It has a population of around 9,615. The multiview postcard of Caernarfon, of around 1920, emphasises the castle, constructed by Edward I, and also shows views of this medieval walled town. However, the area has historical connections dating back to the ancient Britons and their hill fort; the Romans and their fort; and the Normans, whose castle previously occupied Edward I's site.

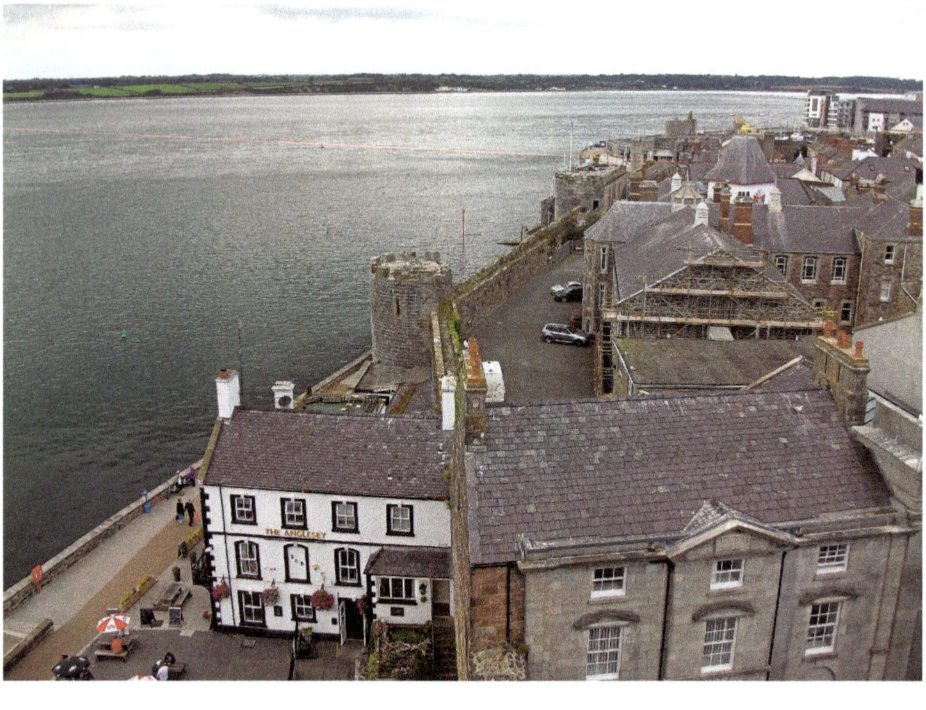

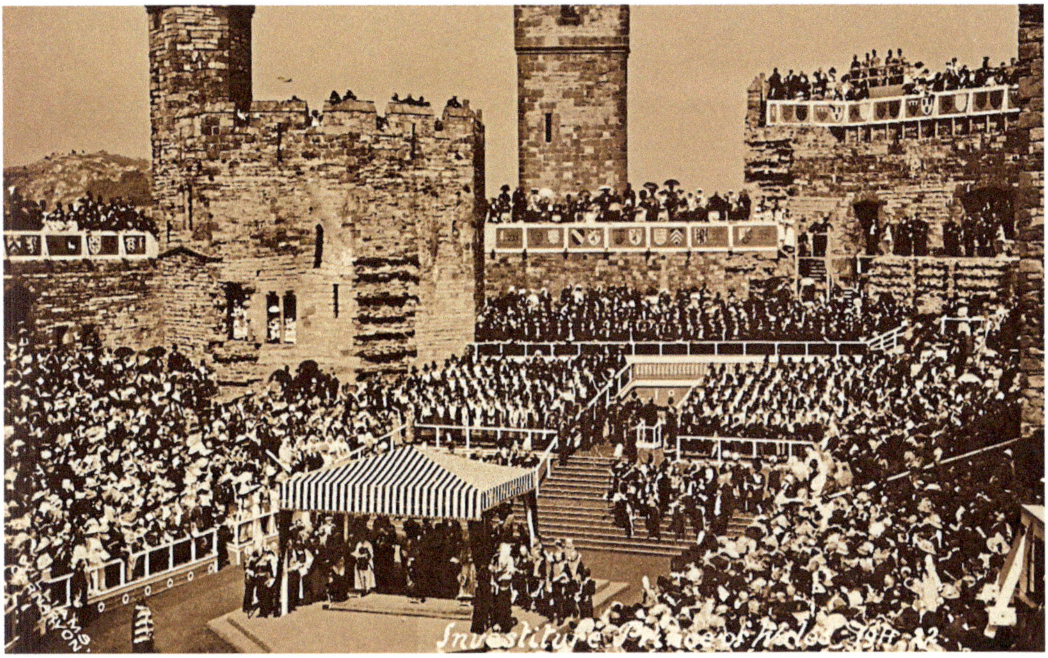

Investiture of the Prince of Wales, 13 July 1911

In 1911 the MP for Caernarfon boroughs, David Lloyd George, agreed to the Royal Family's suggestion that the Investiture of the Prince of Wales should be held at Caernarfon Castle. The ceremony was held on 13 July, with the future King Edward VIII being invested. The Investiture of Prince Charles also took place at Caernarfon Castle, on 1 July 1969. In the build-up to the 1969 ceremony there were terrorist threats and protests, although the Investiture itself went ahead without incident.

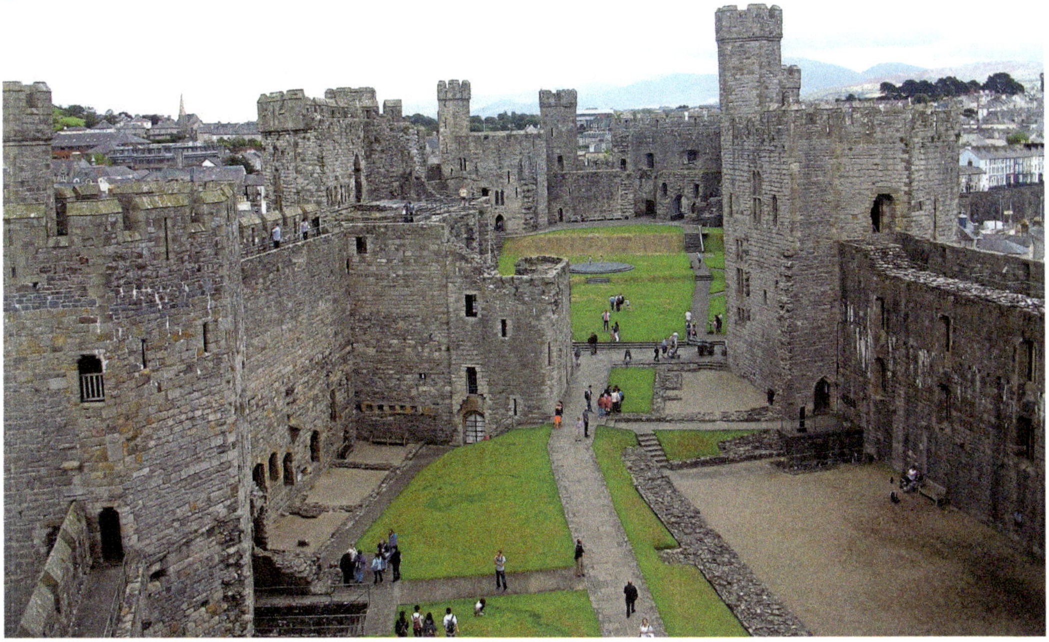

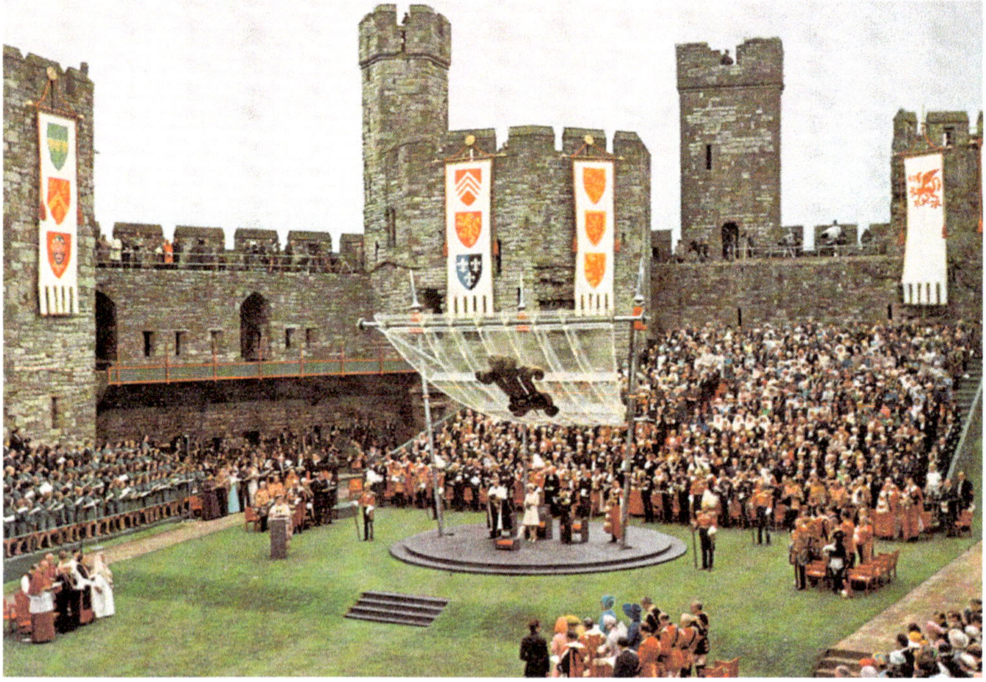

Investiture, Caernarfon Castle, 1 July 1969

The Investiture of Prince Charles was completed without controversy. However, in the weeks leading up to the ceremony there had been threats and terrorist activity, with a bomb at Abergele, two in Caernarfon, and one at Llandudno Pier. Two members of Mudiad Amddiffyn Cymru (Welsh Defence Movement), Alwyn Jones and George Taylor, were killed when their bomb exploded prematurely. It was intended for the railway line at Abergele to stop the Royal train. Their leader, John Jenkins, was sentenced to ten years' imprisonment.

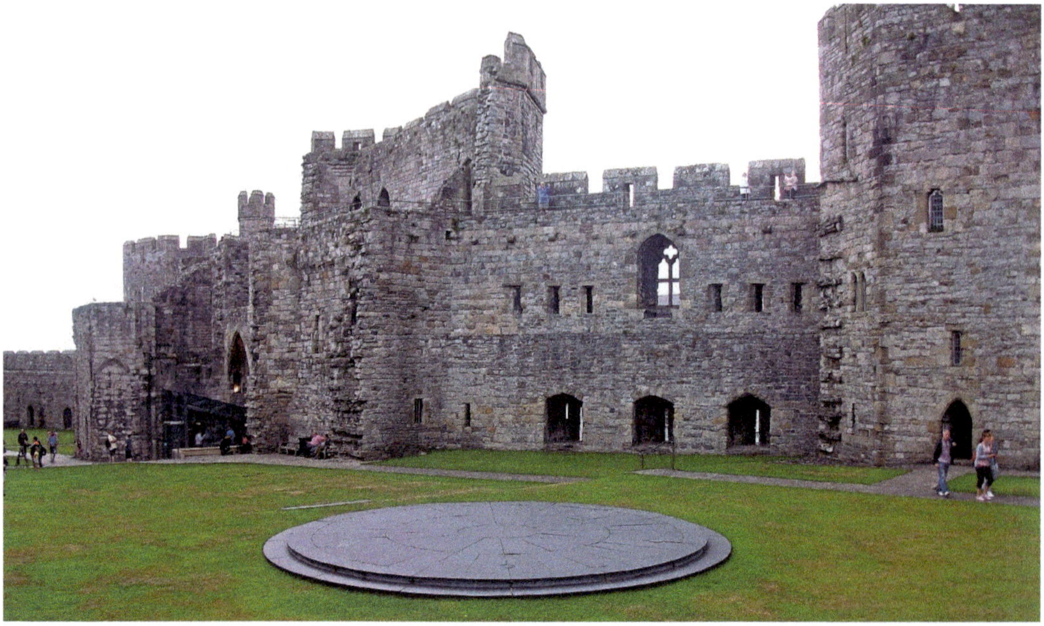

The King's Gate Entrance to Caernarfon Castle, Pen Deitsh (Castle Ditch), *c.* 1900
The King's Gate is a monumental, twin-towered gateway, forming the entrance to Caernarfon Castle from the walled town. It was not completed, but is still an impressive three-storey construction. There is now a new entrance pavilion here, built to deal with the 200,000 visitors who flock to see this historic monument annually. The new modern structures are located within the existing archway of the King's Gate entrance and the old hall site. Access is via two sets of steps, or a ramp.

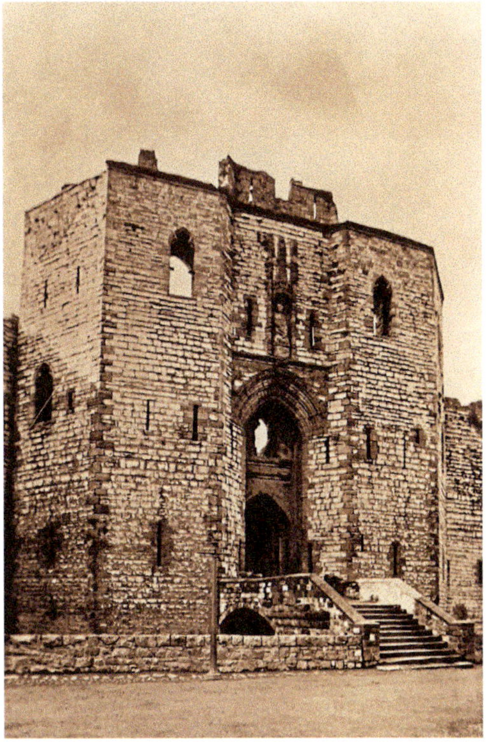

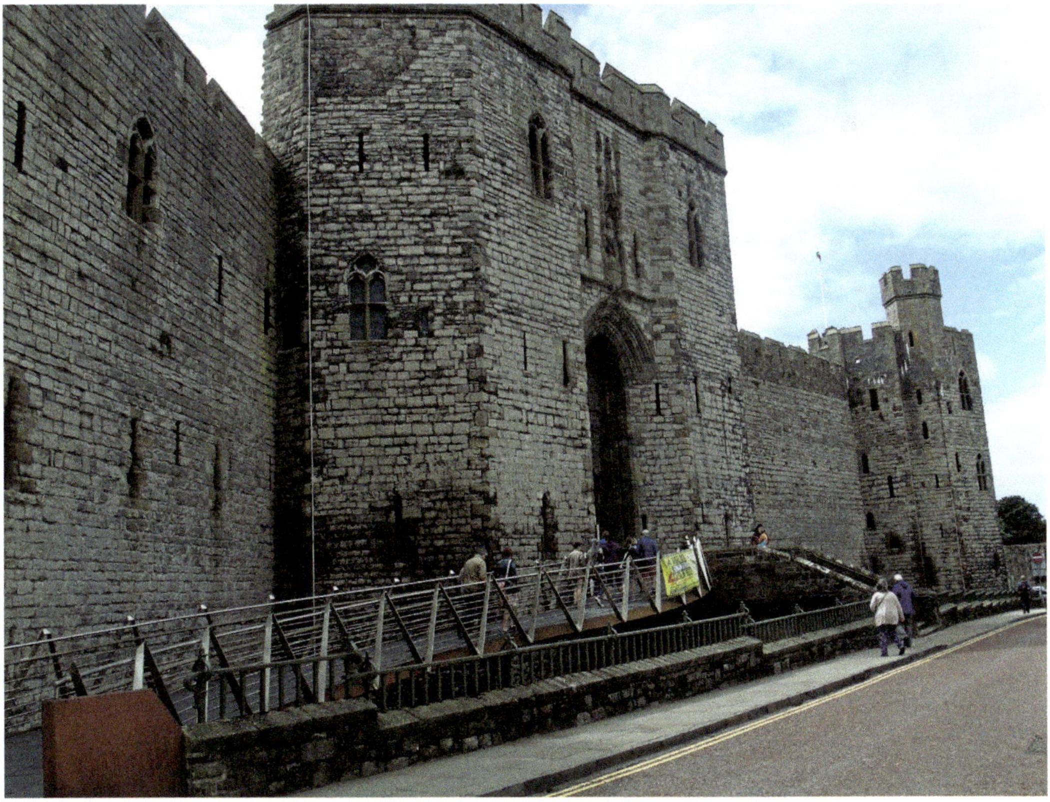

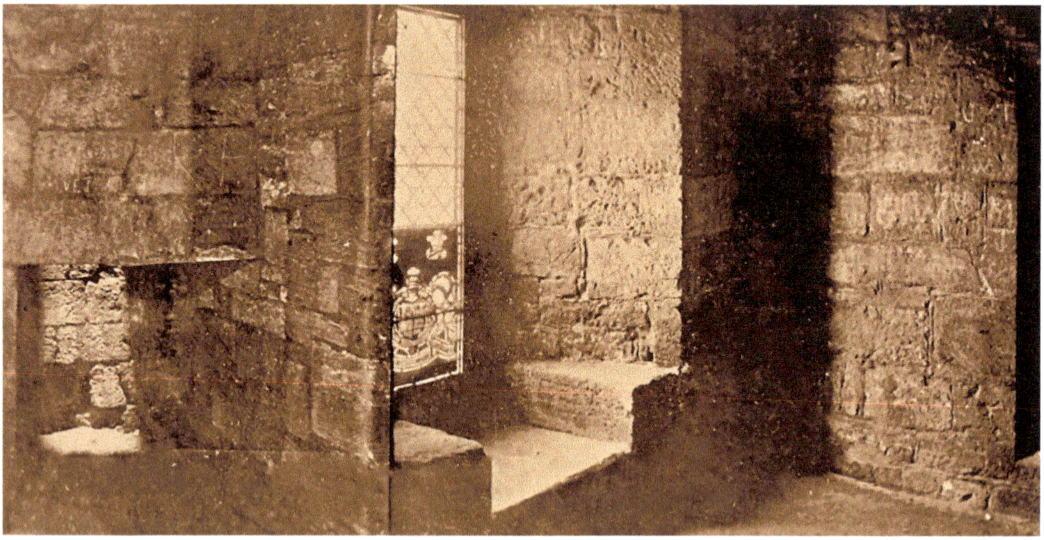

Birth Chamber of the First Prince of Wales (Caernarfon Castle), *c.* 1910

Edward I was eager to emphasise the symbolic superiority of Caernarfon Castle at every available opportunity; so much so that he ensured his son, the first English Prince to hold the title 'Prince of Wales', was born there. Shown is the birth chamber of Edward's fourth son, Edward of Caernarfon, later Edward II of England, who was born at the castle on 25 April 1284 and made Prince of Wales in 1301. Edward I died in July 1307; Edward (his son) became King, his three brothers having died before him.

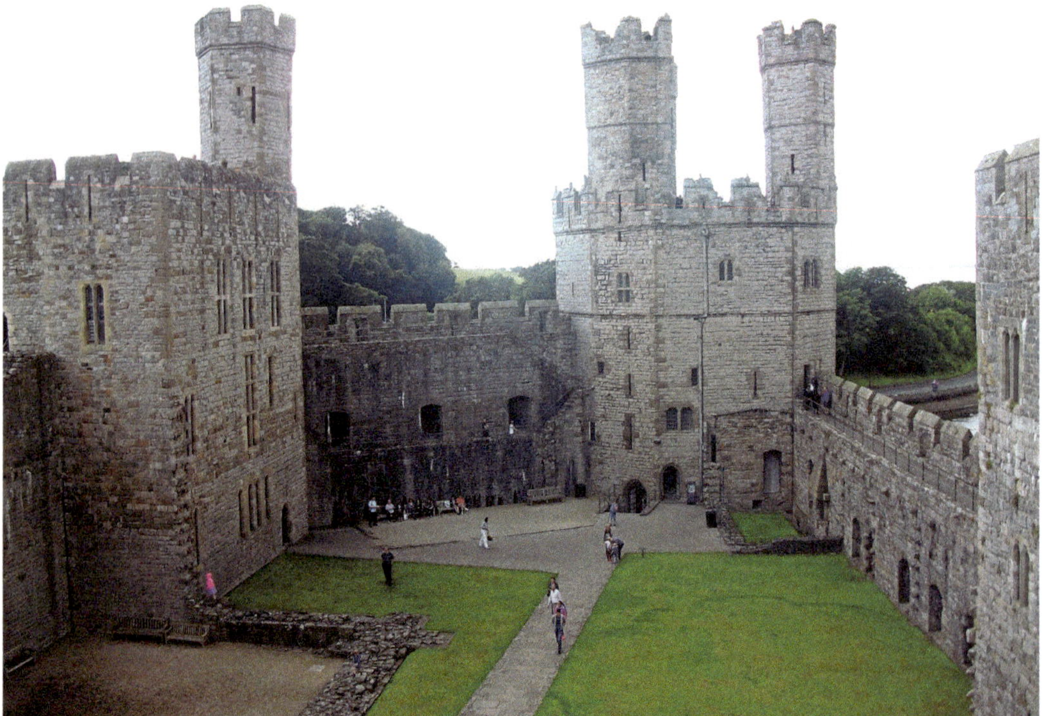

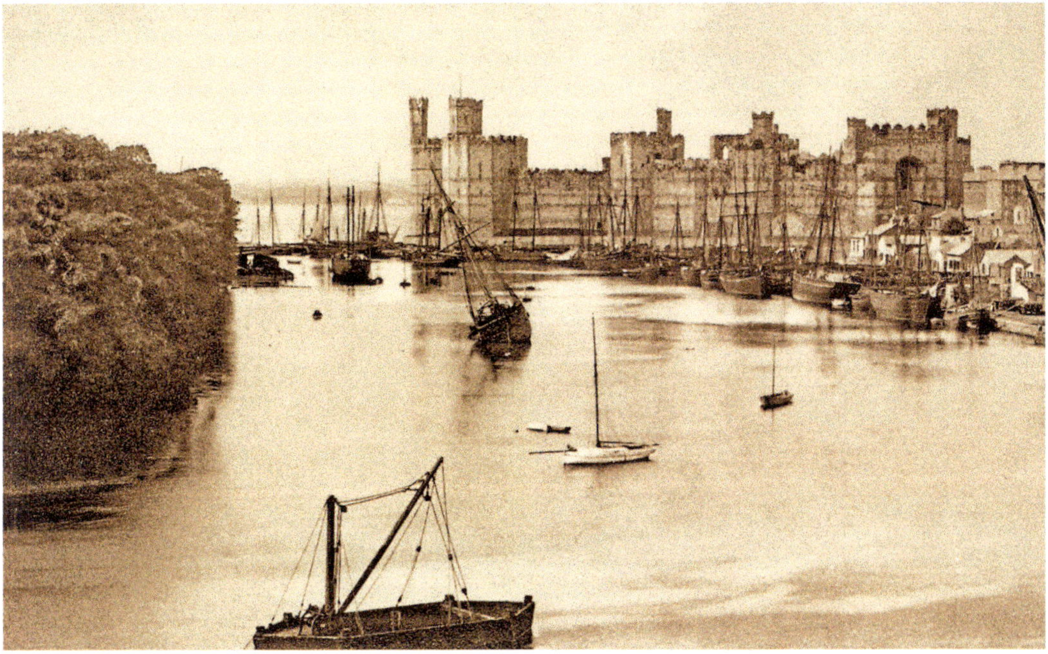

Caernarfon Castle and Slate Quay, *c.* 1880

Caernarfon was at one time an important port, exporting slate from the Nantlle Valley quarries. Today the town has a small marina and a Blue Flag beach at Victoria Harbour. The town established itself as a maritime economic centre in medieval times, trading from locations on the Afon Seiont, where the Slate Quay exported local slate, and Afon Cadnant, where the Victoria Dock (Doc Fictoria) served general coastal trade. Locally mined copper and lead-ore were also exported from the Slate Quay.

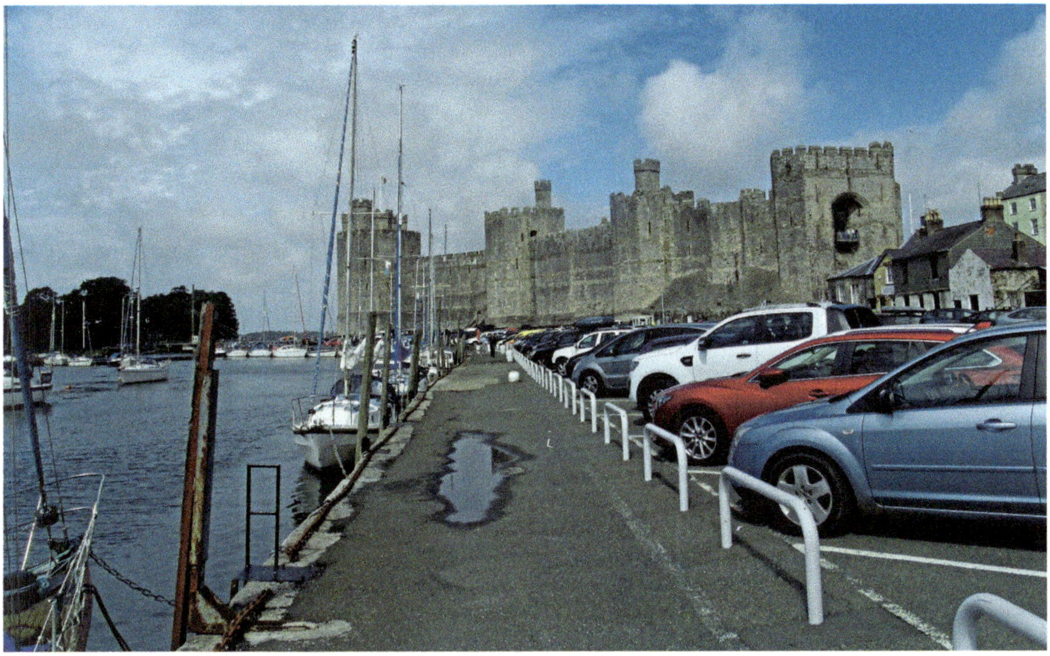

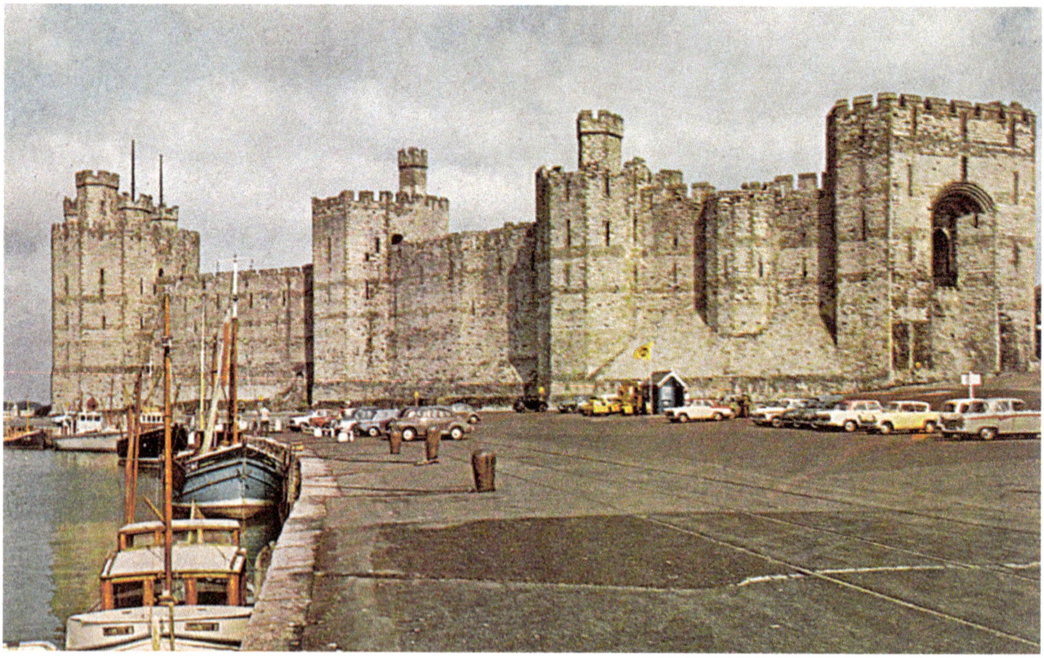

Caernarfon Castle from the Slate Quay, 1966

Caernarfon's slate export trade was further enhanced by the construction of the Nantlle Railway in 1826. This encouraged other heavy industries to grow in the area, including railway engine construction and its related trades, and shipbuilding. However, the construction of the Slate Quay meant that the view of the castle alongside the waterfront, enjoyed by Caernarfon's earliest tourists, no longer survived. In 1840 the harbour office was constructed, as were some of the buildings around Y Maes; both remain today.

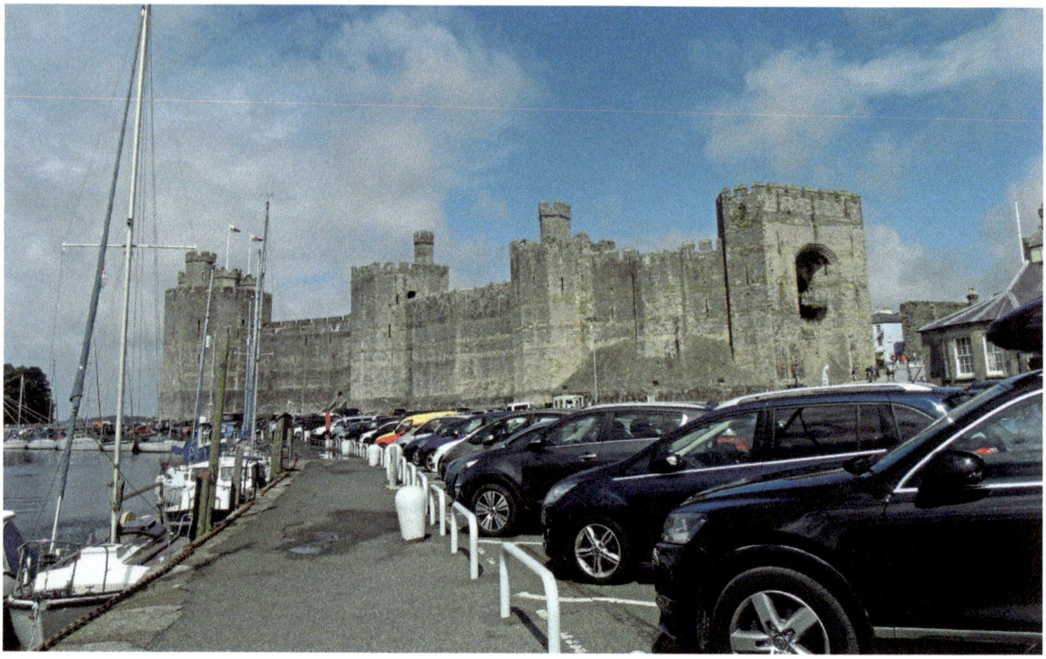

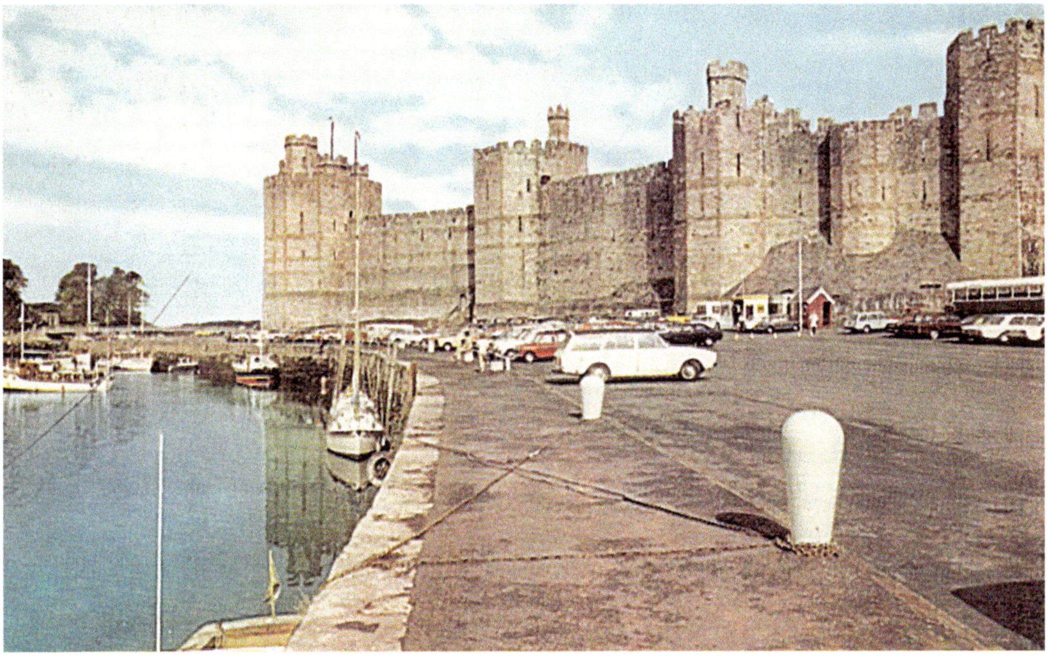

Caernarfon Castle from the Slate Quay, *c.* 1965

The first three decades of the nineteenth century saw new wharves constructed along the Afon Seiont, in order to process the increasing output of slate and other minerals produced by local quarries; this was then transported to its destination, at home and abroad, by ship. In 1817 the quay was enlarged, with earth being removed from the bank which once led down to the shore from Y Maes. High retaining walls were then constructed to take the bank's place.

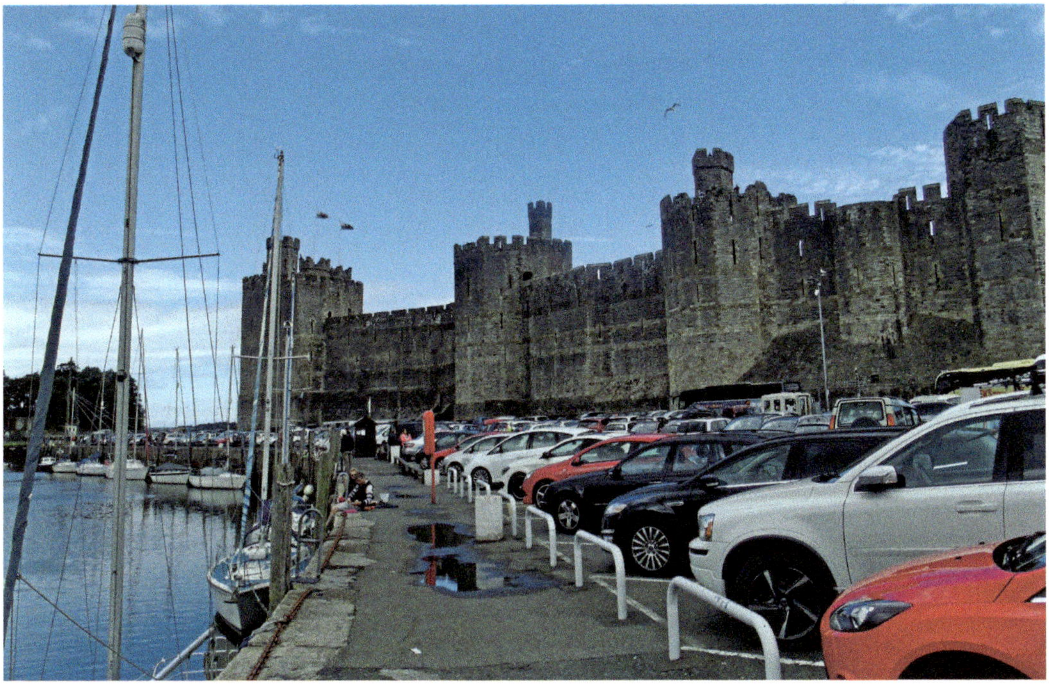

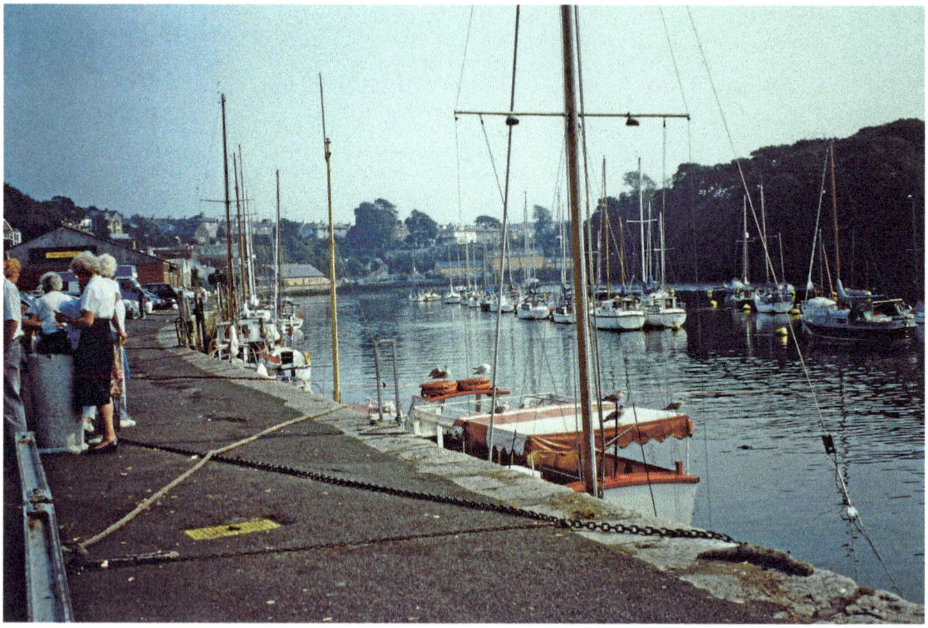

Afon Seiont and Slate Quay, Caernarfon, 1990

The Afon Seiont runs into the Menai Strait at Caernarfon. Its source is at Llyn Padarn, near Llanberis, from where it flows in a roughly north–west direction to the sea. Between Llyn Padarn and the village of Llanrug, where it reaches the Pont Rhythallt, it is known as the Afon Rhythallt, changing its name just after the village. The name of the Roman fort of Segontium, on the outskirts of Caernarfon, is based on the Latin form of the name 'Seiont'.

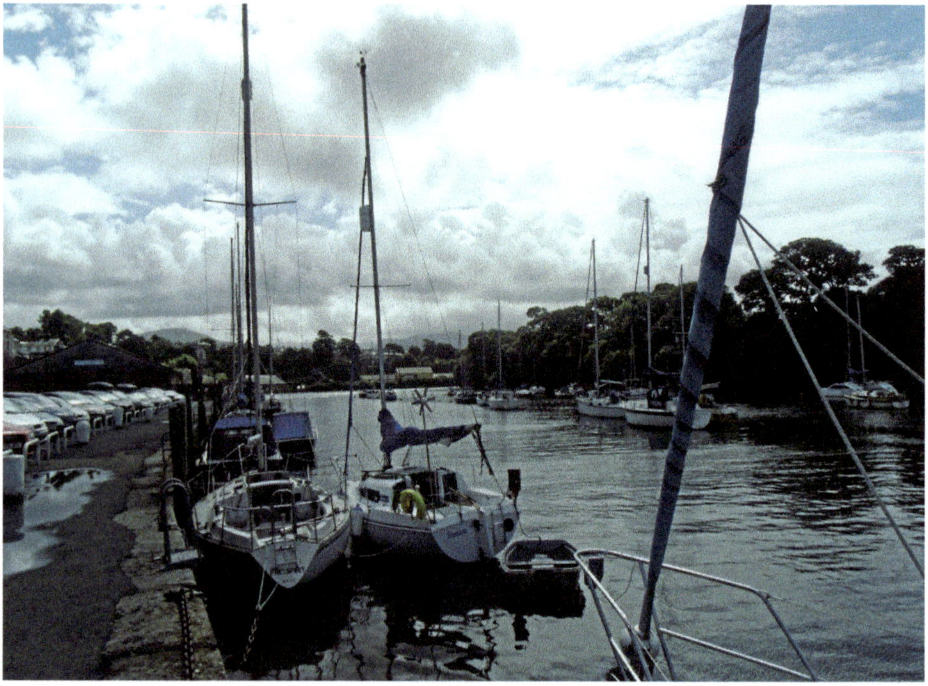

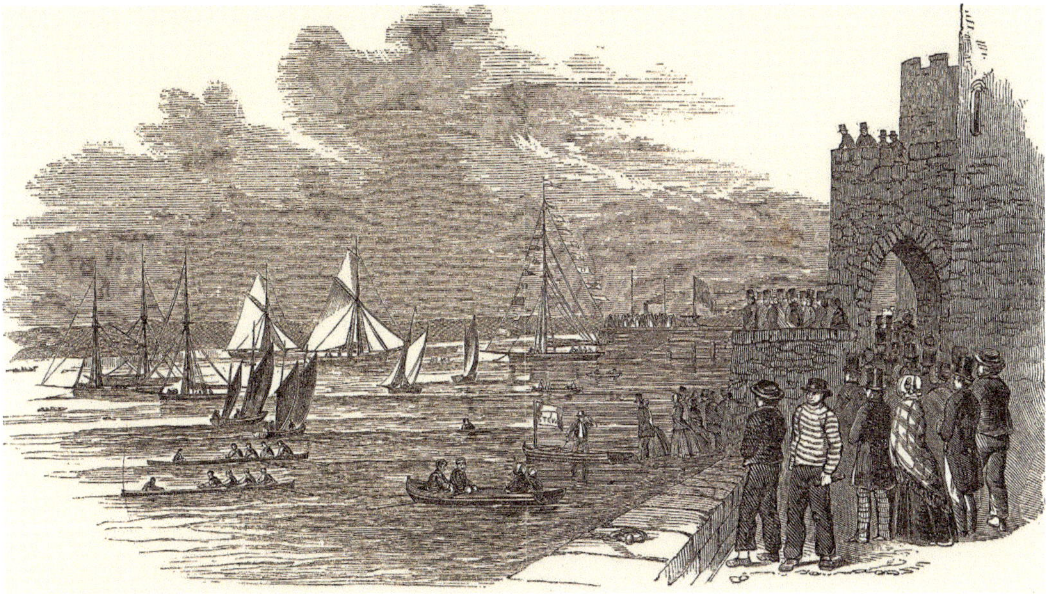

Caernarfon Regatta and Porth-Yr-Aur (Golden Gate), 1849
The Royal Welsh Yacht Club was founded in 1847 and is situated within the medieval town walls of Caernarfon, overlooking the Menai Strait. The club's headquarters are in Porth-Yr-Aur (Golden Gate), built around 1284 as the West Gate, or Watergate, of the walled town. It claims to be the oldest yacht club premises in the world. In the late eighteenth century it housed a battery of seven canons and today houses starter canon for sailing regattas.

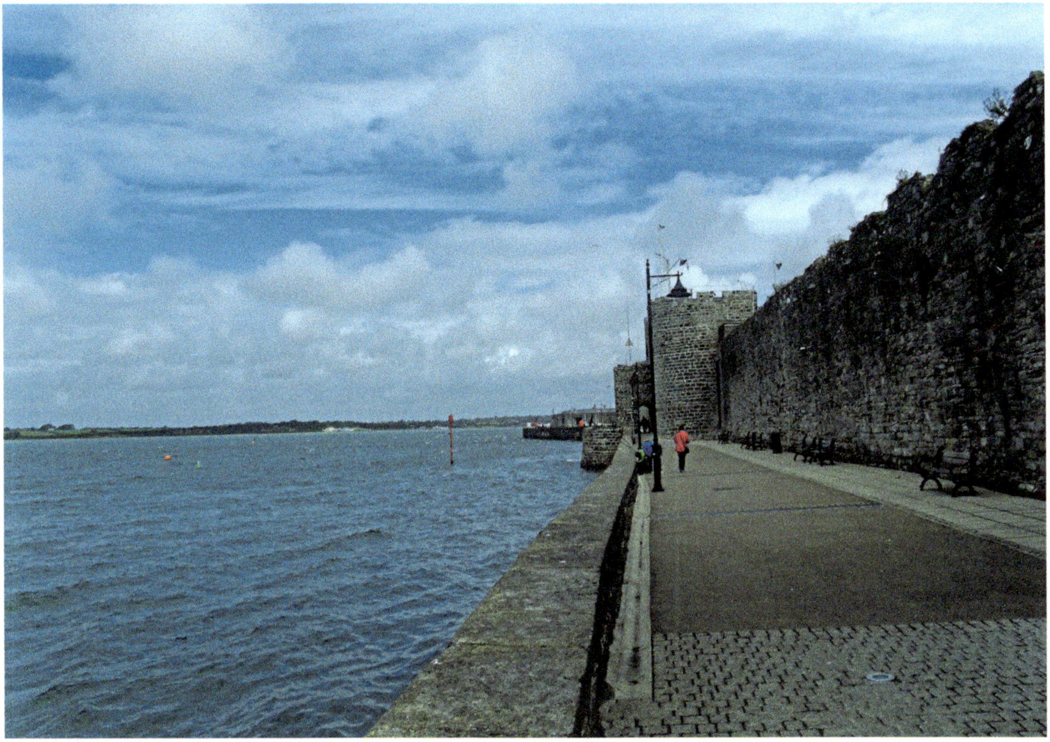

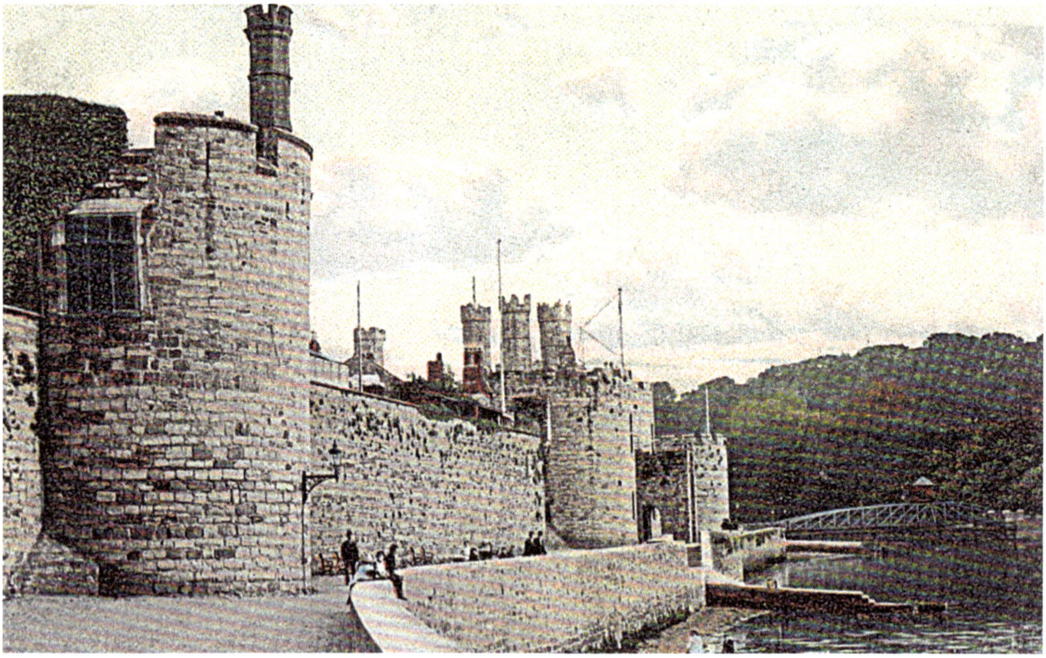

Caernarfon Promenade, Town Walls and Pont Yr Aber, *c.* 1900

The Promenade dates to the early nineteenth century and runs between the Slate Quay and Victoria Dock (Doc Fictoria). Today, this is the location of the Galeri, a cultural development which has won many awards, and incorporates an art gallery, theatre, cinema and restaurant. There are panoramic views to be had from along the Afon Seiont of the Menai Strait, Caernarfon Castle, the harbour and the medieval walled town. It is well worth taking the time to walk along the Promenade.

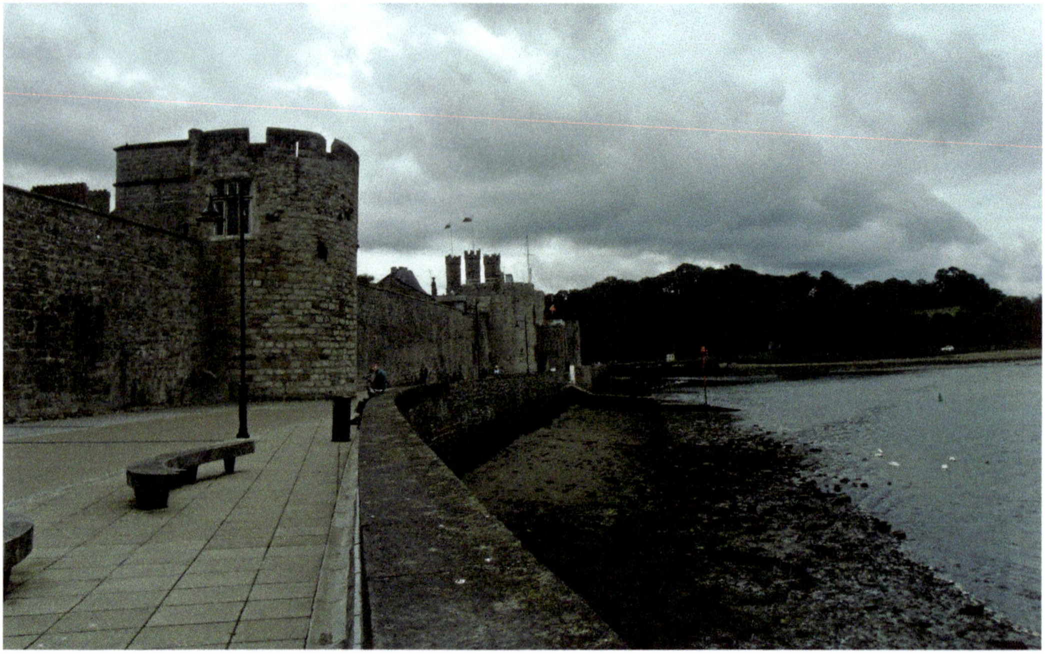

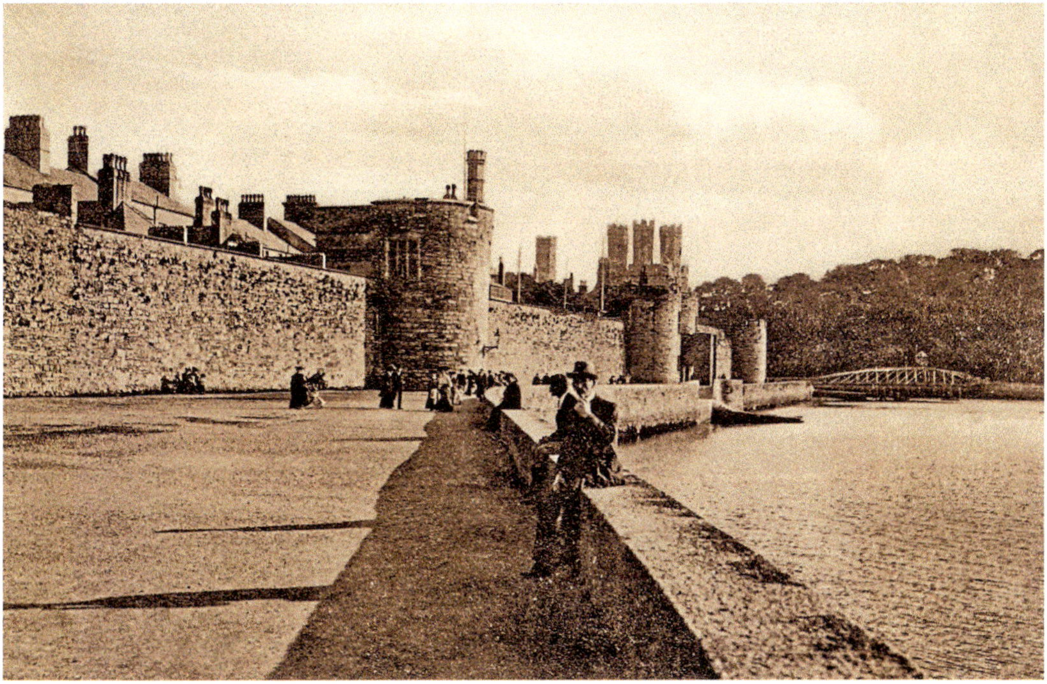

Caernarfon Promenade, Town Walls and Pont Yr Aber, *c.* 1910
The medieval walls of Caernarfon and the turrets of the Eagle Tower are clearly visible in this photograph from around 1910. From the position of the shadows cast on the Promenade by the sun, it is evident that those pictured are out for their evening stroll. Apart from a new swing bridge, installed around 1970, this view has changed very little in the intervening century. The biggest change has been in the opposite direction, with the construction of Doc Fictoria Marina.

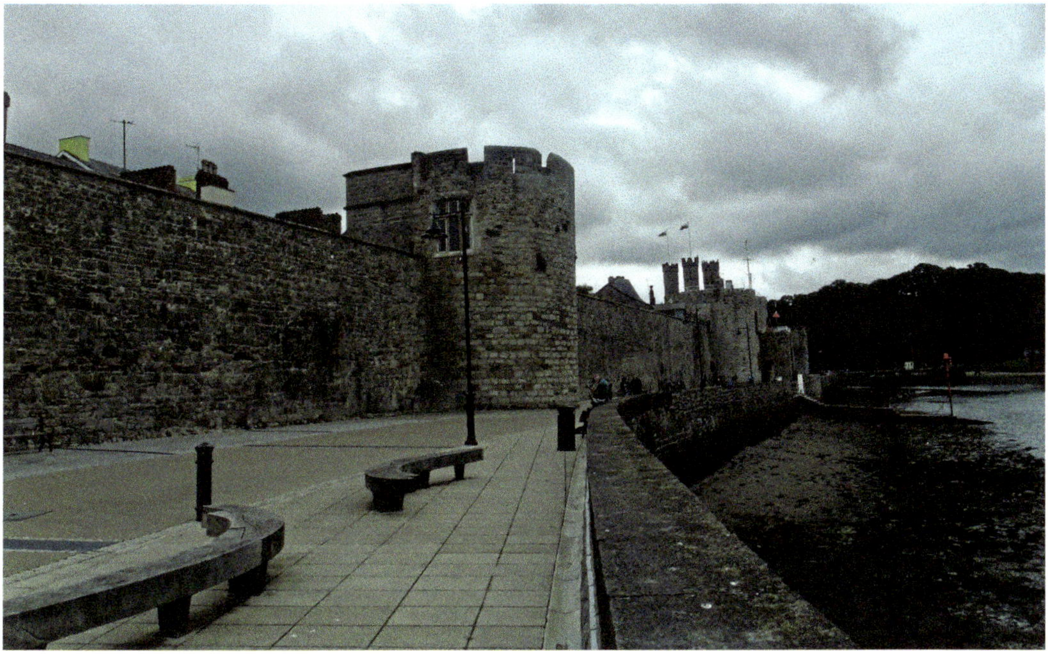

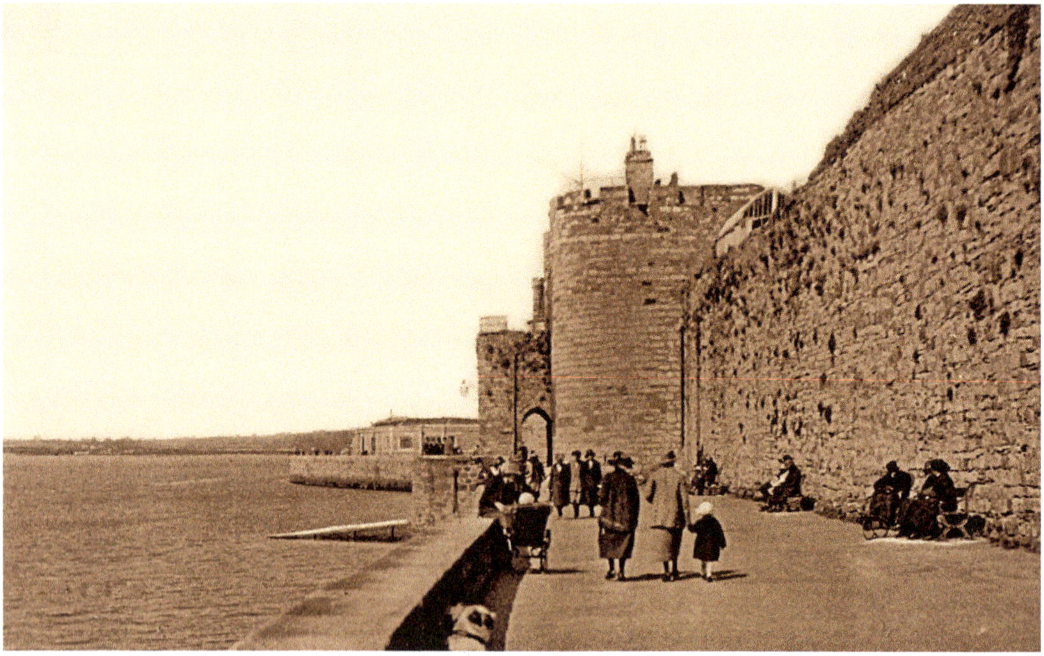

Caernarfon Promenade and Town Walls, *c.* 1920

The medieval town walls, including eight towers and two twin-towered gateways, form a complete circuit of approximately 730 metres (2,394 feet) around the old town, with the first phase completed between 1283 and 1285. Some stone from Segontium Roman fort was re used in its construction. The walls are maintained by Cadw, but only a small section can be accessed by the public. The town walls and castle at Caernarfon were declared part of a World Heritage Site in 1986.

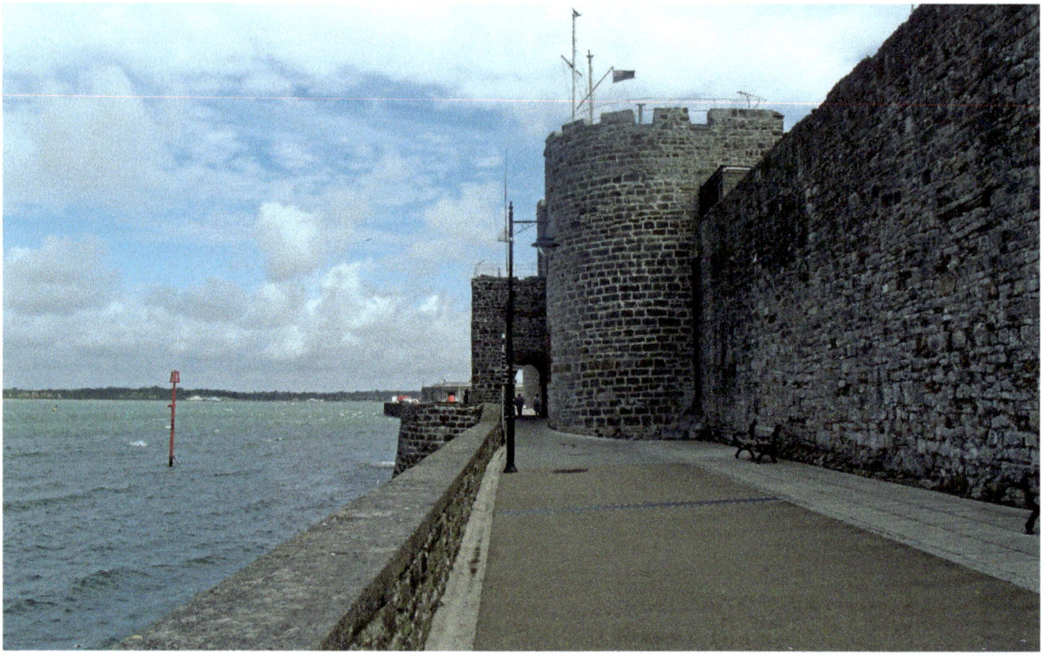

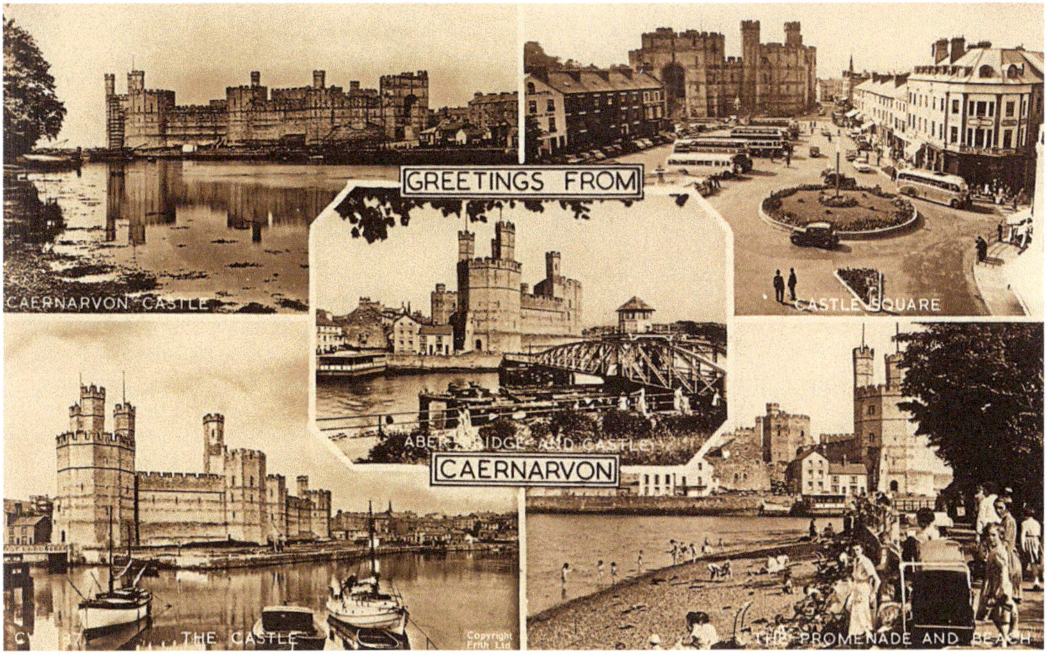

Caernarfon Promenade and Beach, 1960

The historic waterfront at Caernarfon was established as a maritime trading centre in medieval times. In the nineteenth century Doc Fictoria, on the Afon Cadnant, served general coastal trade, while the mouth of the Afon Seiont became home to the historic Slate Quay, which can be seen from the beach on the opposite bank. In 1960 it was a popular location and today it continues to attract holidaymakers to its shores on fine days.

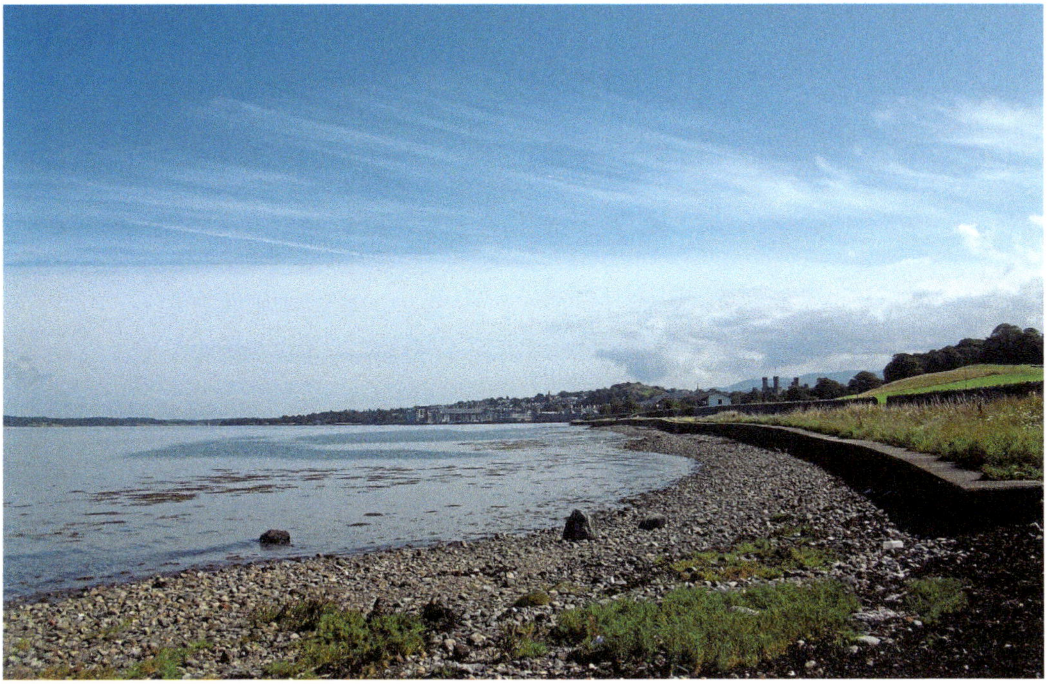

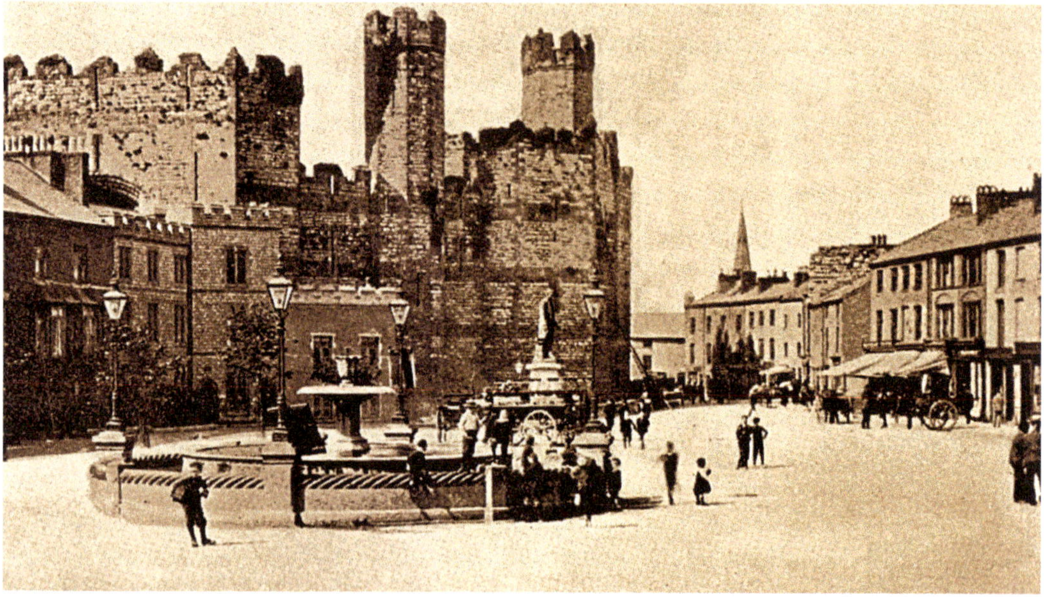

Castle Square (Y Maes), Caernarfon, *c.* 1900

The recently developed Castle Square now emphasises the open environment, which acts as a backdrop to the area. This allows the castle to be viewed within the context of Y Maes, while permitting the space to be used for various functions. This includes a small fairground, market and various exhibitions, which co exist within the same space as pedestrians, tourist coaches and motor traffic. All have access to the various shops, cafés, restaurants and hotels which line its perimeters.

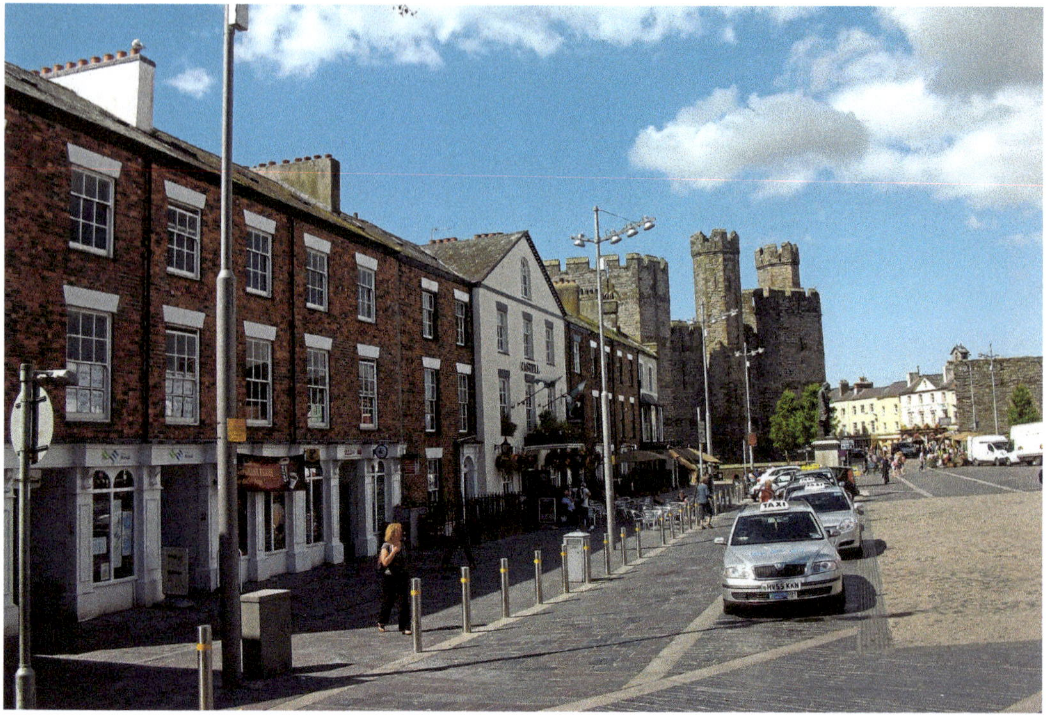

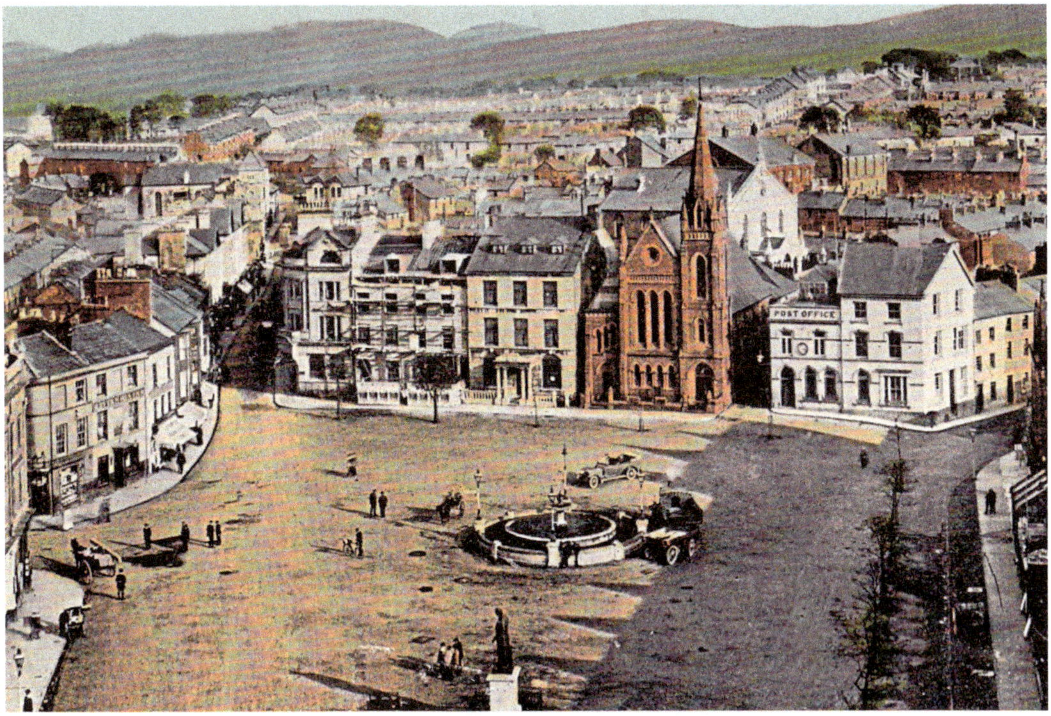

Castle Square from the Eagle Tower (*c.* 1910) and Presbyterian Church, Castle Square, Caernarfon, 2017

The Eagle Tower is the most impressive of Caernarfon's defences. When first constructed in the thirteenth century it became a castle in its own right. Wooden barricades were built to protect the stonemasons from Welsh attacks, but work was often interrupted while they retired to the Eagle Tower for protection. The most westerly of the castle's structures, the Eagle Tower has three turrets which once bore stone eagles. A water-gate allowed provisions to be received by river or sea. Built in 1883, the Gothic-style Presbyterian church is a Grade II listed building, designed by Richard Owen of Liverpool. The contractor was Richard Williams of Bank Quay, Caernarfon.

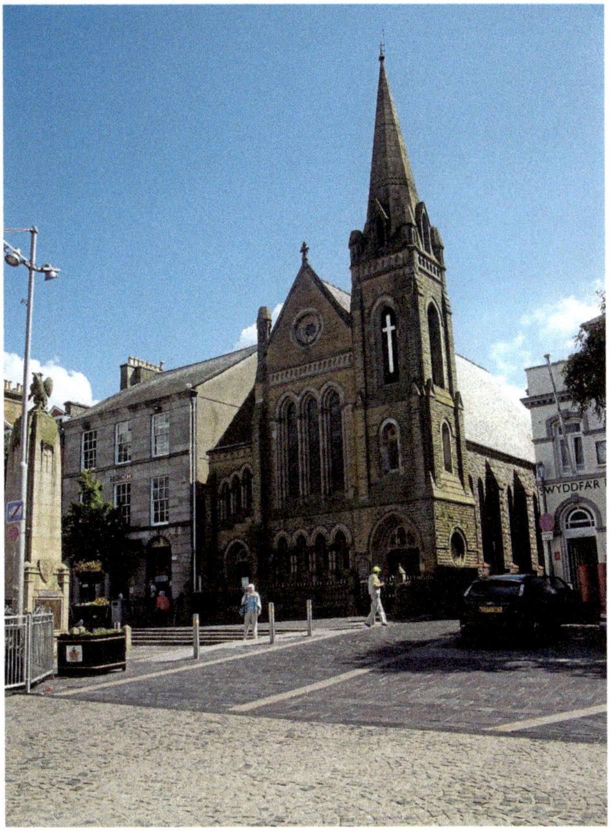

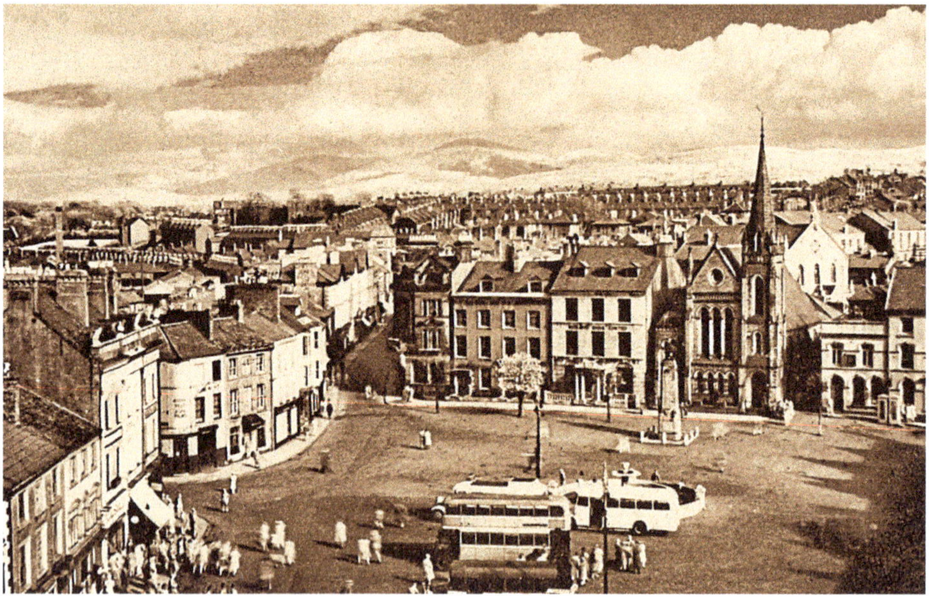

Castle Square, Caernarfon, c. 1950

This photograph of Castle Square in the 1950s shows it in an era when people relied upon public transport to a much greater extent than today. Therefore the whole set-up of Castle Square was geared towards provision for buses, long before the increase in private motor vehicles in the 1960s and 1970s. This means the space has had two separate traffic systems in operation in the last half century. The recent redesign of the Square attempts to readdress these issues.

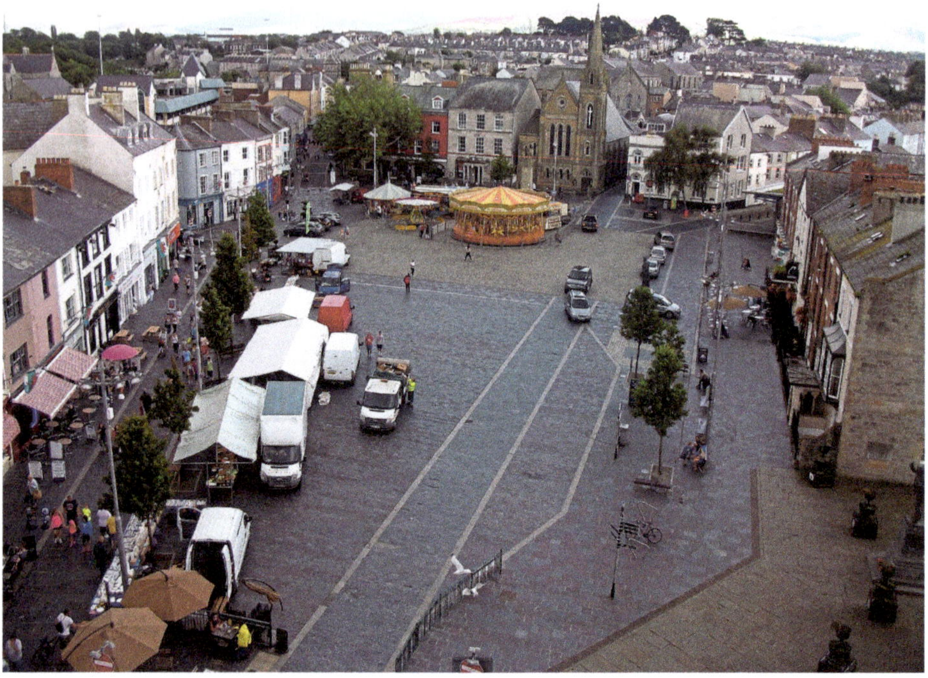

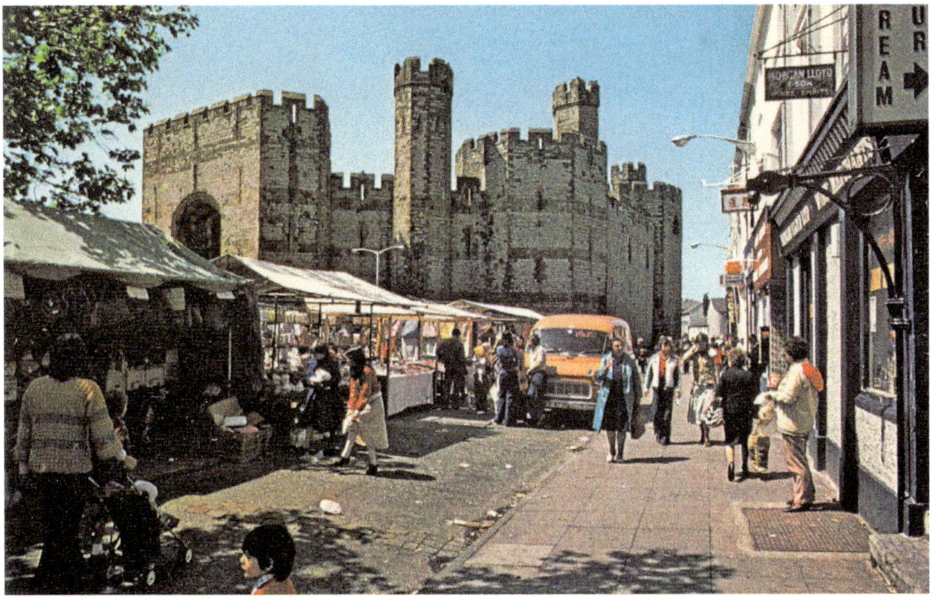

Market Day, Castle Square, Caernarfon, *c.* 1970

This area of Caernarfon is known as 'Y Maes' by local people and, as the photograph from around 1970 illustrates, it is the market square of the town. A market is held here every Saturday throughout the year and also on Mondays in the summer. Caernarfon became a Borough in 1284, although Hugh de Avranches, the Earl of Chester who built a motte around 1090, may also have granted Borough status to Caernarfon. However, it was Welsh occupation which made Caernarfon an administrative centre.

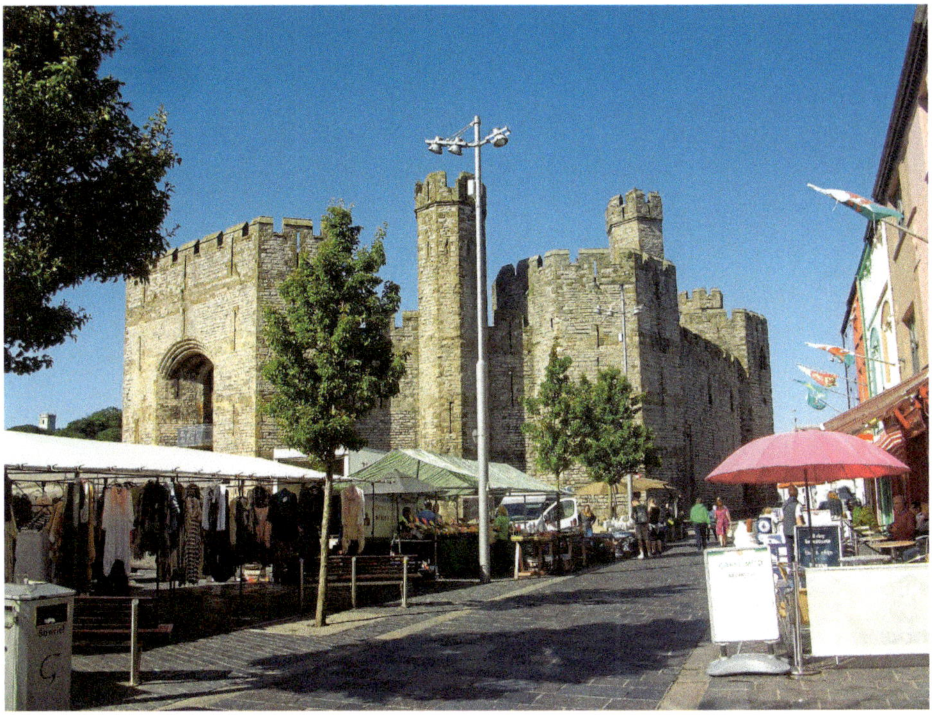

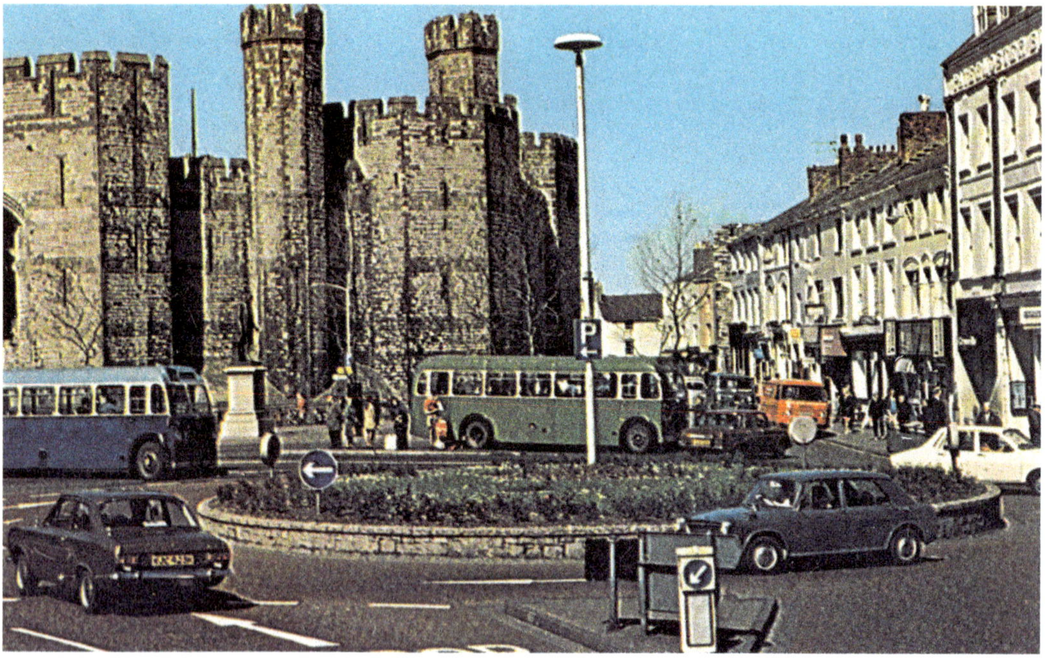

Castle Square and Roundabout, Caernarfon, *c.* 1970

Once the town became more established, a small suburb beyond the Eastgate was developed by the early fifteenth century. However, this was destroyed during the Glyndwr revolt in 1400. Despite these early setbacks, Caernarfon's importance as a commercial centre continued to outweigh its political influence. Apart from the aforementioned market, within and without the town walls, there were four annual fairs after 1352. In more recent times it has become a centre for the modern Gwynedd County Council and the National Assembly for Wales.

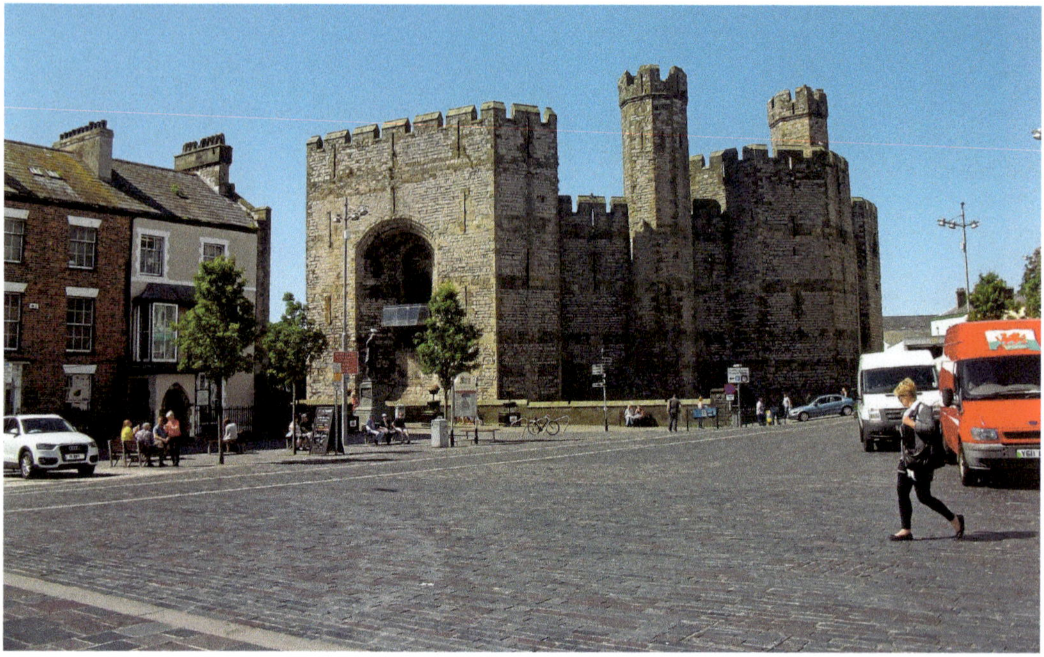

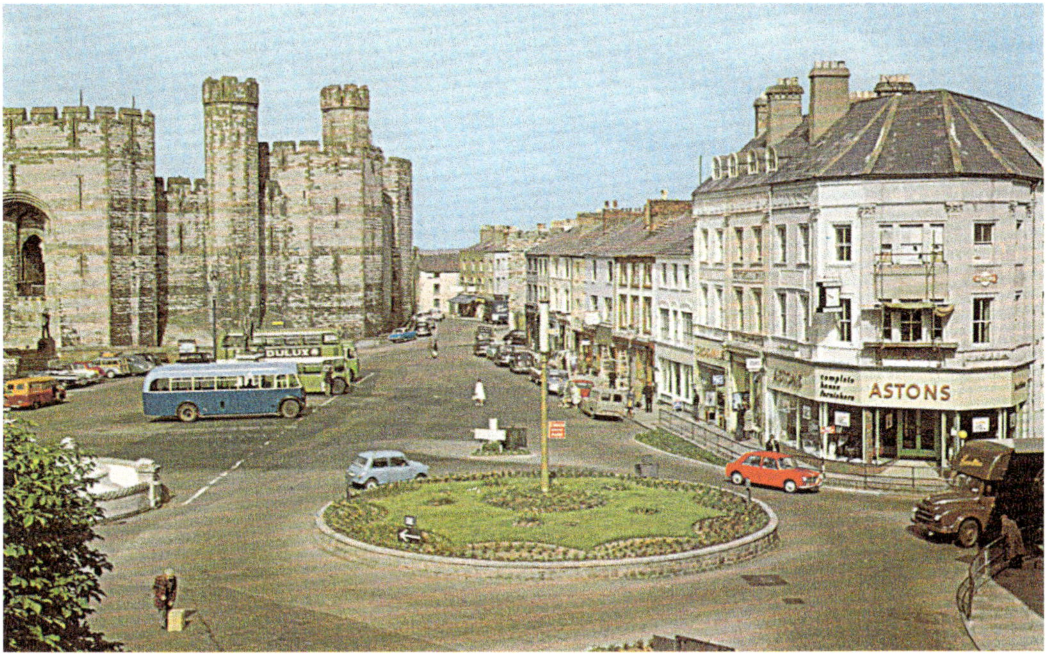

Caernarfon Castle, Castle Square and Roundabout, *c.* 1970
The roundabout which managed the busy traffic streams that passed through Caernarfon is again evident here. The changes that have taken place in the intervening years have led to clearer views of Caernarfon Castle and the other historic buildings located within the Square. The unique architectural importance of the Presbyterian church, the adjacent banks and the War Memorial counter the dominance of the castle. A new fountain and a stepped area help to 'soften' the view.

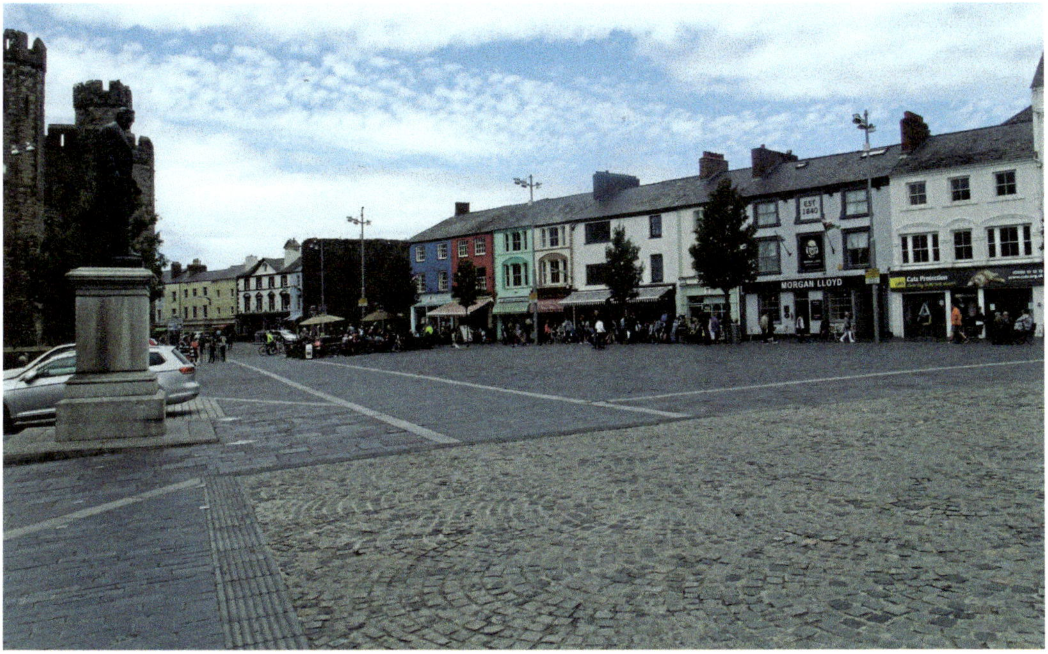

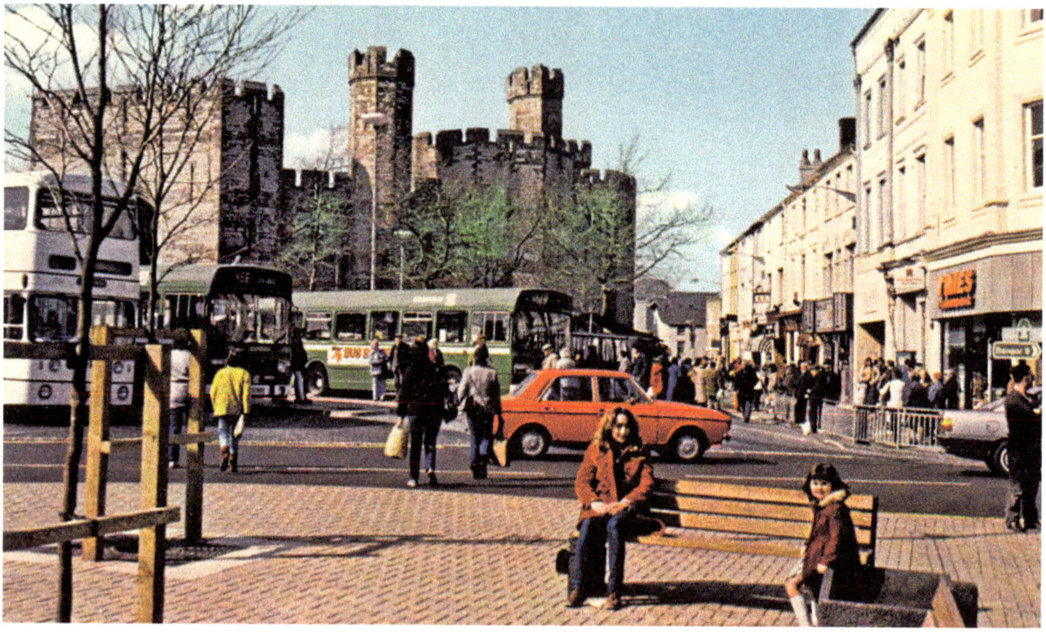

Caernarfon Castle and Castle Square, *c.* 1970

The town's main Square is part of a World Heritage Site and was previously dominated by roundabouts which managed the busy traffic streams that passed through Caernarfon; it was also a terminus for the various public bus services which worked Caernarfon's routes. Therefore, as can be seen in this photograph, the view of Caernarfon Castle from the Square was rather restricted. Guard-rails, as seen on the right side of the photograph, hemmed in pedestrians and constrained their access to the Square.

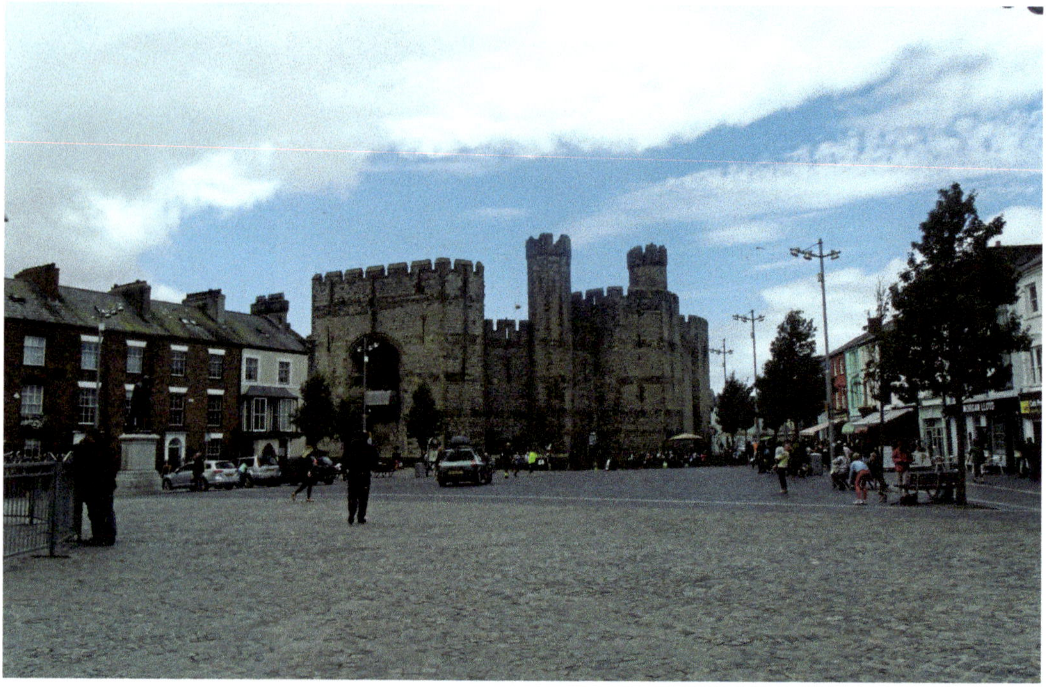

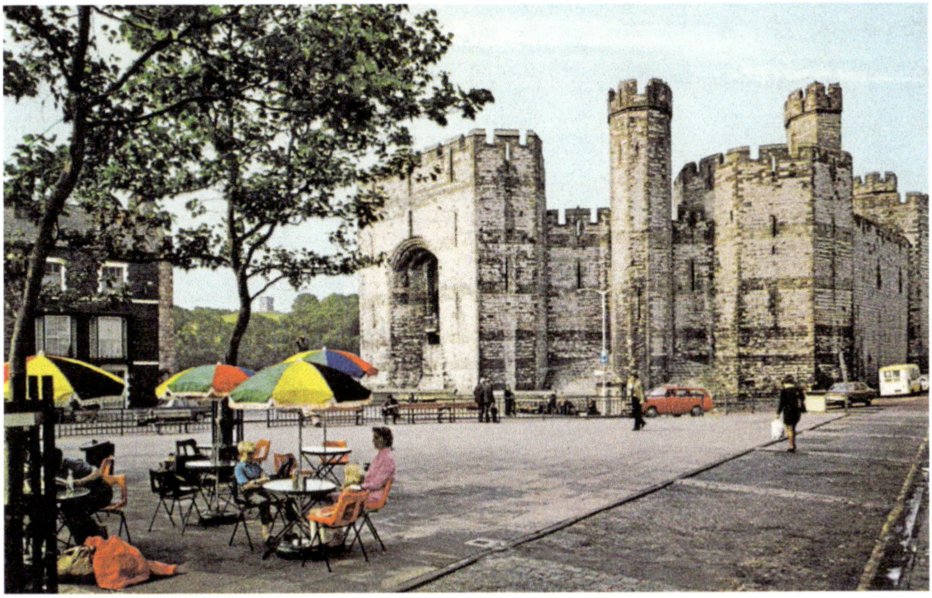

Caernarfon Castle and Castle Square, *c.* 1975

Existing sculptures have been relocated in the new Square, although that of David Lloyd George remains in its original location, close to Queen Eleanor's Gate and overlooking the town which he served as an MP. The new surfacing materials used in the Square include locally sourced Welsh slate and granite, all from within 48 kilometres (30 miles) of Caernarfon. The photograph shows people relaxing and enjoying the café atmosphere of the Square, which is something that locals and tourists alike continue to do today.

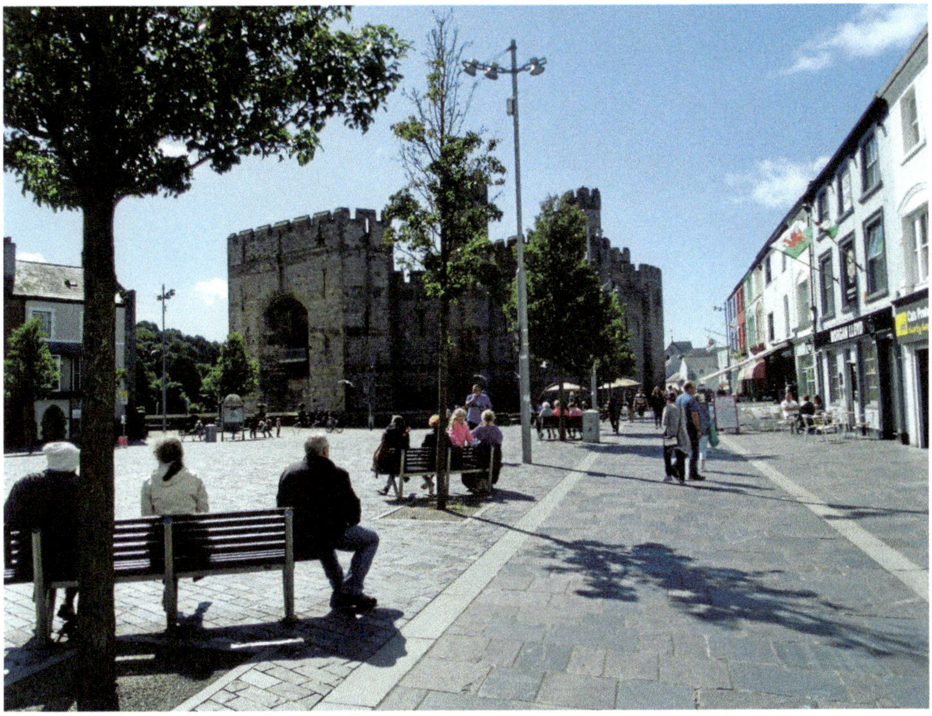

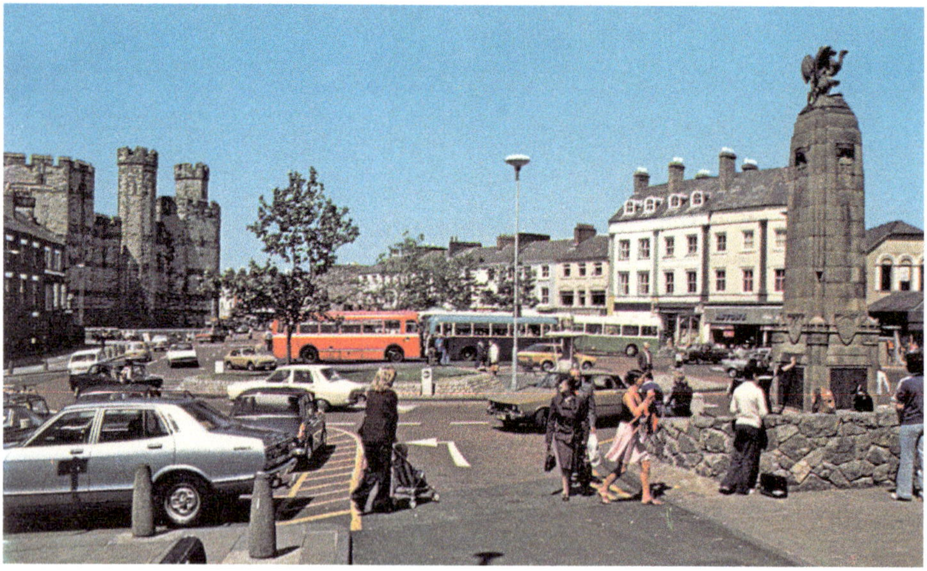

Castle Square and War Memorial, Looking Towards the Market, Caernarfon, *c.* 1976
***Inset*: Old Market Hall, Hole-in-the-Wall Street and Crown Street**

Under Welsh control, Caernarfon became a Royal residence and the administrative centre of Gwynedd. Once military and administrative influence had passed into the hands of Edward I work began on the construction of a new castle and town, in 1283. Caernarfon then rapidly became the administrative and judicial centre of the new Principality of North Wales. Despite an attack and brief Welsh occupation in 1294 the town continued to develop. A small marketplace was established within the town walls (inset) and a larger one without.

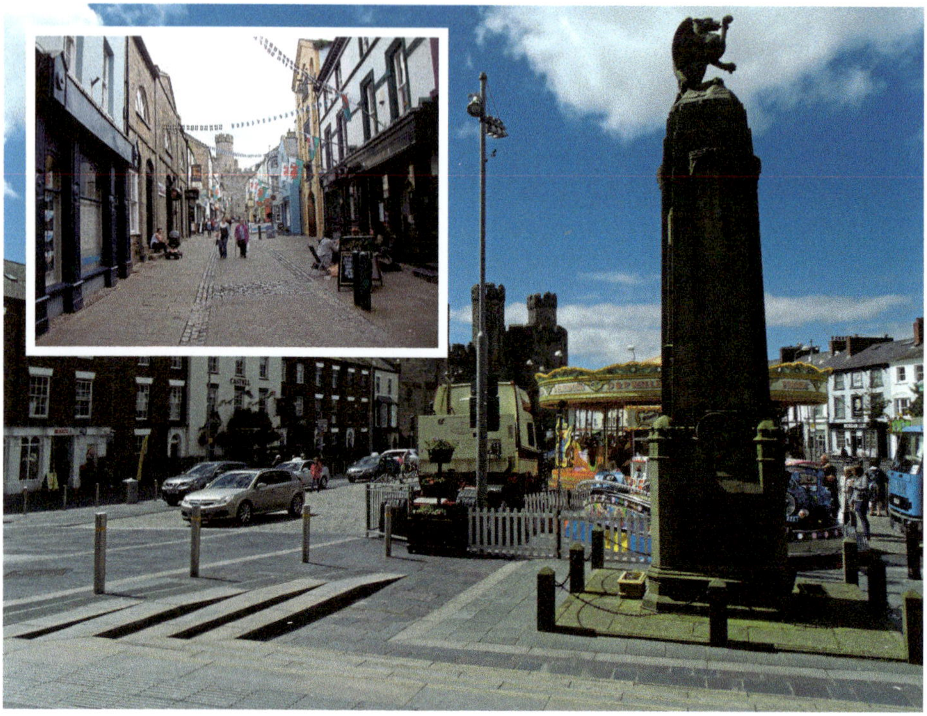

Right: David Lloyd George MP, 1907

Below: Scenes Depicting the Paris Peace Conference, 1919, on the Statue in Castle Square

Inset: Llanystumdwy Schoolroom

The statue of David Lloyd George is located in Castle Square and was sculpted by W. Goscombe John (1860–1952). It was erected in 1921 when Lloyd George was the Prime Minister. He was the Member of Parliament for the area from 1890 to 1945. A Liberal politician, he helped to lay the foundations of the modern welfare state and was influential in the Paris Peace Conference of 1919. Lloyd George was the only Welsh-speaking British Prime Minister to have spoken English as a second language.

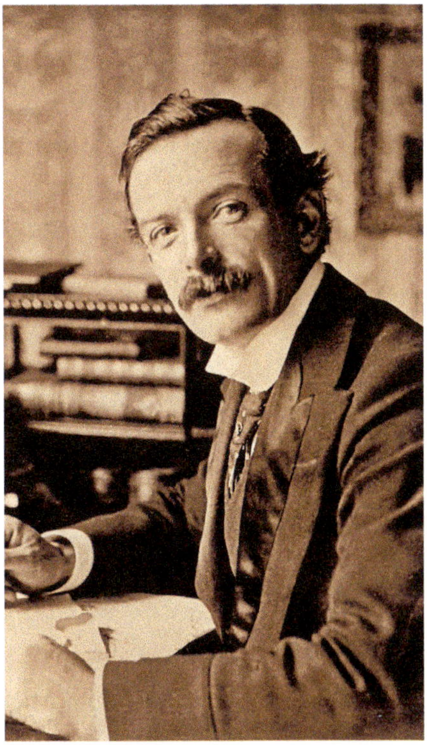

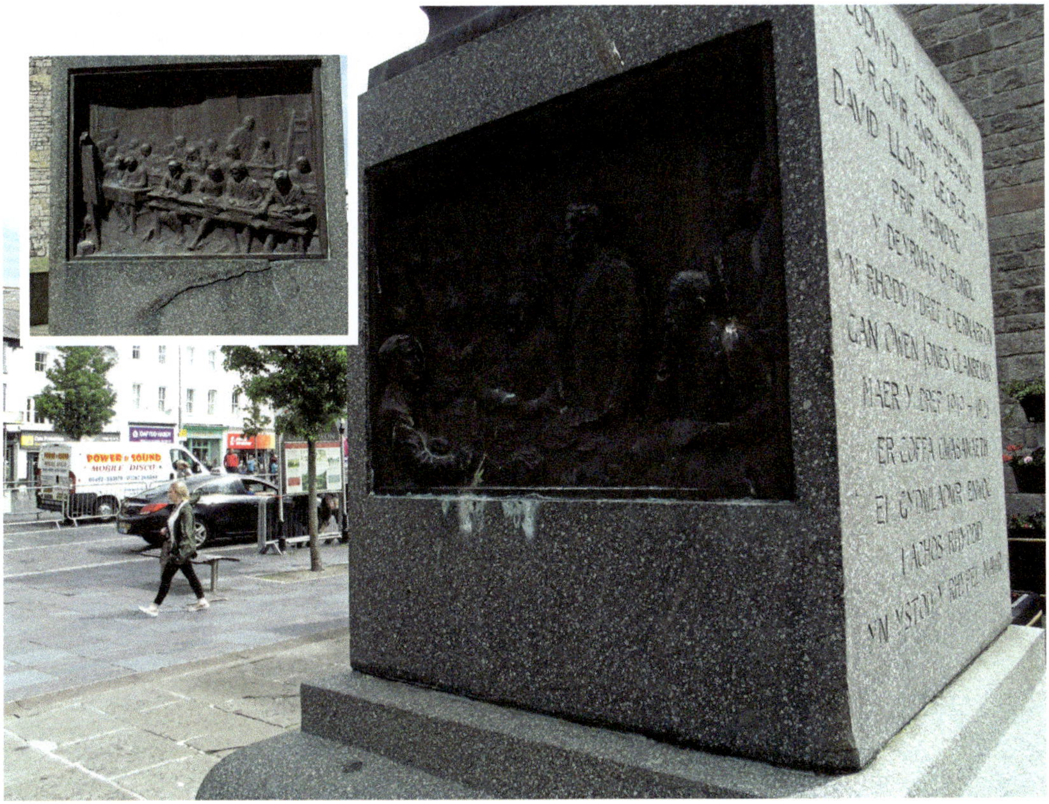

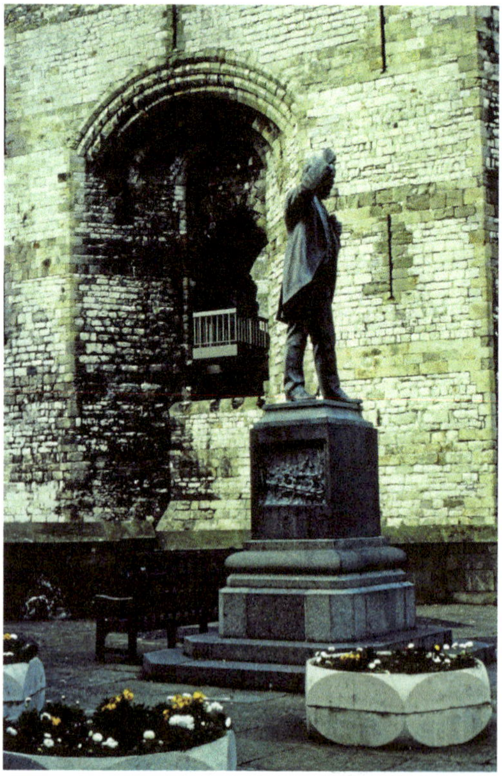

Statue of David Lloyd George MP, Castle Square, Caernarfon, *c.* 1975

Lloyd George was born in Chorlton-on-Medlock, Manchester, in 1863 to Welsh-speaking parents, and died at Llanystumdwy in 1945. The statue is made of bronze and there are two bronze reliefs representing the Peace Conference, Paris, in 1919, and the village school, Llanystumdwy. The statue was unveiled on 6 August 1921 by W. M. Hughes, the prime minister of Australia, whose father came from North Wales. It was a gift to the town from Owen Jones Glanbeuno, Mayor of Caernarfon from 1919 to 1921.

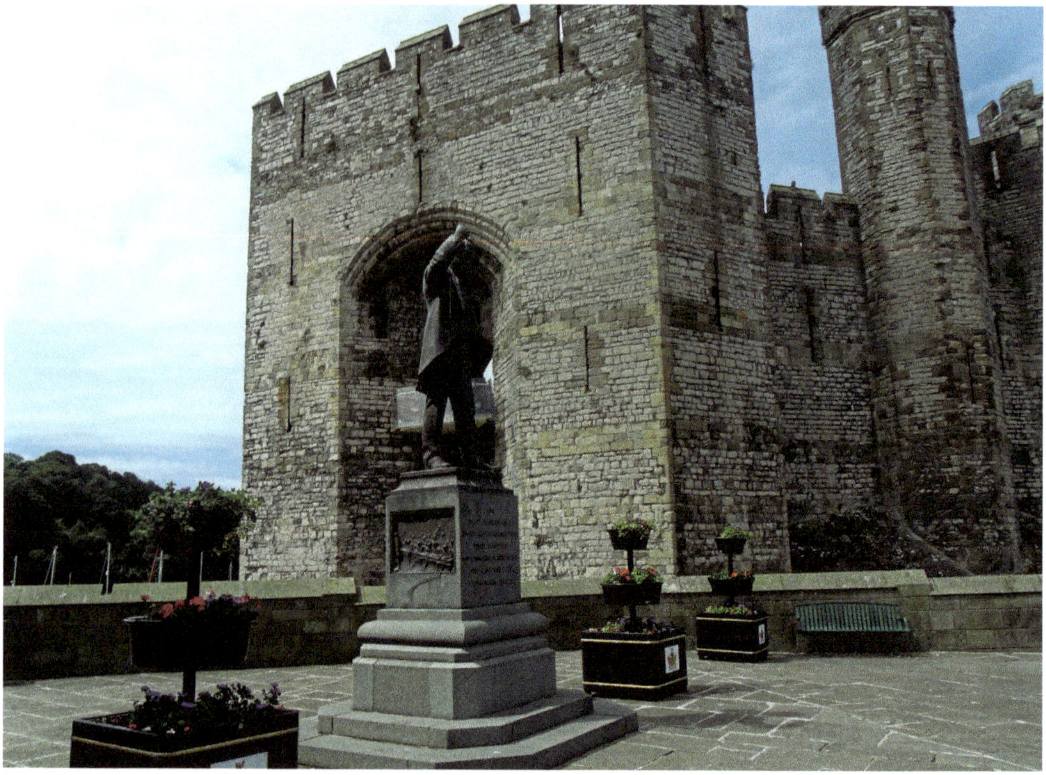

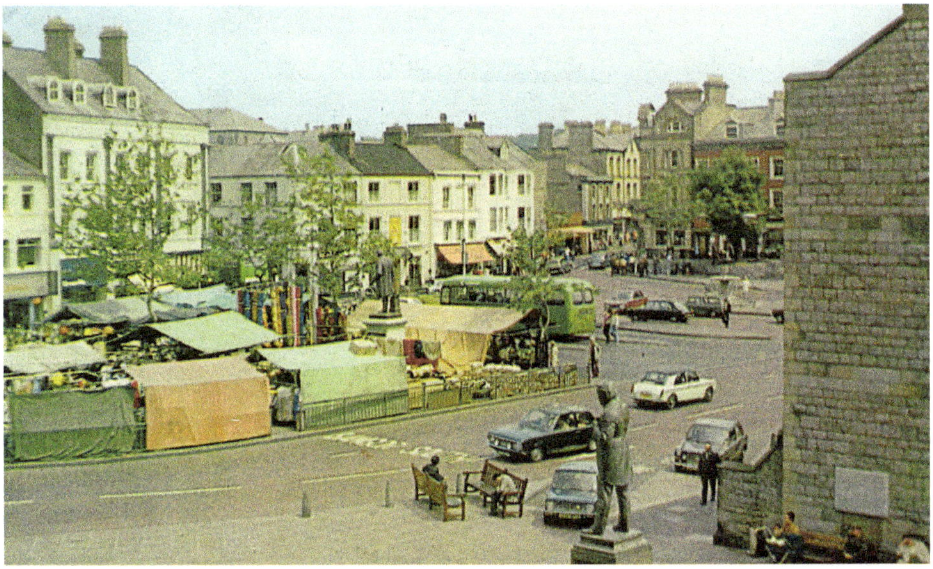

Castle Square and Statues of Sir Hugh Owen and David Lloyd George, Caernarfon, 1975
This view of Castle Square has changed very little since the above photograph was taken, even though Y Maes has been redesigned and updated since 1975. The market is still held at the same spot, the main difference being that the statue of Sir Hugh Owen (1804–1881) – who pioneered higher education in Wales – has been moved further back, in order to open up the Square. Ysgol Syr Hugh Owen, Caernarfon's secondary school, is named after him, as is the main library at Aberystwyth University.

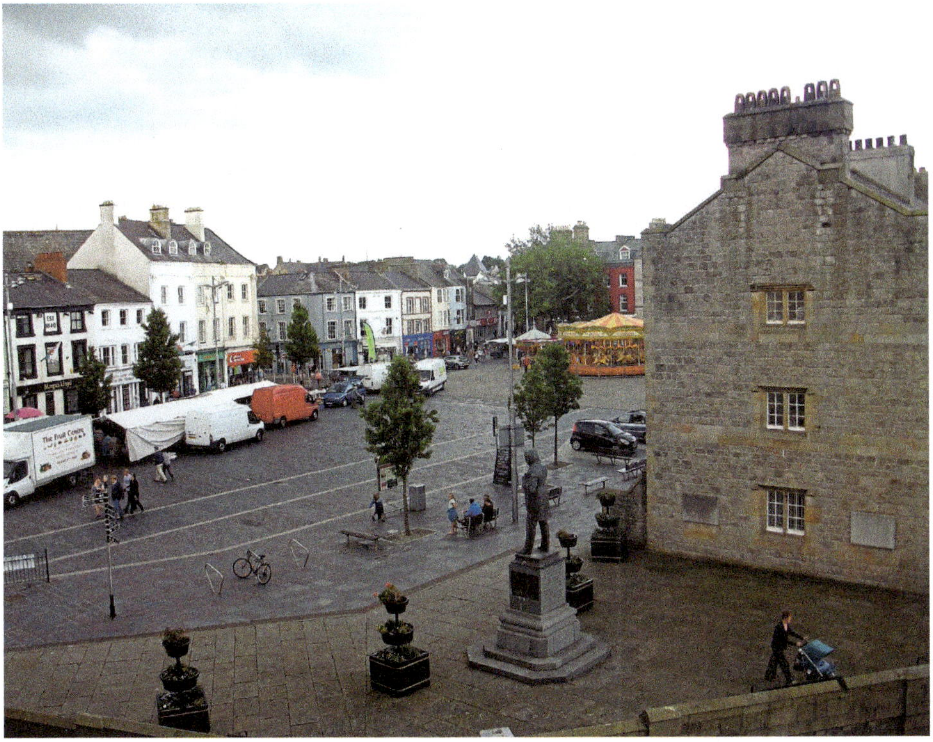

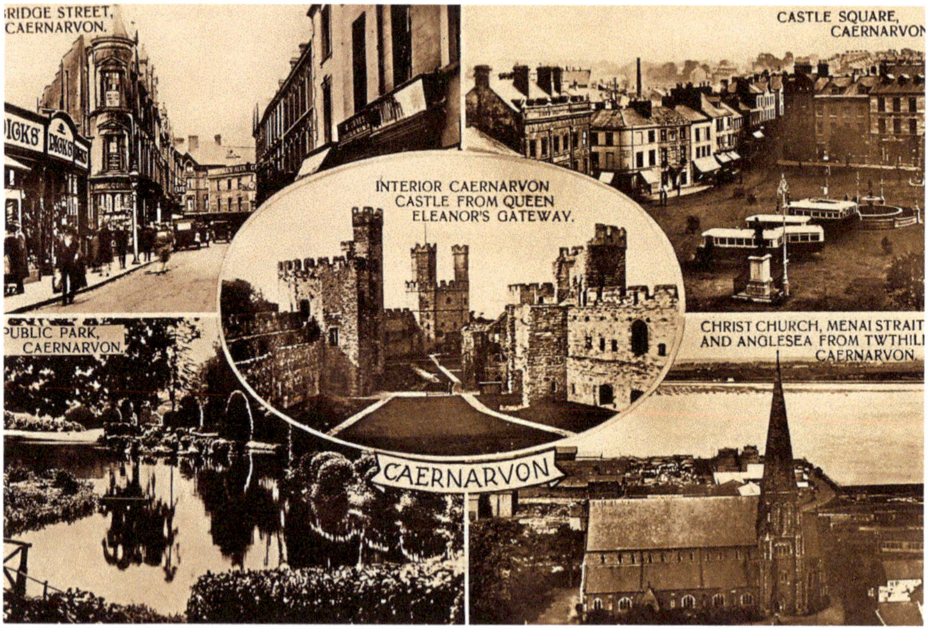

Bridge Street (Y Bont Bridd), Caernarfon, 1930
***Inset*: from Castle Square, 2017**

The distinctive frontages of the retail establishments on the left of Bridge Street (Y Bont Bridd) remain recognisable and intact today. These include the familiar 'spire' in the centre foreground of both photographs (top left of the multi-view). The public house in the centre background of both images is the Harp, located at South Penrallt. Unfortunately, this establishment has fallen upon hard times recently and has been offered for sale, although it remains in a prime location in the town centre.

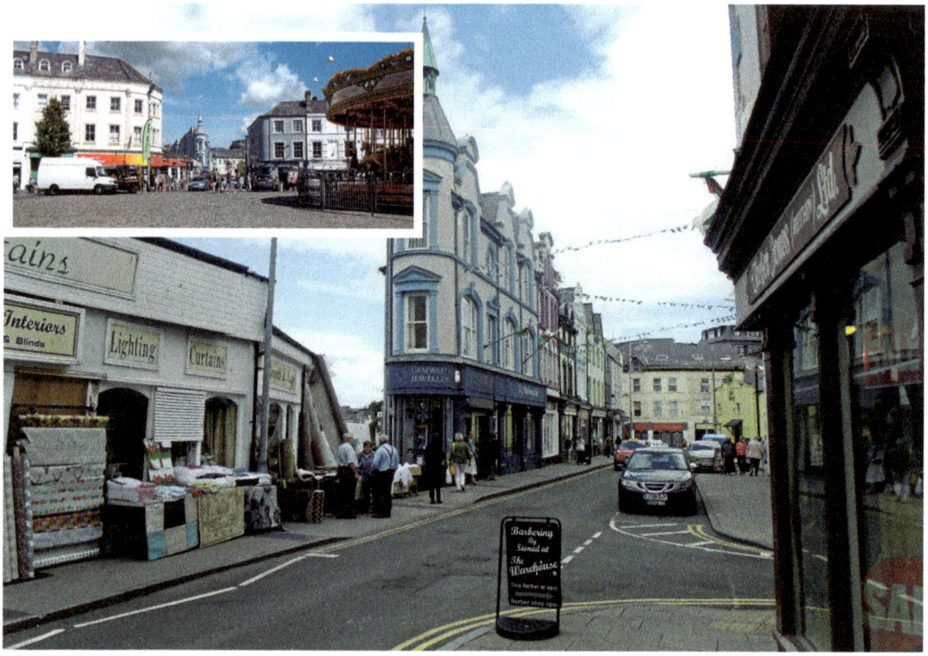

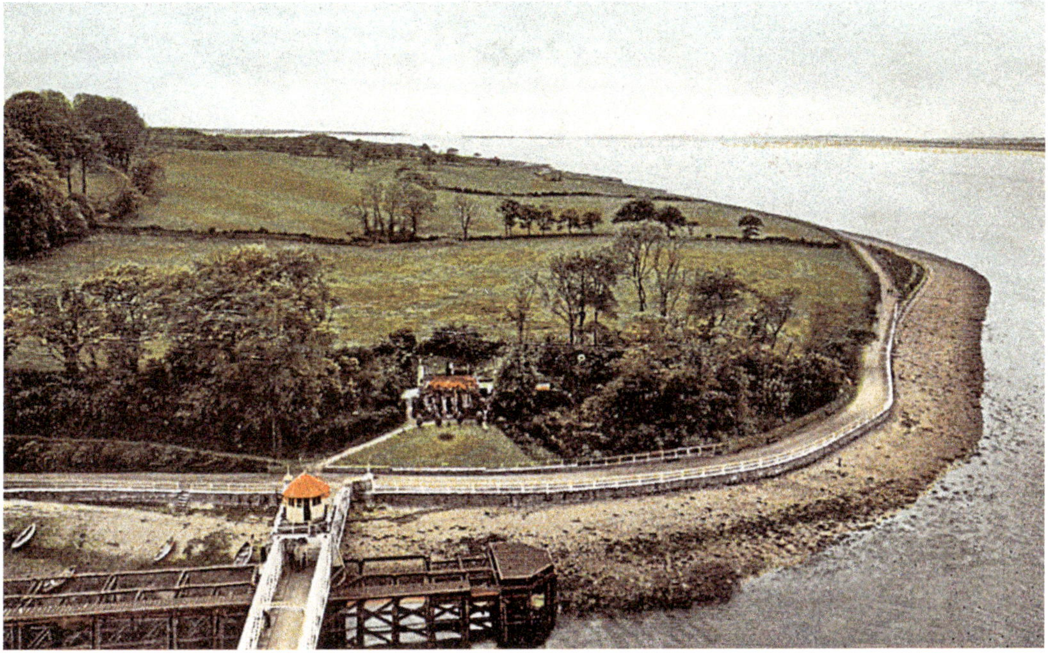

Coed Helen from the Castle, Caernarfon, *c.* 1910

The site is now the location of a holiday park, near to the town of Caernarfon, but set back from general view. There is also a small play area located on adjoining fields. This area has uninterrupted views across the Menai Strait towards Anglesey and inland across the mountains of Snowdonia. The campsite is less than 1.6 kilometres (1 mile) from Caernarfon and less than 8 kilometres (5 miles) from Snowdonia National Park. There are footpaths which follow the coastline and cross the footbridge and Afon Seiont.

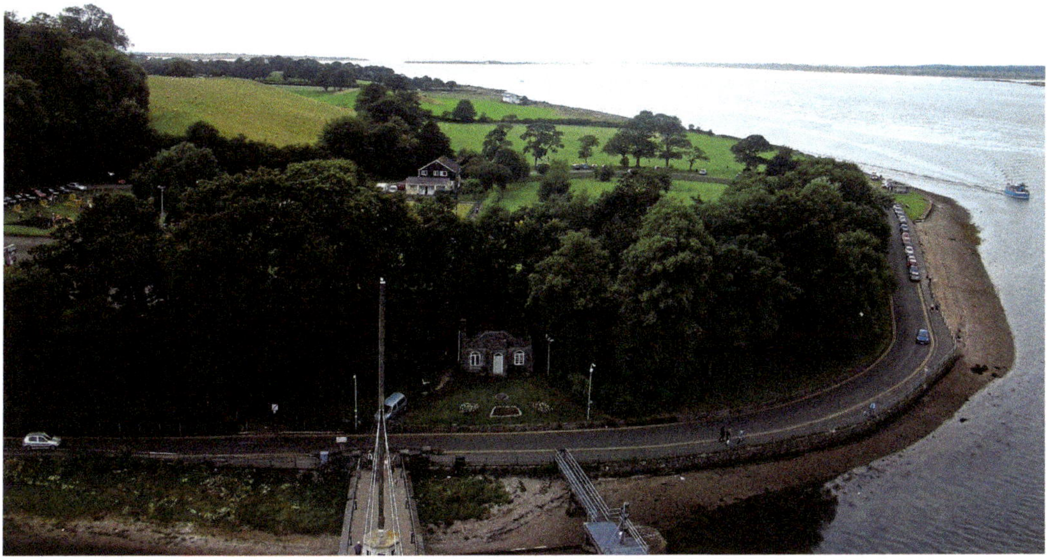

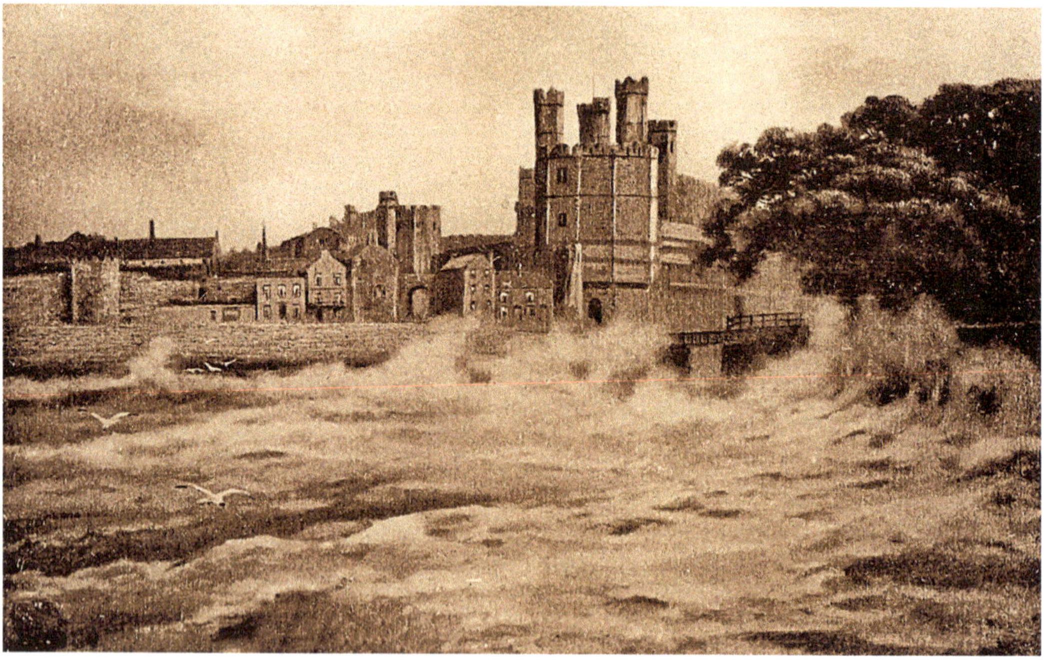

Caernarfon Castle and Rough Sea, *c.* 1900

Caernarfon lies just inside the southerly entrance to the Menai Strait, which is a highly tidal stretch of water. In order to enter the harbour Caernarfon Bar must be crossed, which is a dangerous task in onshore conditions. Its reputation, and that of the 'Swellies' in the Menai Strait, is often enough to deter boat owners from visiting the area at all. Sandbanks extend for 4.8 kilometres (3 miles) from the coast and are constantly shifting, with tides in the vicinity capable of reaching 5 knots.

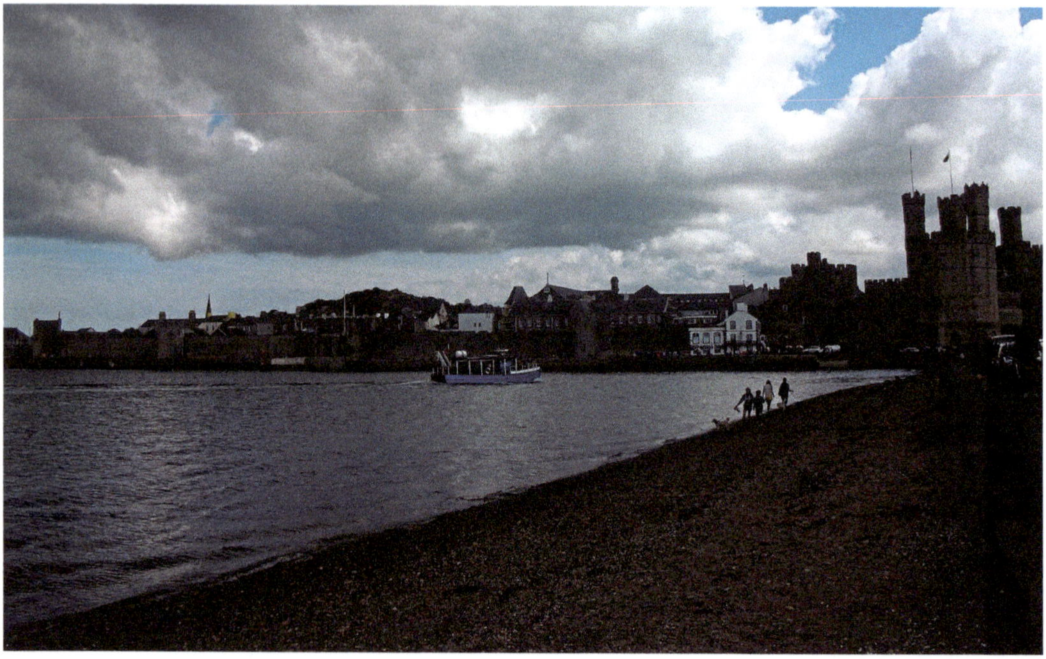

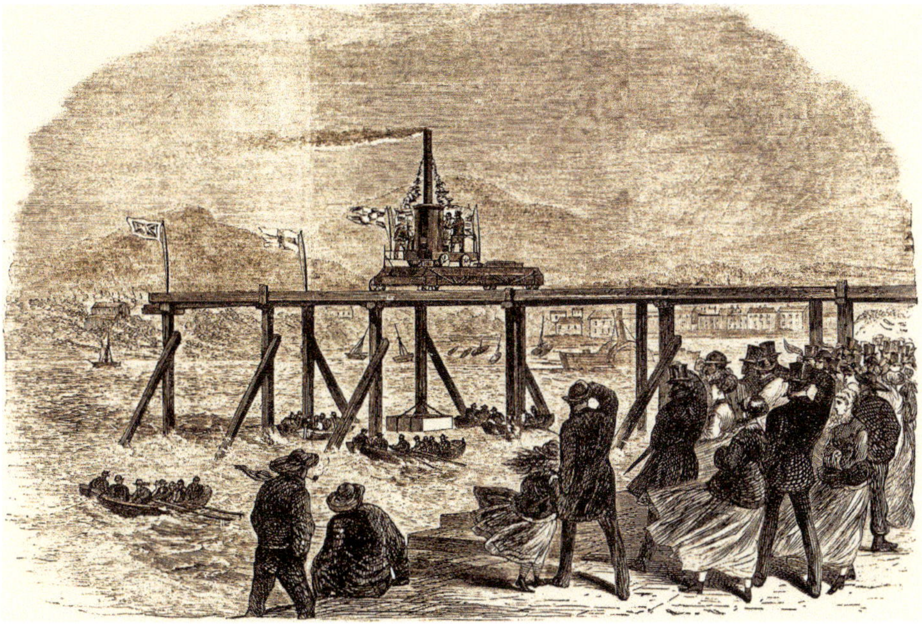

Laying the Foundation Stone of the New Harbour Works, Victoria Dock (Doc Fictoria), Caernarfon, 1868

The Victoria Dock was built in 1868 and originally intended for the import of mostly timber from Scandinavia. However, it was the arrival of the railways that heralded the steady decline of commercial shipping and saw the Victoria Dock decline as a result, eventually ceasing its commercial activities. In 1997 it was purchased by Gwynedd Council, who transformed the site into the Victoria Dock Marina. Complete with berths for sea-going private boats and yachts, the Marina also has extensive coastguard facilities.

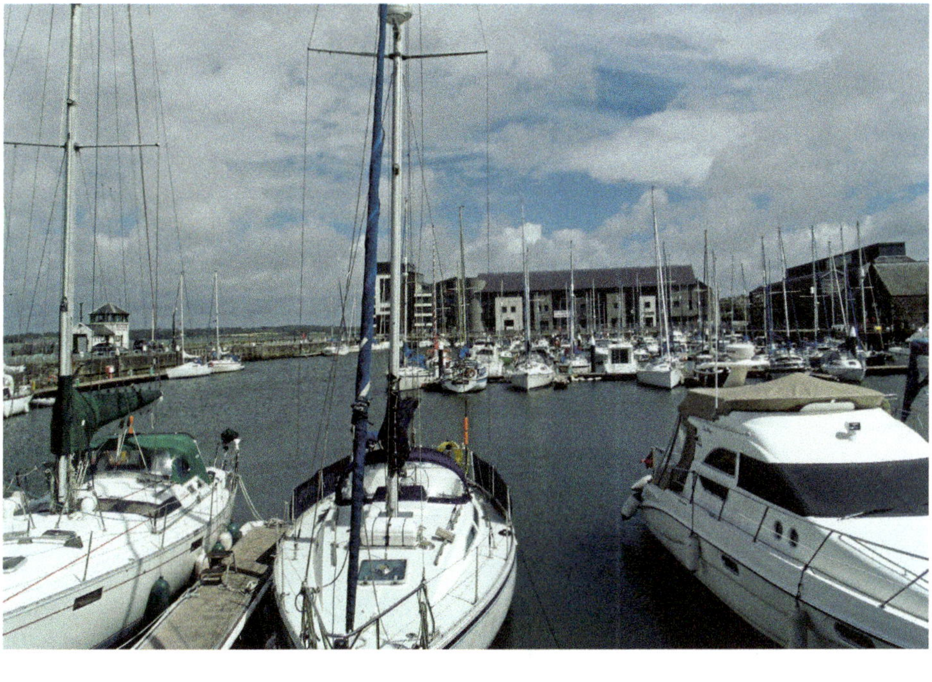

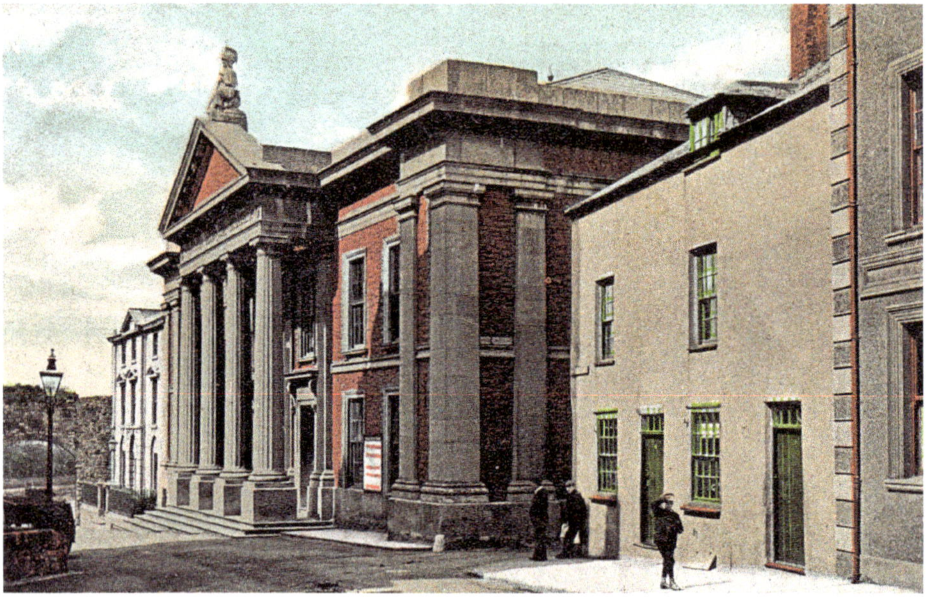

County Hall, Pen Deitsh (Castle Ditch), Caernarfon, 1906
The County Hall was built in 1863 and later became the County Court. It is a neoclassical style columned building and was Grade I listed in 1953. It is adjacent to the Anglesey Arms Hotel and the Gwynedd County Council buildings. The old buildings adjoin what used to be Caernarfon gaol, which has been closed since the early twentieth century and has now been converted into further council offices. The old County Court building recently underwent refurbishment as a private dwelling.

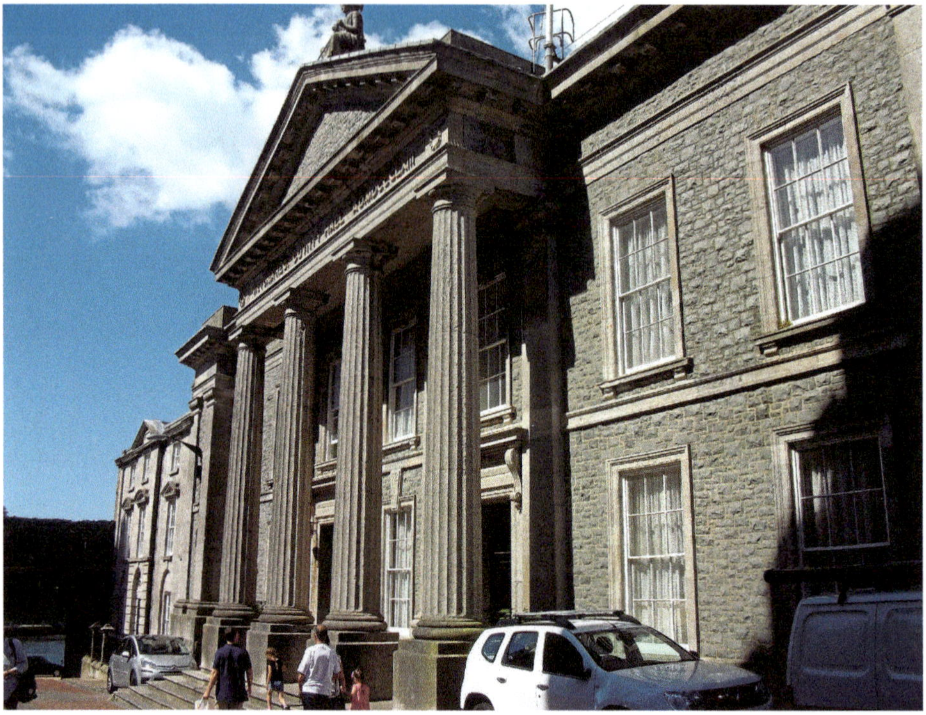

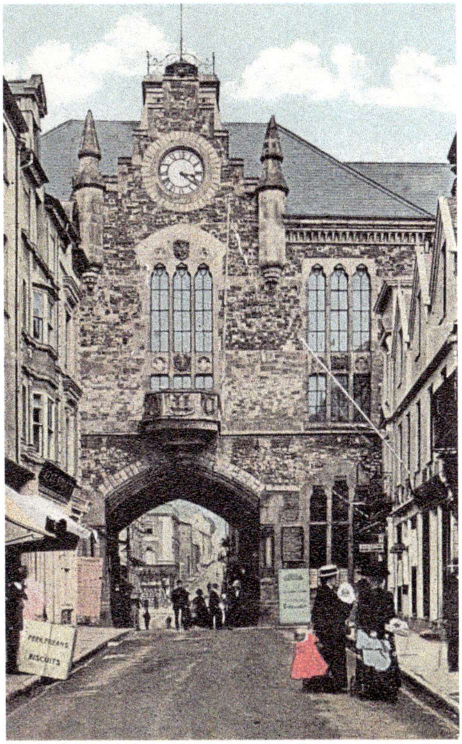

The Guildhall, Looking Towards Bridge Street (Y Bont Bridd), Caernarfon, *c.* 1900

The modern view is from Bridge Street, due to building work. The main entrance to the old-walled town was once a lock-up and watch-house. The rooms above the gateway were used by the Exchequer in 1284 and it was the site of the town's curfew bell. In 1767 it became the Guildhall. There was a large, gas-lit, illuminated clock with four faces housed within its high tower. However, it had to be removed because it was dangerous to vessels sailing at night.

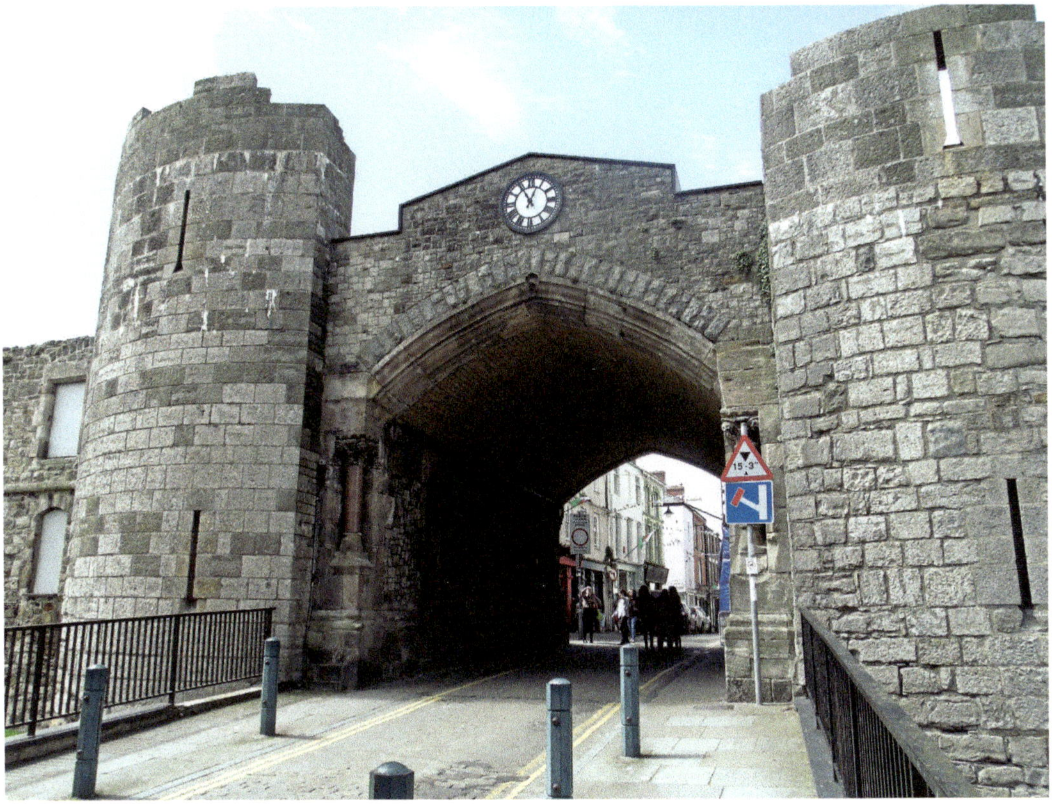

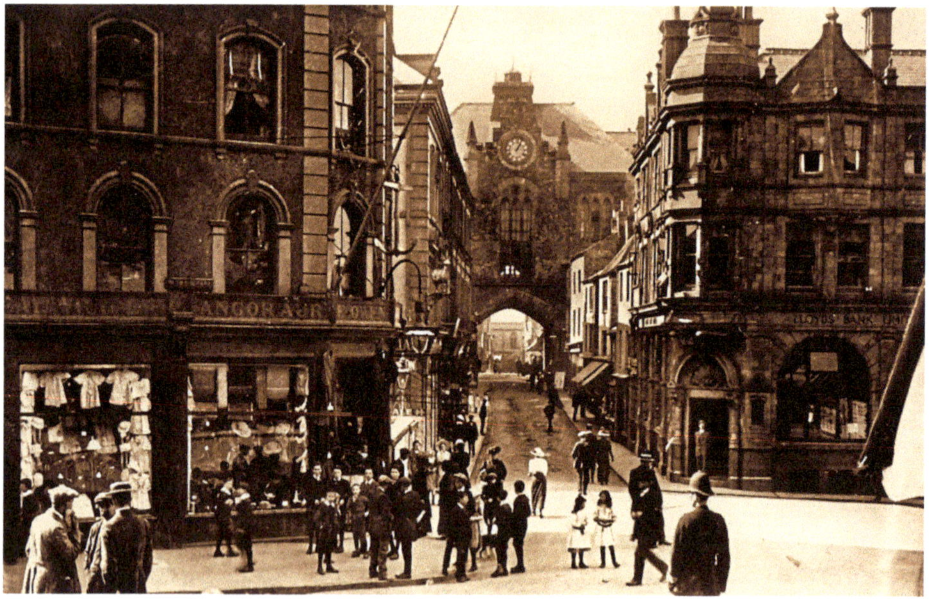

Guildhall (y Cloc Mawr or Eastgate), from Bridge Street, Caernarfon, 1914

The original photograph was taken from the junction of High Street (Stryd Fawr) and Bridge Street (Y Bont Bridd), where there is a policeman on 'point duty' at this busy crossroads. While the buildings on the left and right of the photograph are still here today, I have moved the modern view towards the right (Turf Square) in order to emphasise the changes that have taken place to the former Guildhall and surrounding buildings, which were once council offices in the twentieth century.

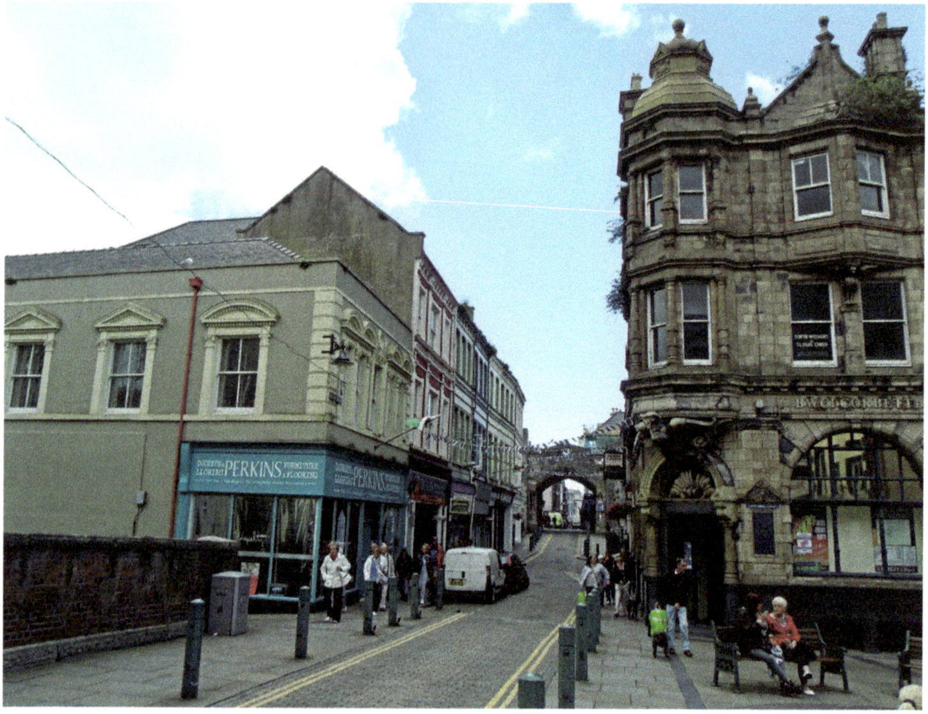

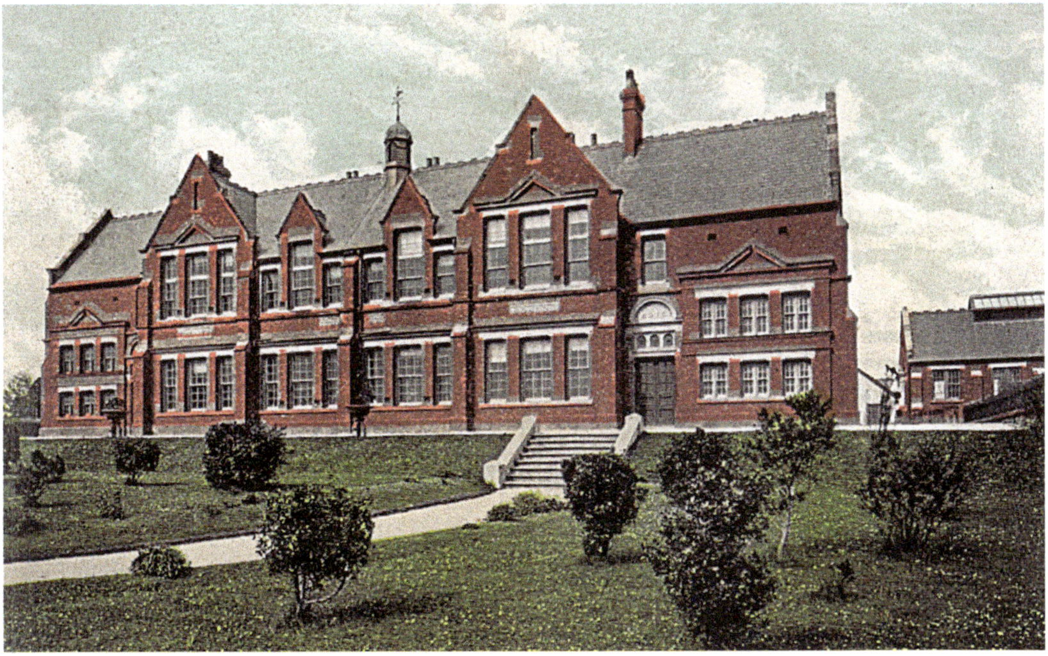

Caernarfon County School, Bethel Road, 1907

The first intermediate school was established in Caernarfon and received Royal assent in 1893, opening in February 1894. Originally known as Caernarfon County School, it was later renamed in honour of Sir Hugh Owen. He was an advocate of educational reform, supporting the idea of non-denominational day schools, the establishment of intermediate schools, the training of more teachers to staff them, and the need for more universities to facilitate their training. He was influential in the Welsh Intermediate Education Act of 1889.

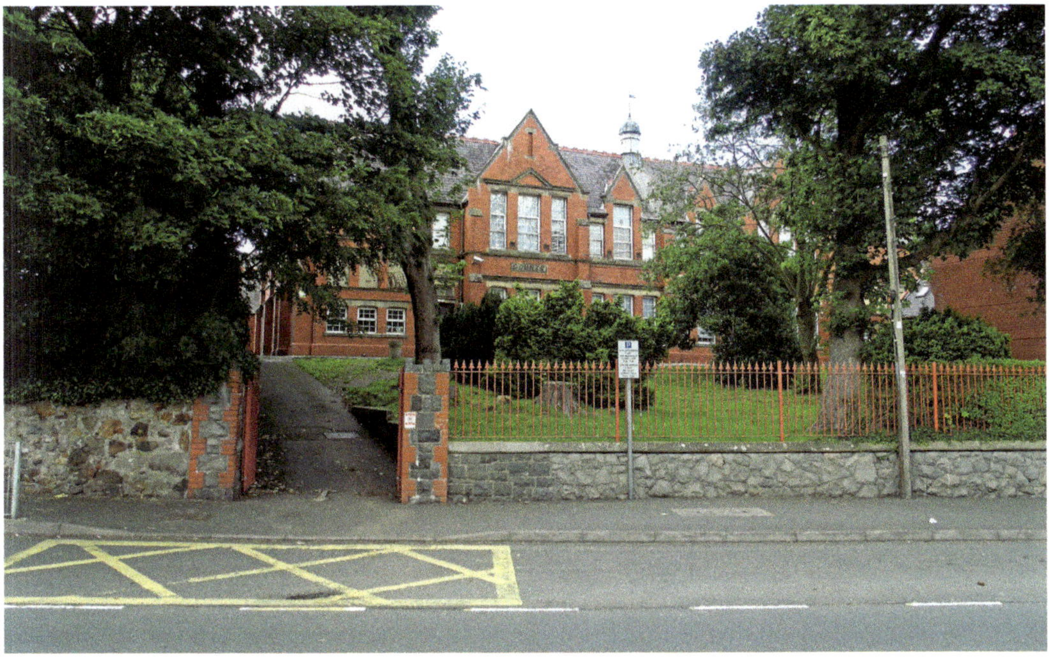

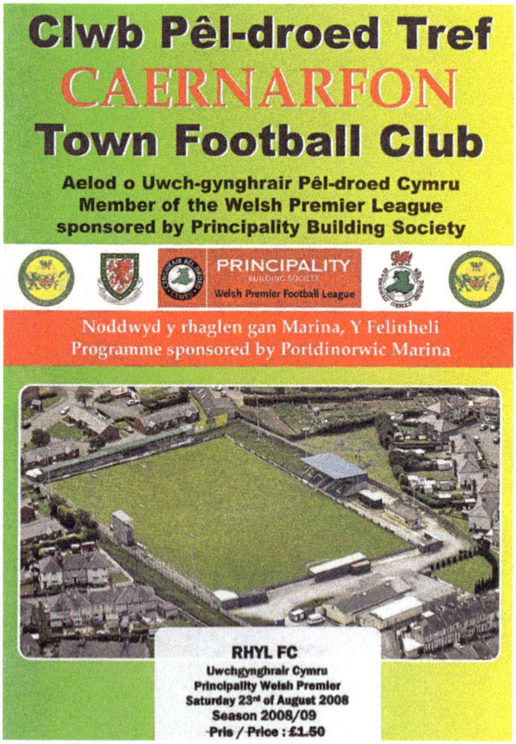

Caernarfon Town FC *v.* Rhyl FC, 2008/09

Caernarfon Town FC were founded in 1937, entering the Welsh League (North) Division One, where they were to remain for thirty-nine years. They won the championship in the 1946/47 and 1965/66 seasons. However, in 1976 the club withdrew from the league after only six matches, only to re-form and return to league football just twelve months later. Caernarfon Town FC then won the title in the 1977/78 and 1978/79 seasons, losing only one game in total, and leading to their joining the Lancashire Combination League.

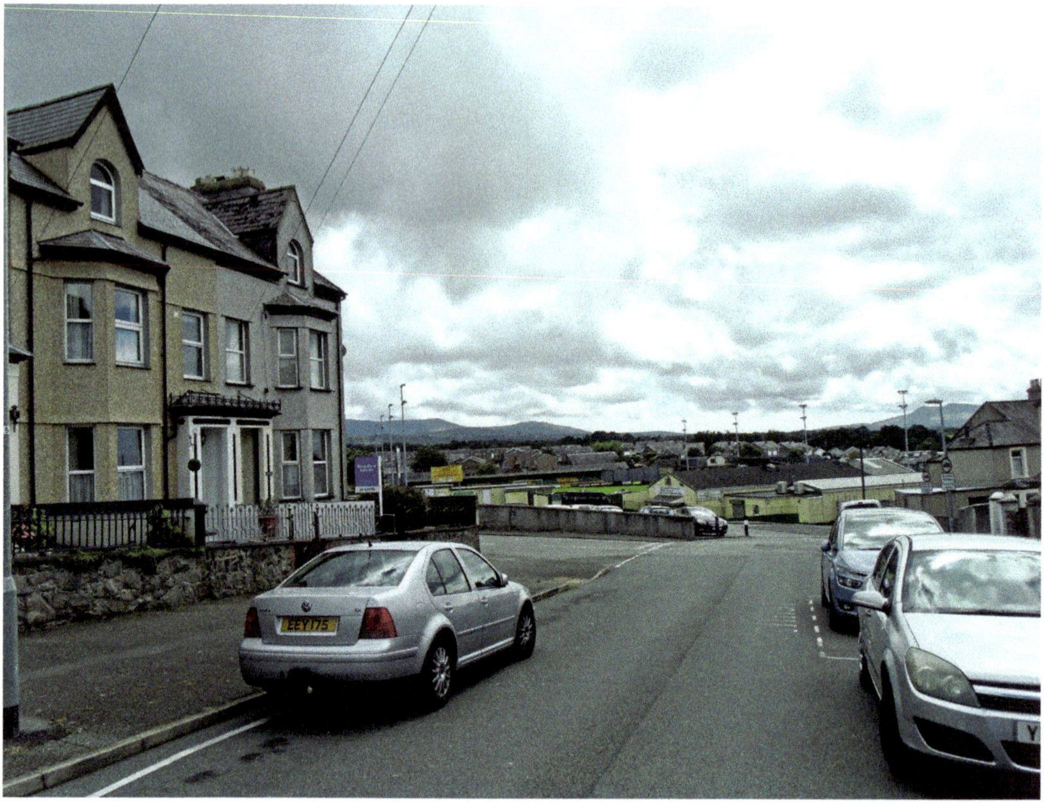

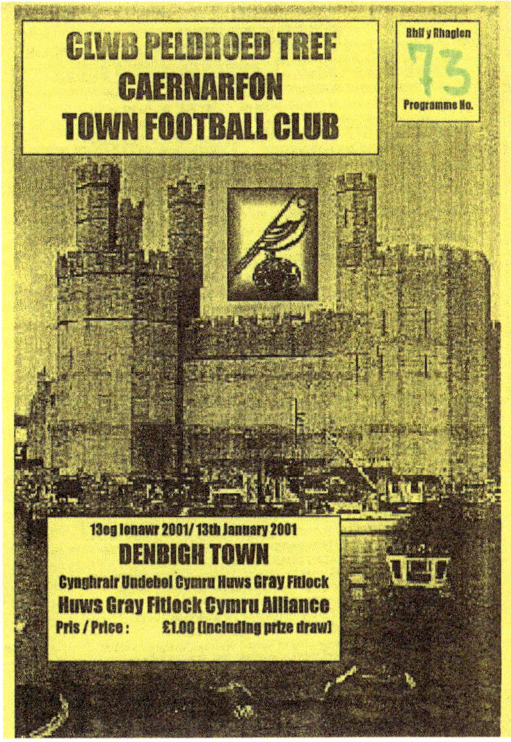

Caernarfon Town FC *v.* Denbigh Town FC, 2001

Caernarfon Town FC won the Combination Cup in 1981, followed by the League Championship in 1981/82. This success led to their competing in the Northern Premier League. They returned to the League of Wales in August 1995. The team play in a yellow and green strip, and have been nicknamed the Canaries since 1895. They play at the Oval, where the club's fans are known as the 'Cofi Army'. Their stadium accommodates 3,000 (500 seated) and at the time of writing they are playing in the Cymru Alliance in 2017/18.

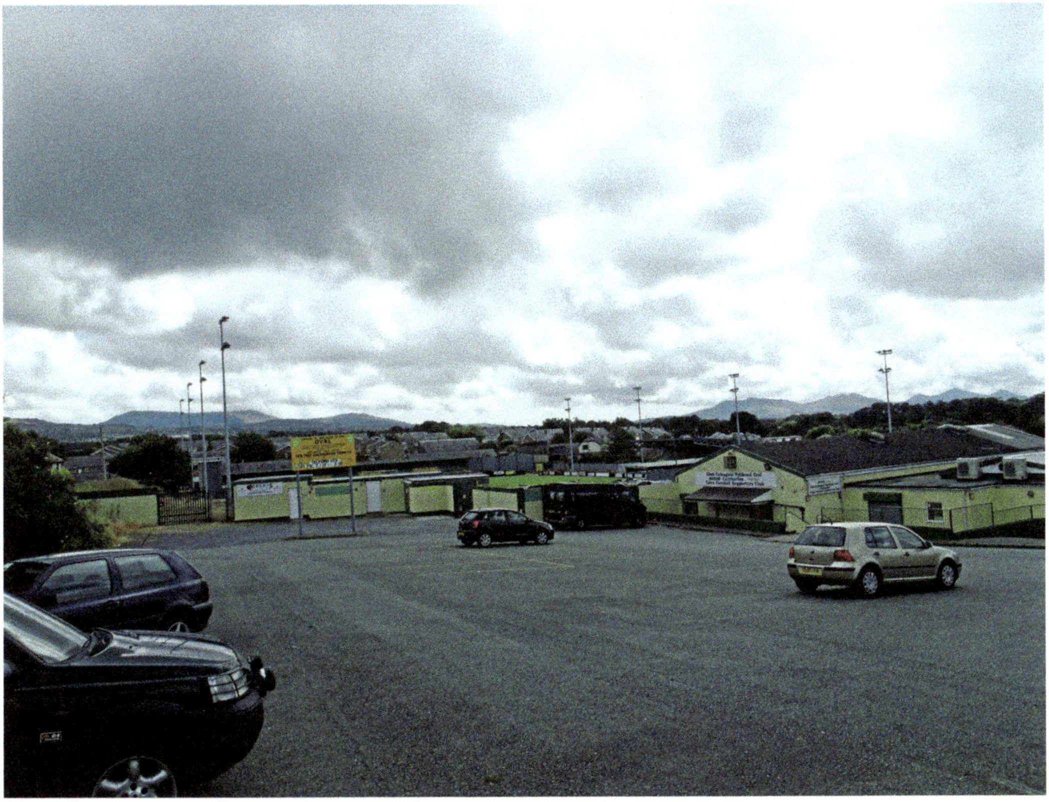

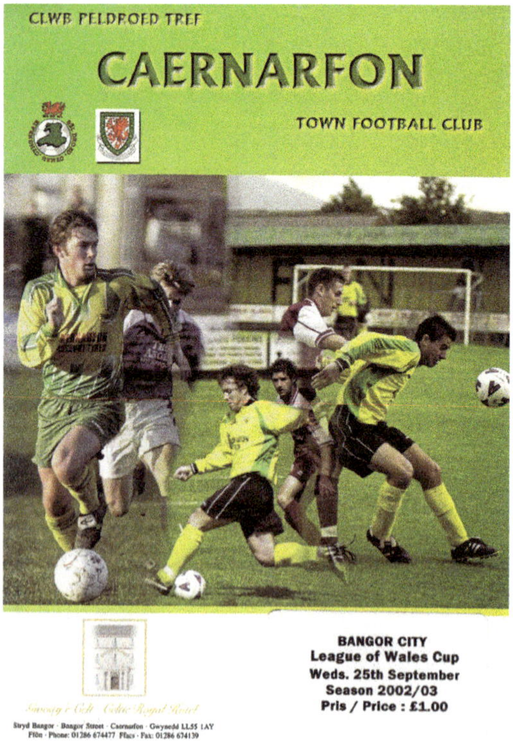

Caernarfon Town FC *v*. Bangor City FC, 2002/03

Caernarfon Town FC's main rivalries are with Porthmadog, Bangor City and Rhyl. Notably, on 13 April 2013 the football club defeated Kilvey Fords FC of Swansea in the 2012/13 FAW Trophy final. They won by a 6–0 scoreline; it was their first FAW Trophy victory since 1978. Caernarfon Town FC's margin of victory was the biggest final-winning result in the competition's 123-year history. The club remain an integral part of the town, emphasised by the fact that they are extremely well supported.

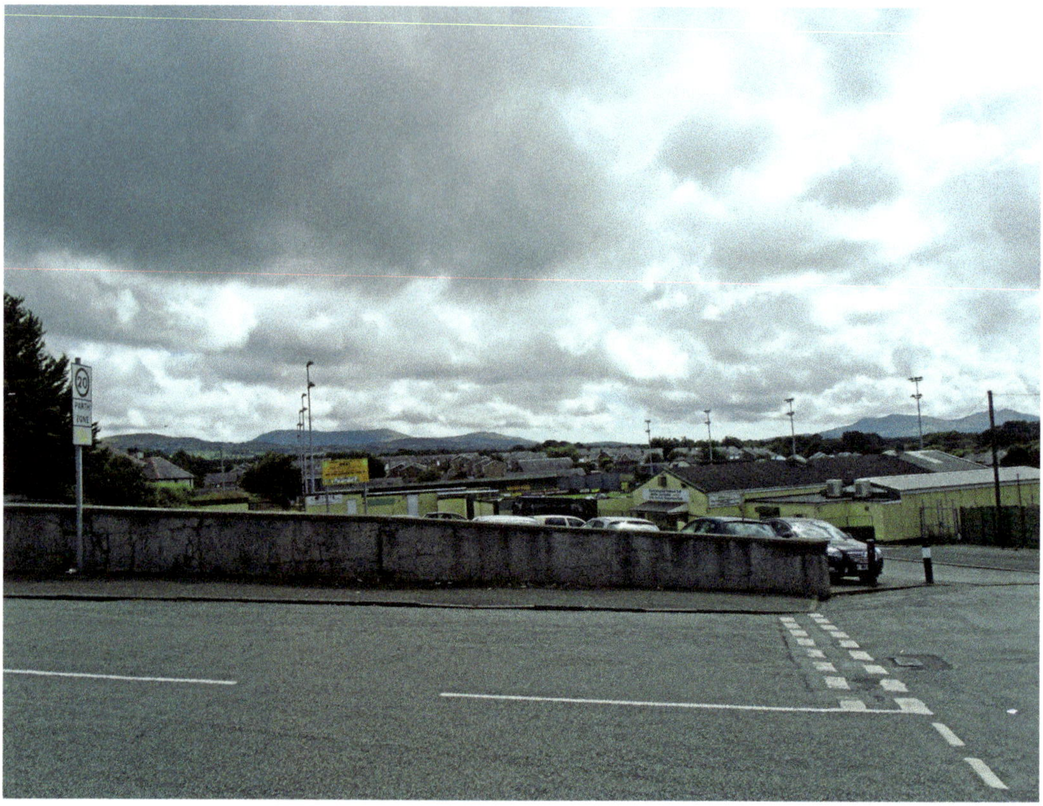

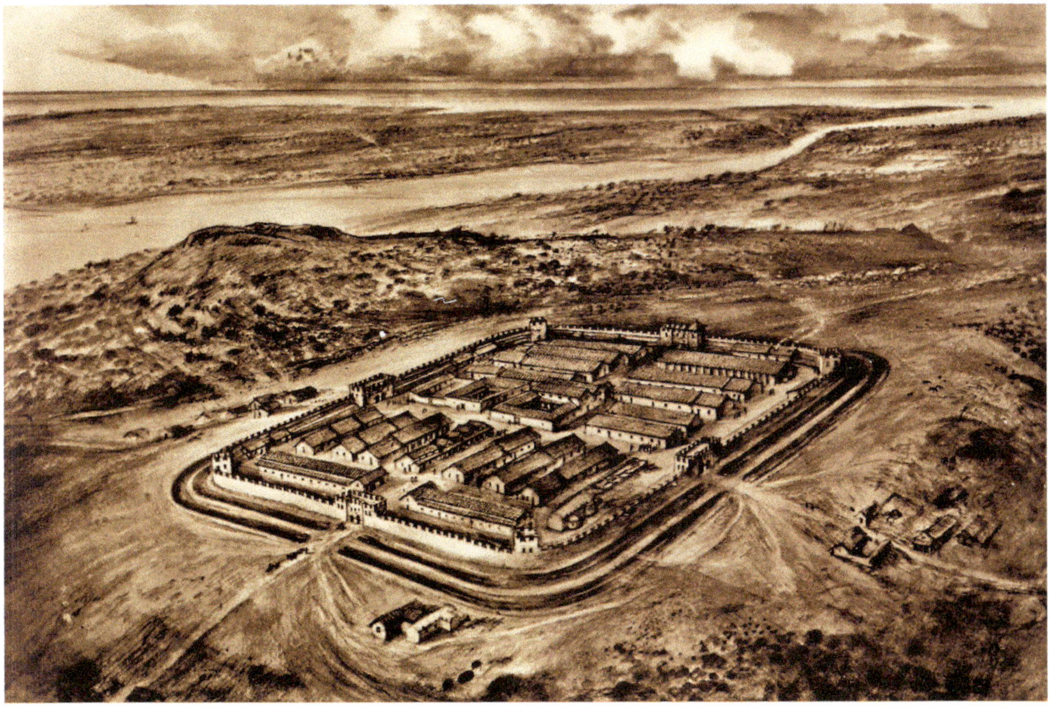

Segontium Roman Fort, Llanbeblig Road. View from the South, Third Century AD

The ruins of Caernarfon's Roman fortifications form the foundations of the modern town and are found on its outskirts. It was built by Agricola around AD 77–78, following the defeat of the Ordovices, and is strategically placed overlooking the approach to the Menai Strait. A Roman road was constructed from Segontium, linking it to Deva Victrix (Chester). The Roman garrison remained until around AD 394. After their withdrawal, much of the original fortification was reused as building material by the local population.

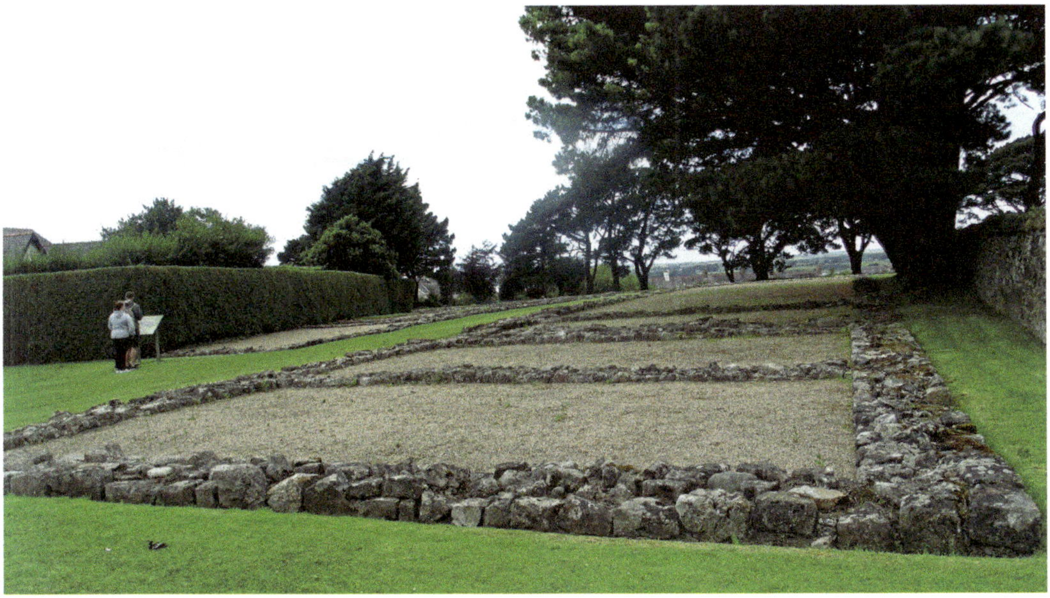

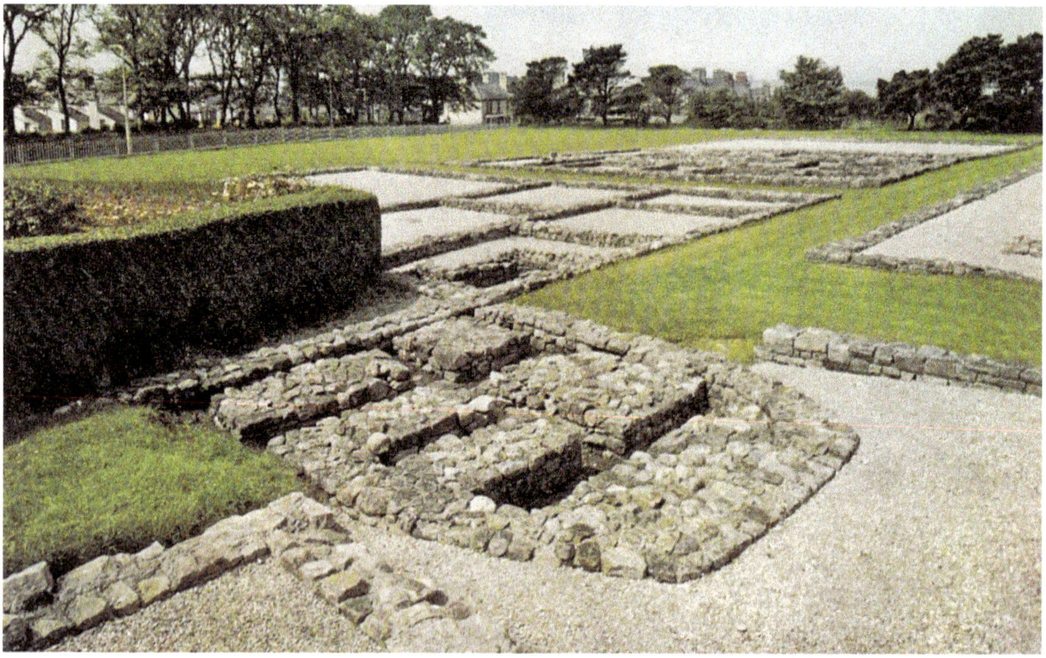

Segontium Roman Fort, Llanbeblig Road: View Looking South-West, with the HQ Building in the Foreground

The headquarters building (Principia) succeeded an earlier timber structure and consisted of an enclosed courtyard and an assembly hall. There was also a regimental place of worship, where the standard was kept; an underground strong room; and a room to store records, with an inbuilt hypocaust to avoid ingress from damp. The fort lies in a well-defended position at the tip of a ridge between the Afon Seiont and Afon Cadnant; the Roman name Segontium means 'forceful river'.

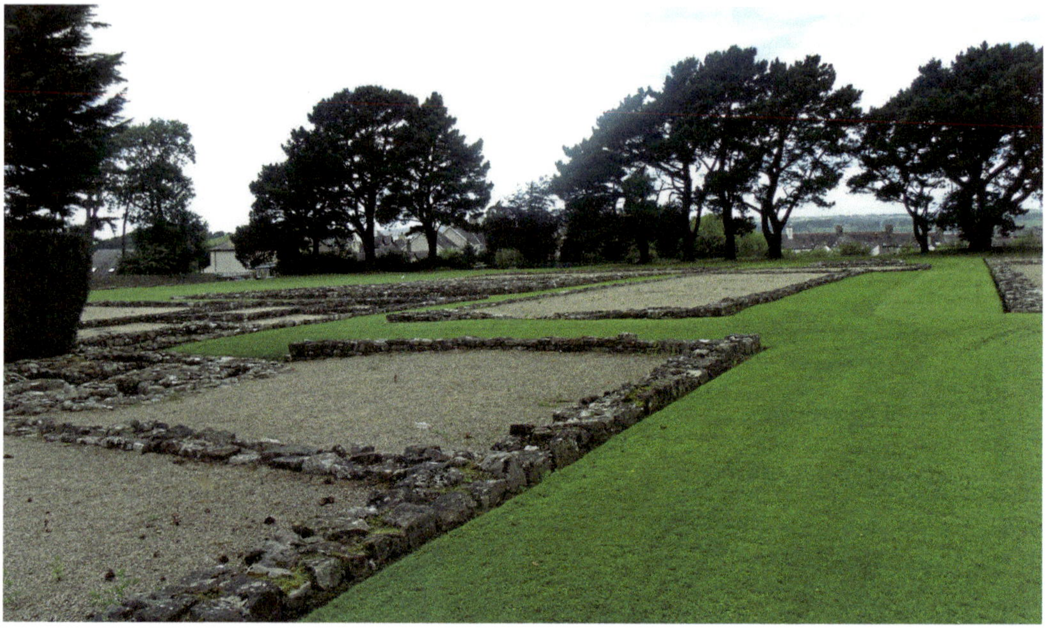

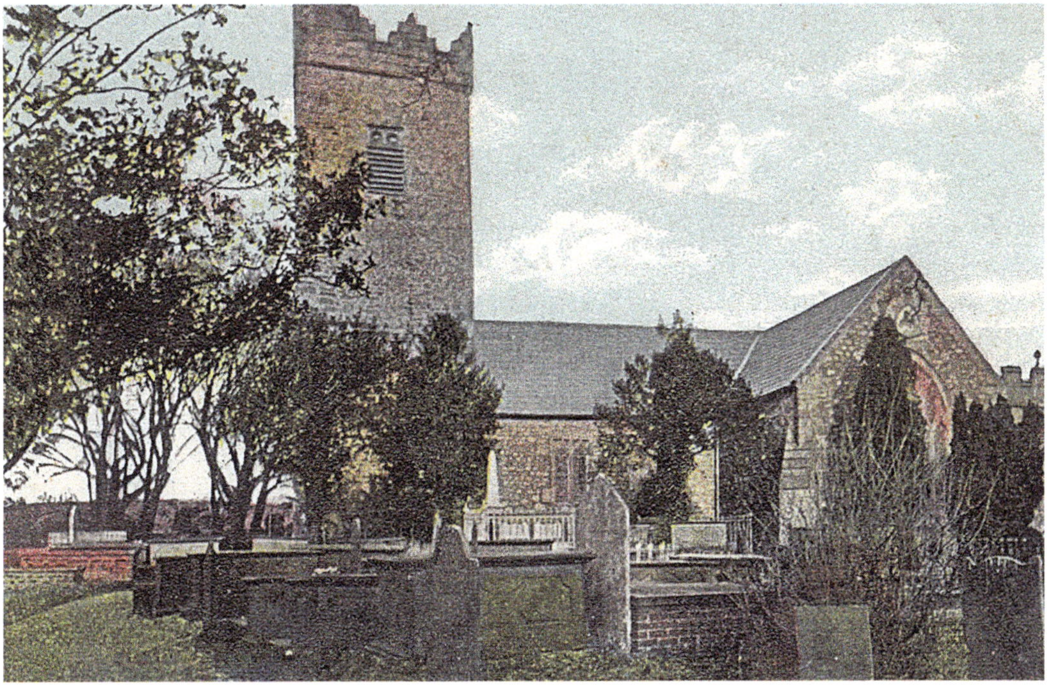

St Peblig's Parish Church, Llanbeblig Road, Caernarfon, *c.* 1910
The church is dedicated to St Peblig (Publicius), the son of St Elen and Macsen Wledig (Magnus Maximus). It has been built over an important early Christian site, which was itself built on a Roman Mithraeum, or Temple of Mithras, close to Segontium Roman Fort (during nineteenth-century restoration work a Roman altar was found in one of the walls). The present church was constructed in the fourteenth century and is a Grade I listed building. The tower was added in the fifteenth and sixteenth centuries.

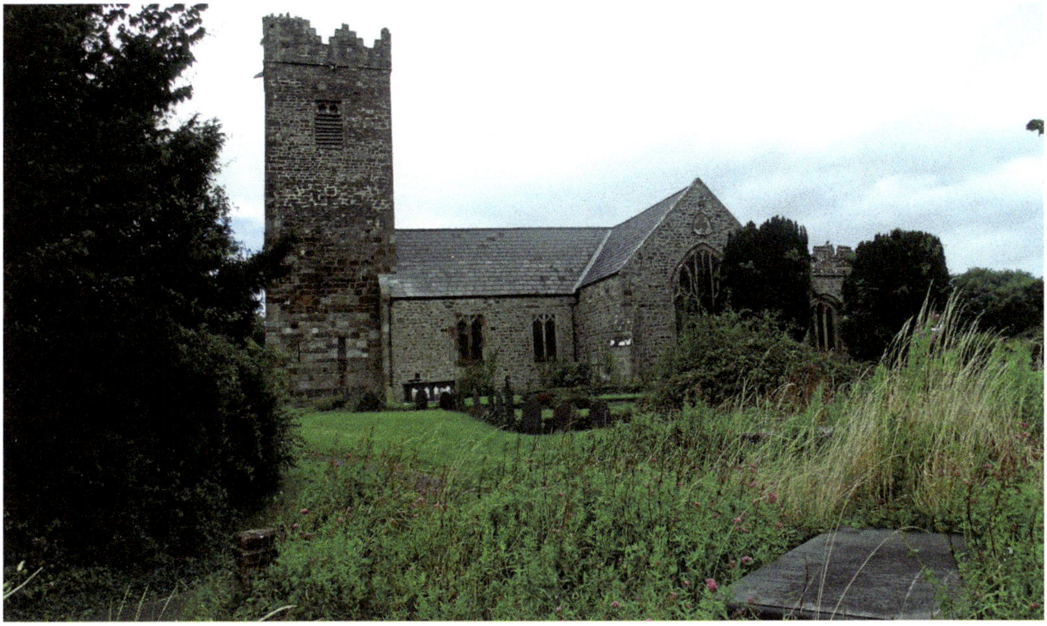

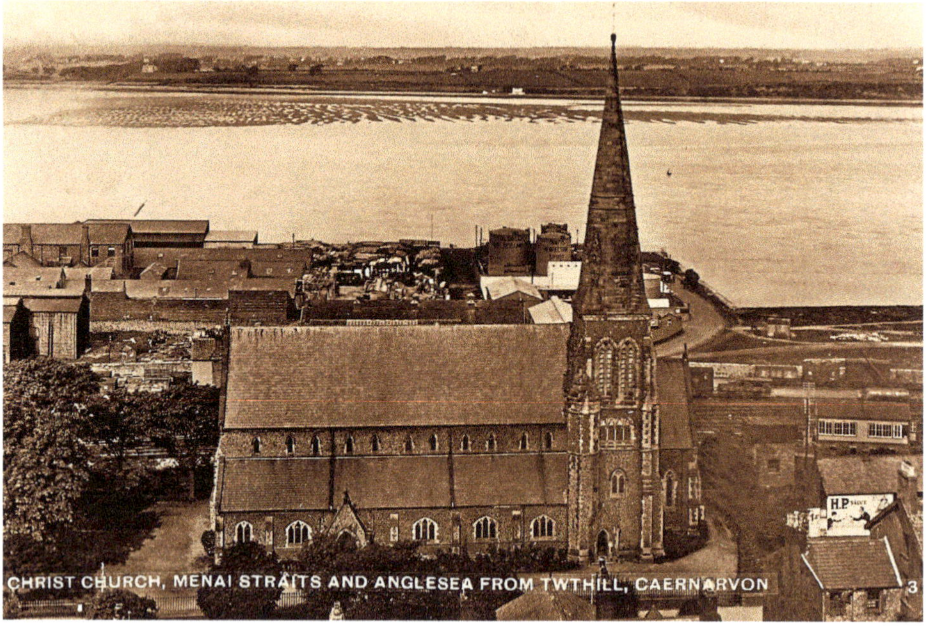

Christ Church, Menai Strait and Anglesey, from Twthill, Caernarfon, 1934
Located on North Road, Caernarfon, this large, mid-Victorian former church was built in Geometrical Style in 1862–64. Designed by architect Anthony Salvin of London, with drawings by Norman Shaw, it was built by contractor Richard Parry, of Menai Bridge, and cost £7,610. The spire was added later, in 1886, by Evan Jones of Groeslon. Christ Church closed for worship in 1982 and was converted for leisure activities in 1999. In its heyday the church provided English language services.

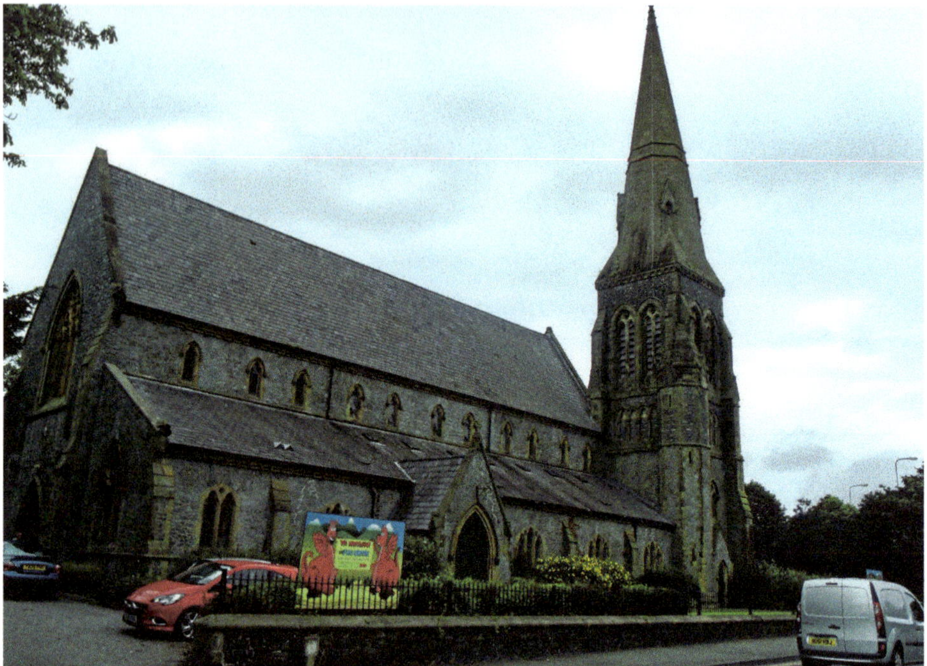

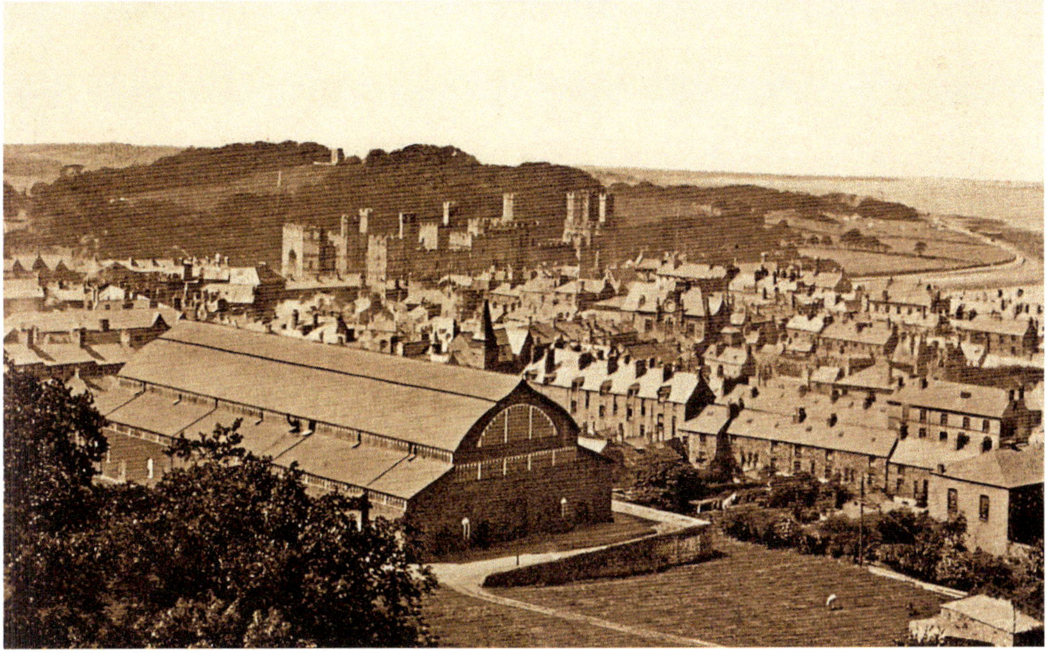

Caernarfon Pavilion from Twthill (*c.* 1920) and View of Caernarfon's Rooftops and Stryd y Castell (Castle Street) from Caernarfon Castle, 2017

The Pavilion's foundation stone was laid on 26 May 1877; it was completed three months later. Its first public meeting was the opening ceremony of the National Eisteddfod on 21 August 1877, with six more held there. It was an ideal venue for shows, concerts, political and religious meetings. It seated 8,000 and was the largest of its kind in Wales. It's decline in popularity coincided with the advent of the cinema, and it was later used a warehouse, being demolished in 1961. The site is now beneath the busy A487.

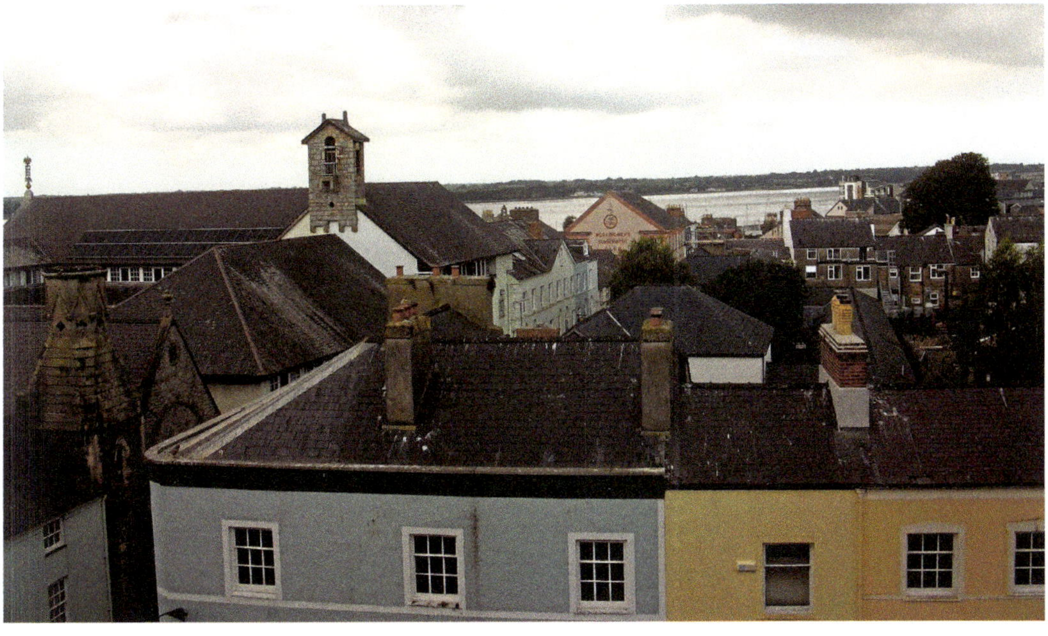

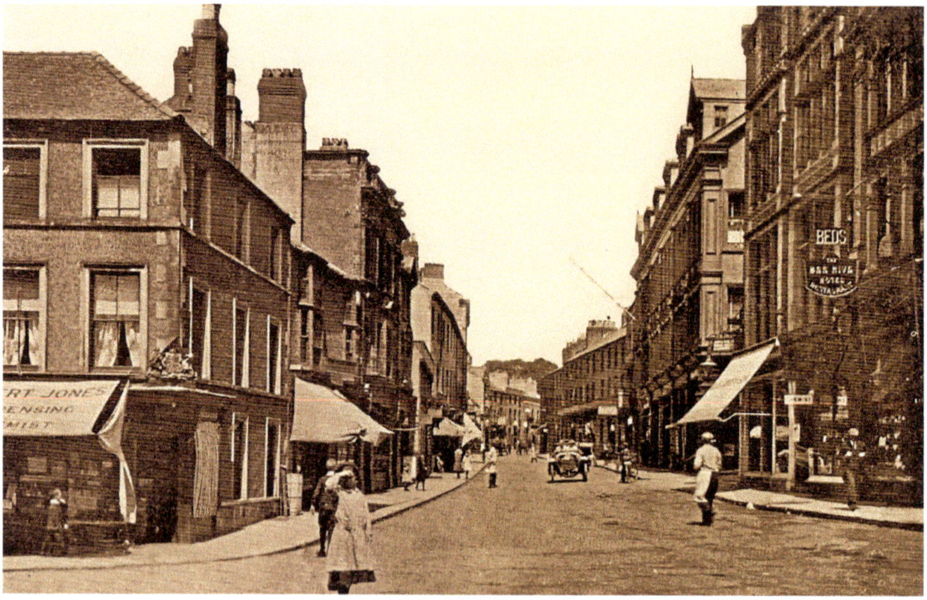

Bangor Street, Caernarfon, *c.* 1920

Today, Bangor Street is a well-established neighbourhood consisting of private residences and commercial properties. This photograph from around 1920 shows that this main route between Caernarfon and Bangor still has the same mix of property use as today, but the roads are much busier in modern times. This is reflected in the fact that there has been a great deal of road-widening and upgrading in recent years, with the creation of roundabouts to ease the movement of traffic.

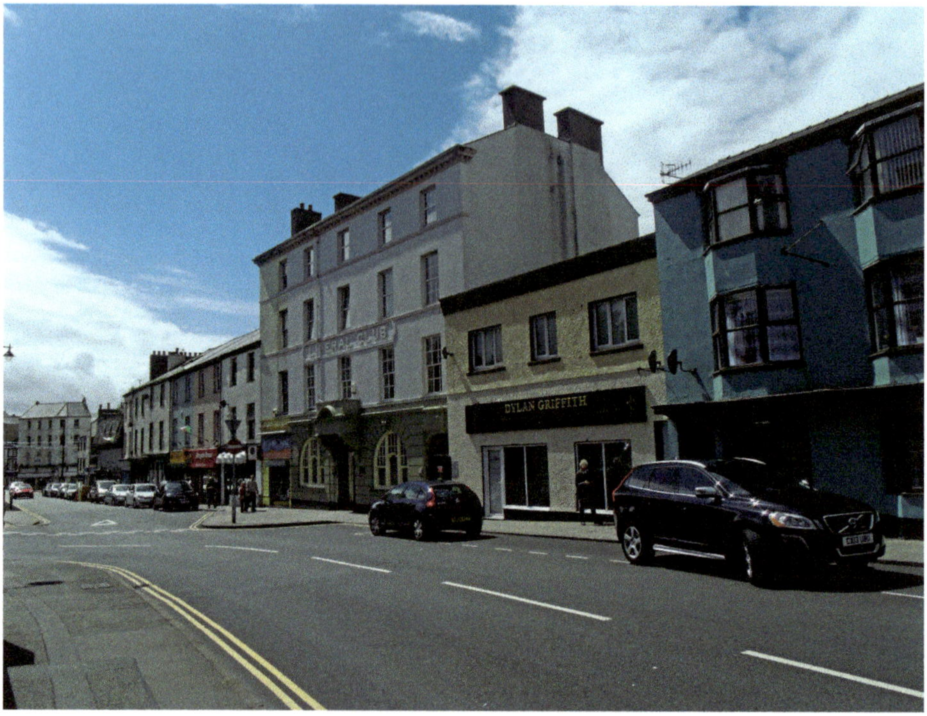

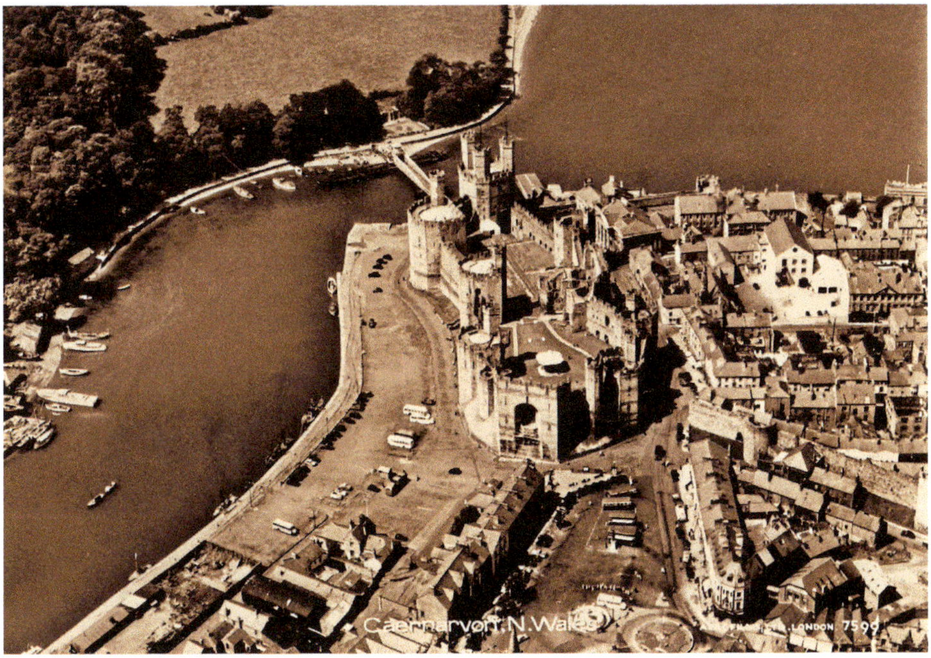

Aerial View of Caernarfon, Showing the Harbour Office (below left), *c.* 1940

Built in 1840, the Harbour Office was the main focus of Caernarfon's shipping activity. It was the office of the Caernarfon Harbour Trust, which remains its occupant. The Trust was formed in 1793, when an Act of Parliament authorised the improvement and enlargement of Caernarfon Harbour, which was then located mainly to the west and north of the walled town. The Act also allowed for new moorings at the mouth of the Afon Seiont, located to the south of the castle.

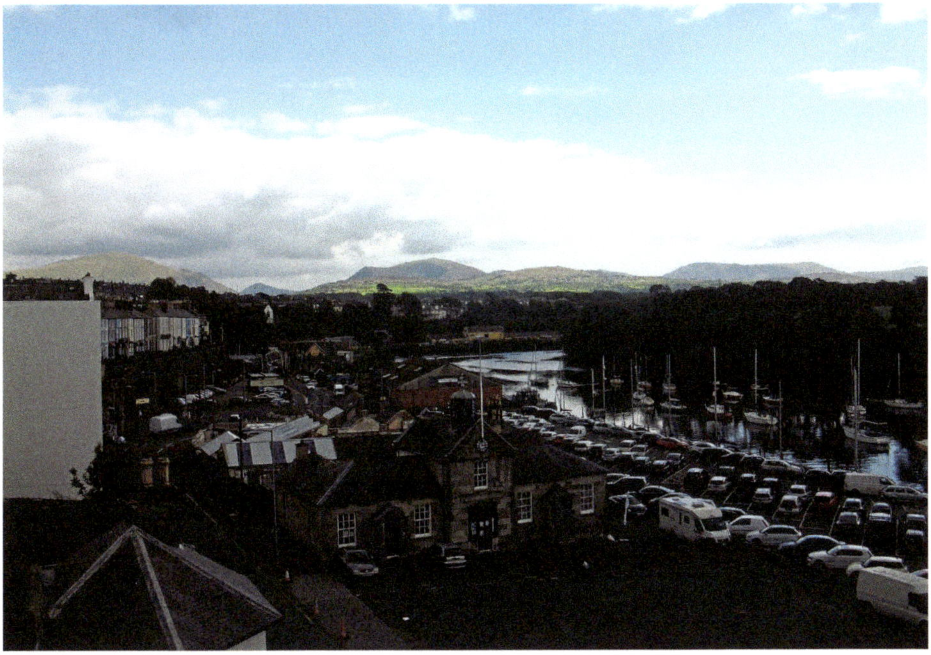

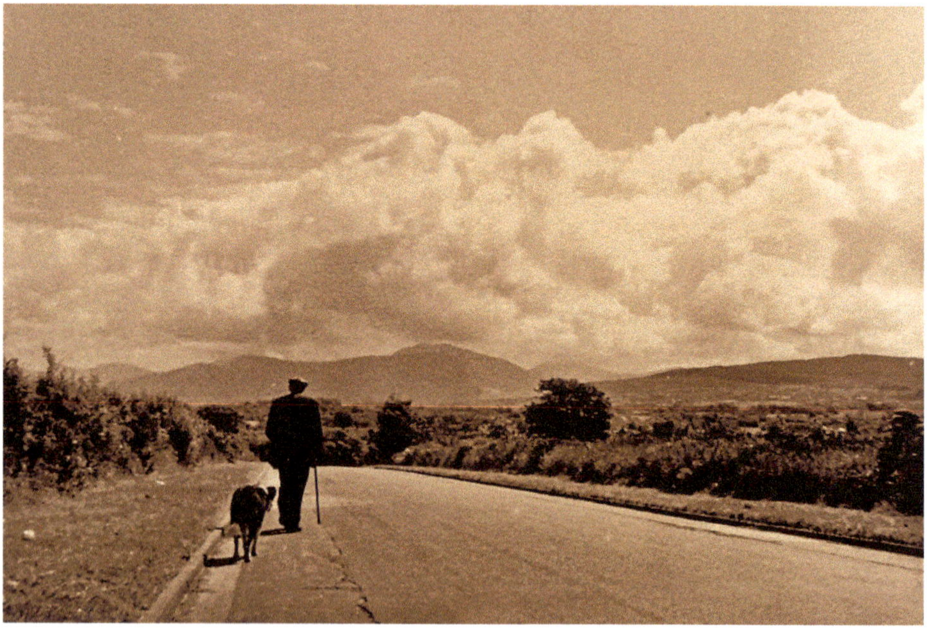

Out of Caernarfon on the road looking towards Snowdonia, 1958, and Mynydd Drws-y-Coed (Door of the Wood), Rhyd Ddu, on the Caernarfon-Beddgelert Road, 2017
Today, this road is known as the A4085. Starting at Caernarfon, it passes a relatively flat stretch, giving views of the Snowdonia mountain range and its surrounding peaks. It then passes through Rhyd Ddu (Black Ford), providing some impressive panoramas of the natural beauty of North Wales, which few other roads can surpass. The above photograph of 1958 shows the Snowdon massif and a clear road. Today it is a popular tourist route for those heading to Beddgelert, at the foot of Snowdon.

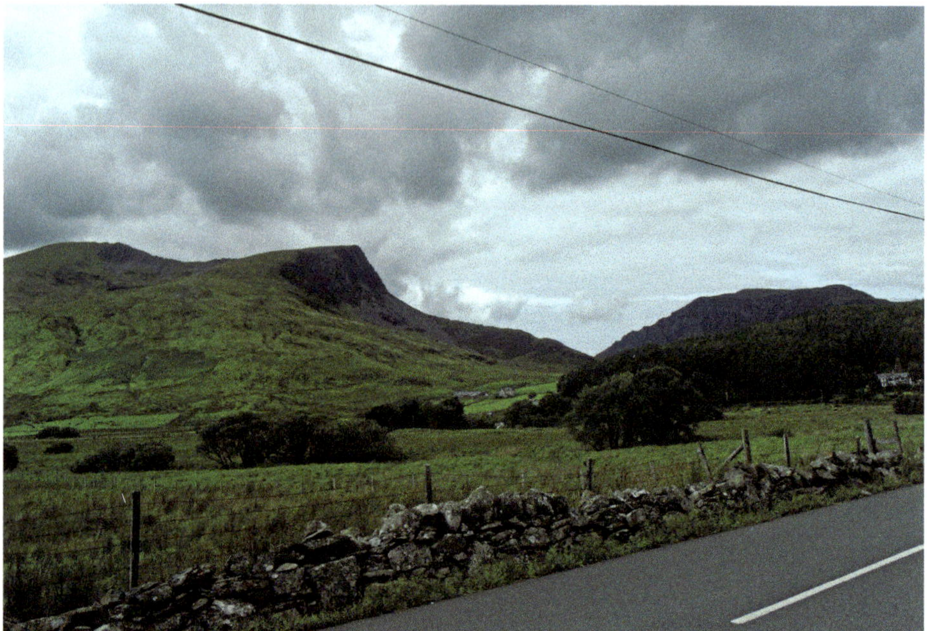

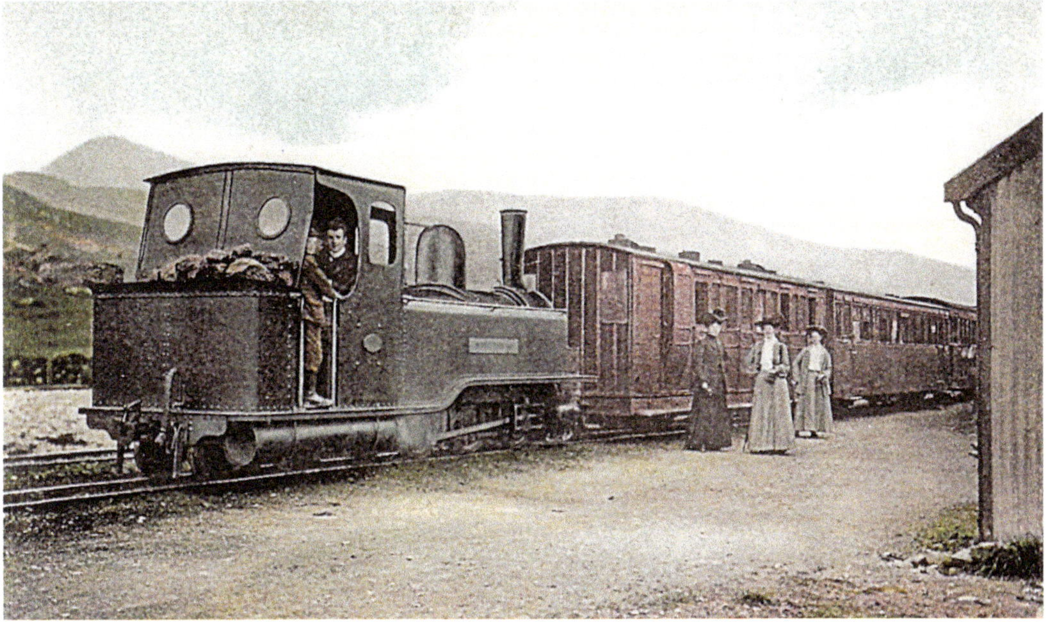

Snowdon Station for Beddgelert, Rhyd Ddu, *c.* 1910
***Inset*: Rhyd Ddu Sidings**

Rhyd Ddu station was built in 1881, as the North Wales Narrow Gauge Railways. It was originally named Snowdon, then South Snowdon, and competed with the later line from Llanberis to Snowdon's summit – Beddgelert was beginning to replace Llanberis as the centre for ascending Snowdon. After takeover by the Welsh Highland Railway, the line was extended to Beddgelert and Porthmadog in 1923. The station was renamed South Snowdon, then Rhyd Ddu in 1934, and closed on 26 September 1936, formally reopening on 30 July 2003.

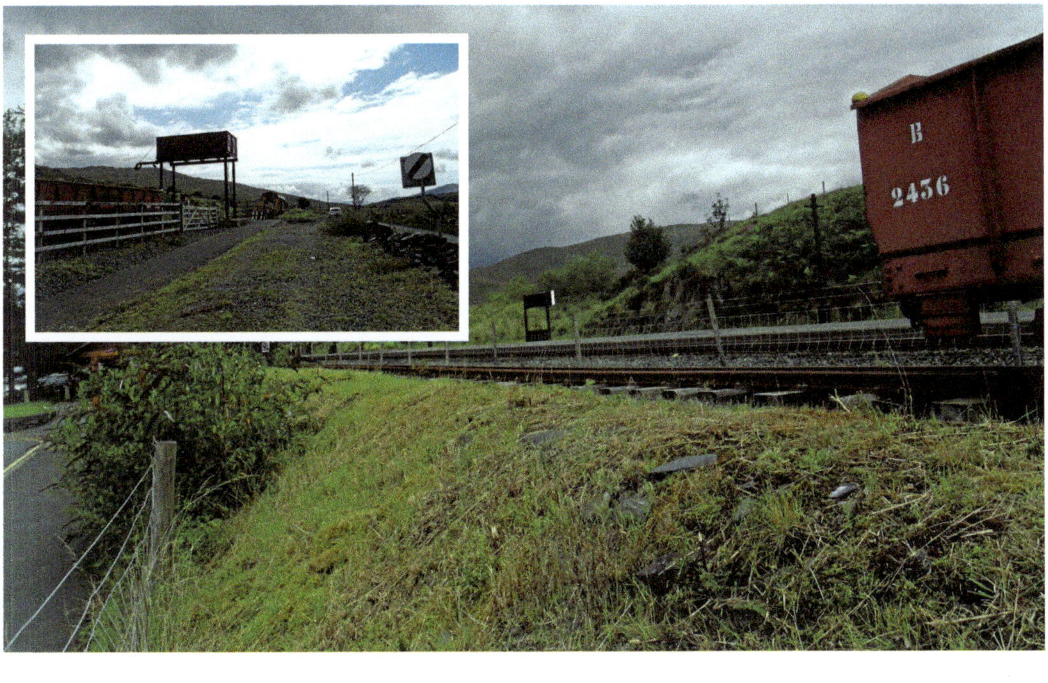

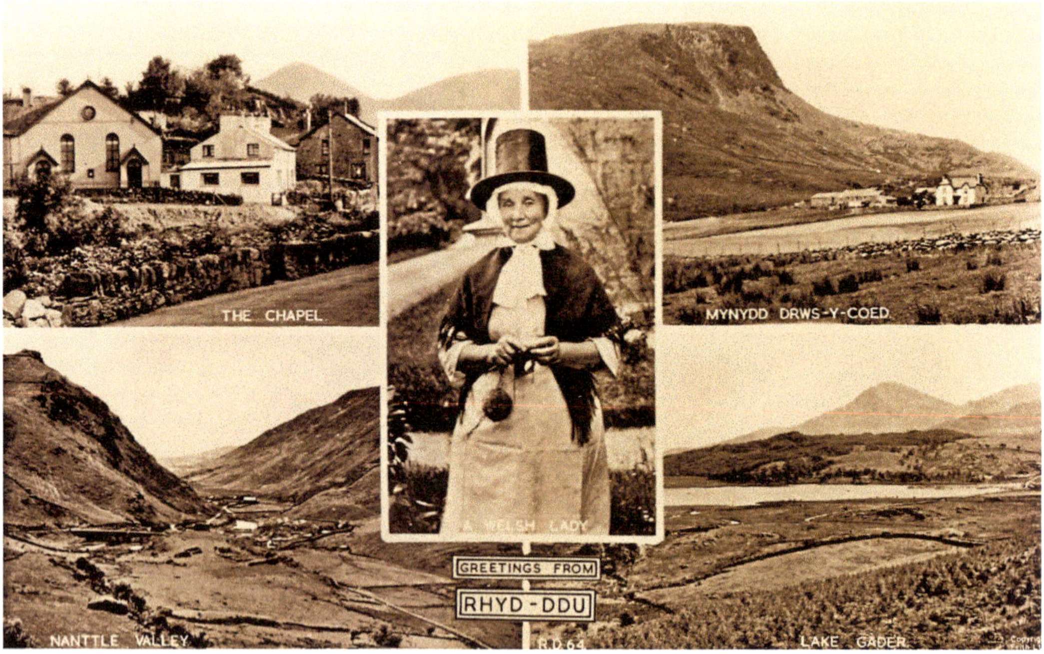

Llyn y Gader, Rhyd Ddu, *c.* 1960

The Welsh Highland Railway's construction to Waunfawr (inset) took about a year to finish and opened in August 2000. Work started on the next section to Rhyd Ddu almost straight away. By early 2003 track was laid from Rhyd Ddu in a northerly direction, to meet up with track being laid from Waunfawr, heading south. The railway was opened for passengers to Rhyd Ddu on 18 August 2003. Here, overlooked by Y Garn II which begins the Nantlle Ridge, is Llyn y Gader, close to Ffridd Uchaf and Beddgelert Forest.

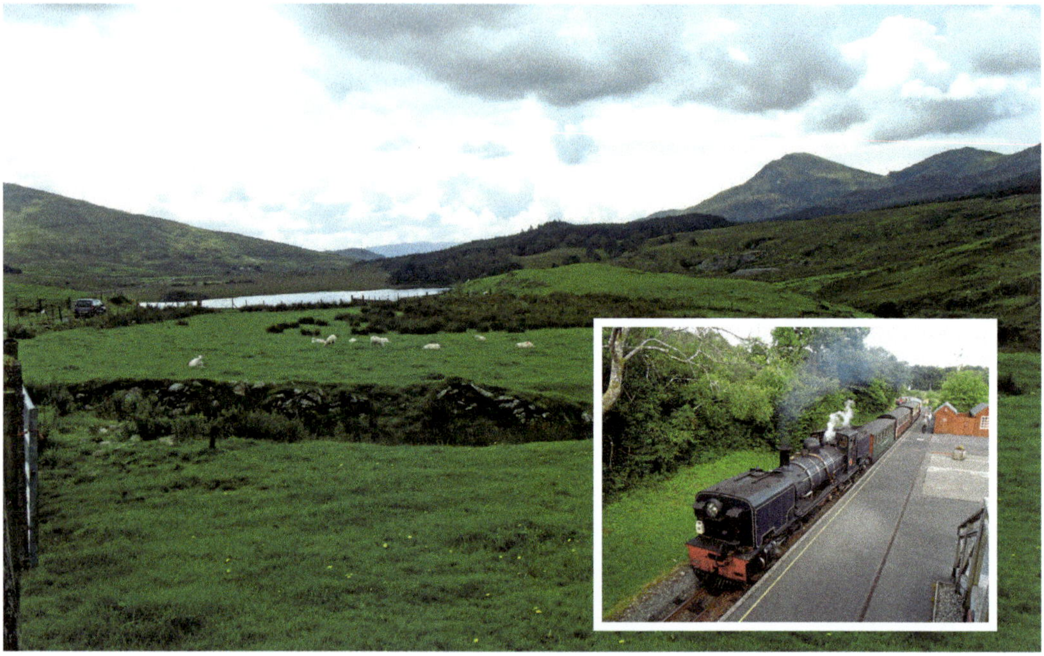

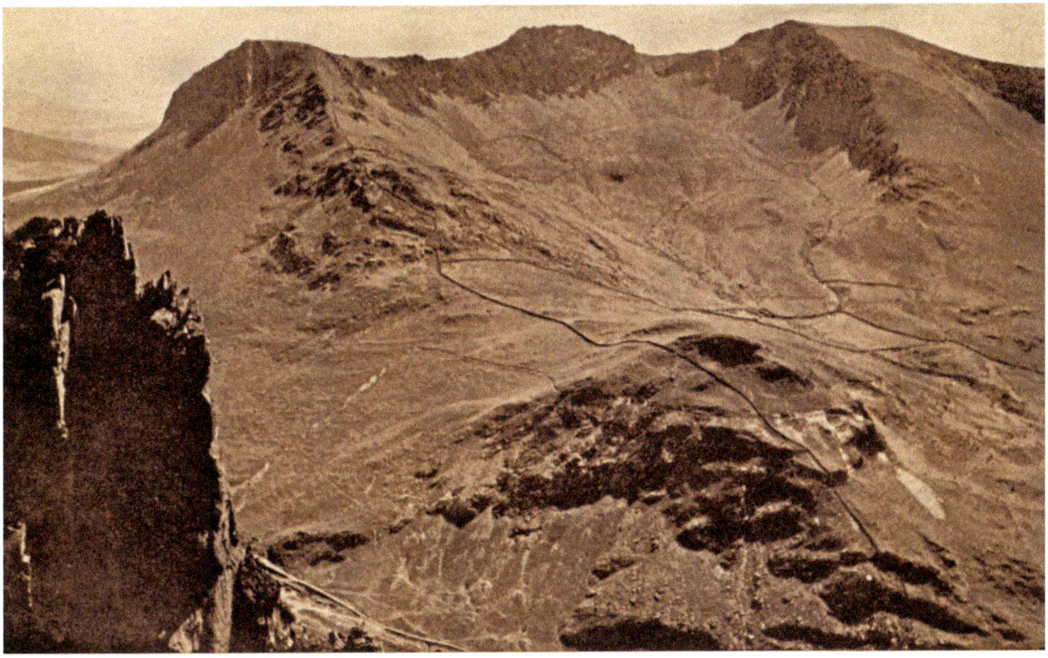

Y Garn II and Trum-y-Ddysgl from Craig-y-Bere, Nantlle Valley, *c.* 1940
Y Garn II (The Cairn, or The Rock), is at the top of Mynydd Drws-y-Coed (Door of the Trees), which is located at the easterly end of the Nantlle Ridge. It is the name of several hills in Wales, including nearby Y Garn (Glyderau Range), in northern Snowdonia. The Nantlle Ridge is very popular with walkers, with Y Garn II rising to 633 metres (2,077 feet) above the valley. The path at Drws-y-Coed was allegedly constructed after the arrival of Edward I.

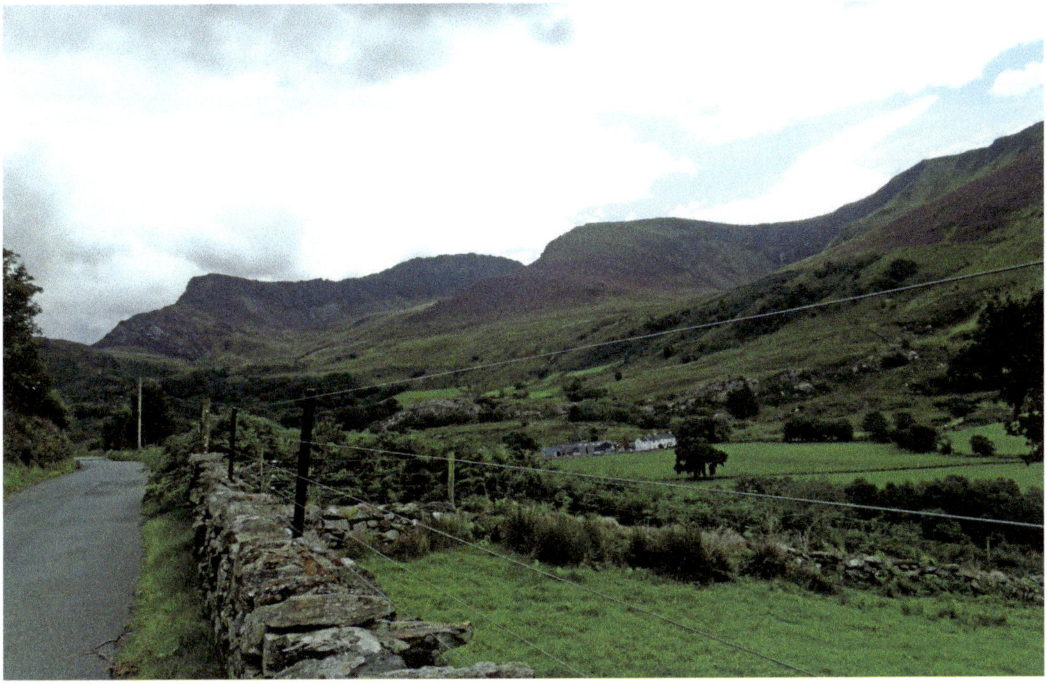

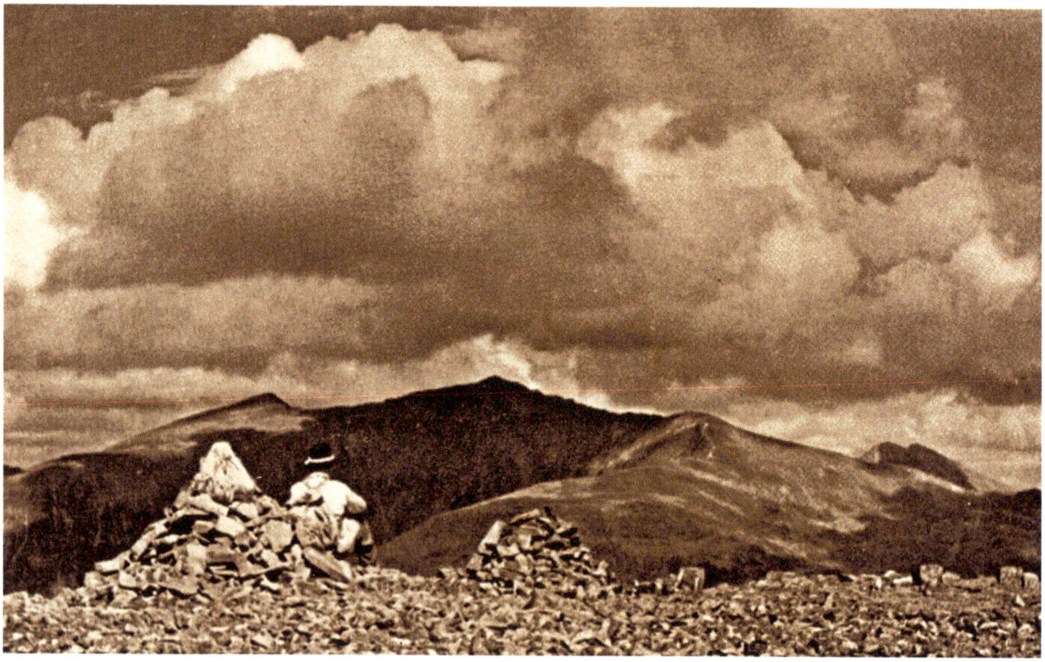

Yr Wyddfa (Snowdon) from Y Garn II, *c.* 1940
Yr Wyddfa means 'tumulus' or 'barrow'. The nearby Rhyd Ddu Path to the summit of Yr Wyddfa, also known as the Beddgelert Path, is considered to be one of the easiest routes to the top. It is also less busy than more popular routes, such as the Watkin Path, with which it meets at a site marked by a large standing stone, a few hundred metres from the peak. The advantage of the Rhyd Ddu route is that the summit is visible from the start.

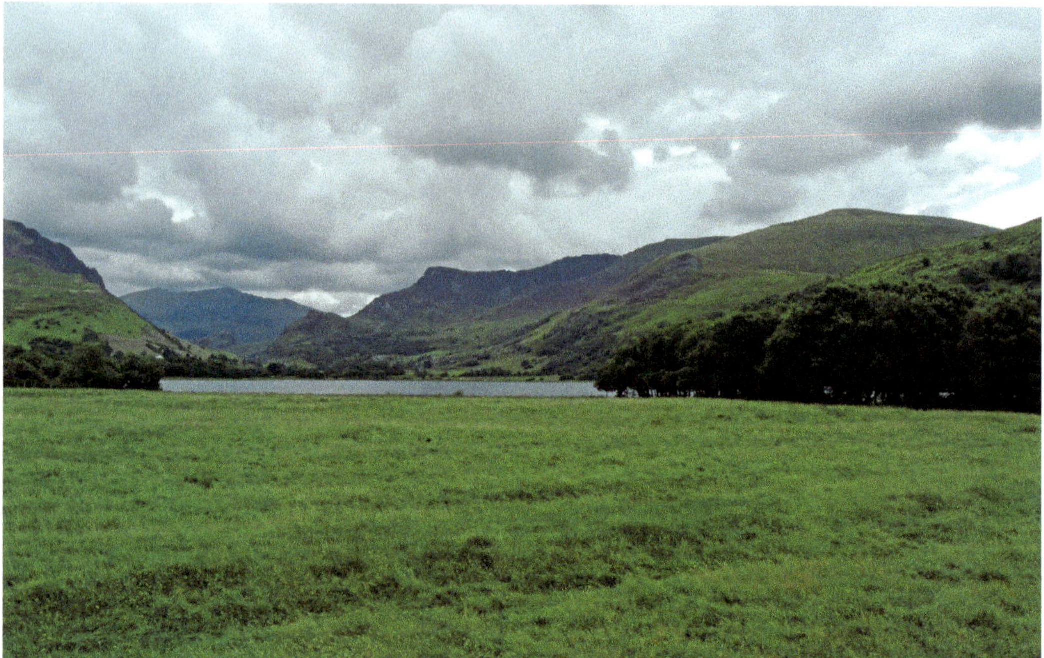

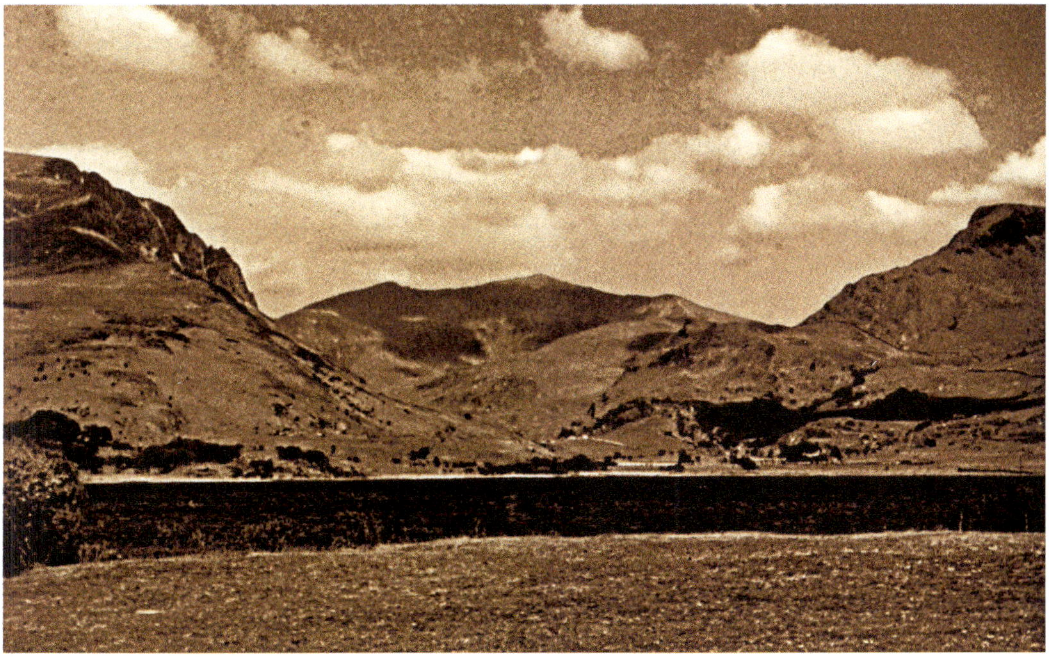

Craig-y-Bere, Yr Wyddfa (Snowdon) and Y Garn II from Llyn Nantlle Uchaf, *c.* 1940
'Upper Nantlle Lake' is located in the Nantlle Valley, Gwynedd. The Llyn forms the backing to Richard Wilson's 1765 oil painting entitled 'Snowdon from Llyn Nantlle'. It has an average depth of 4 metres (15 feet) and a total shoreline of 2 kilometres (1 mile). The Llyn is drained by Afon Llyfni. In the nineteenth century the Nantlle Valley saw a dispute between those who believed in the Biblical flood and those who supported the theory of glacial drift, established by studies of Moel Tryfan.

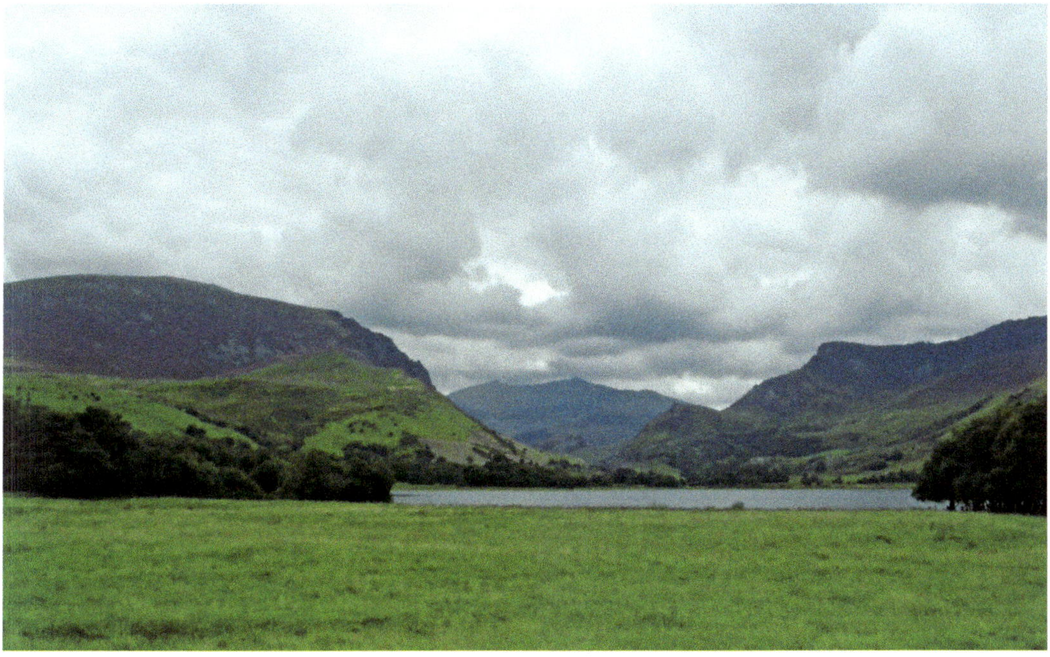

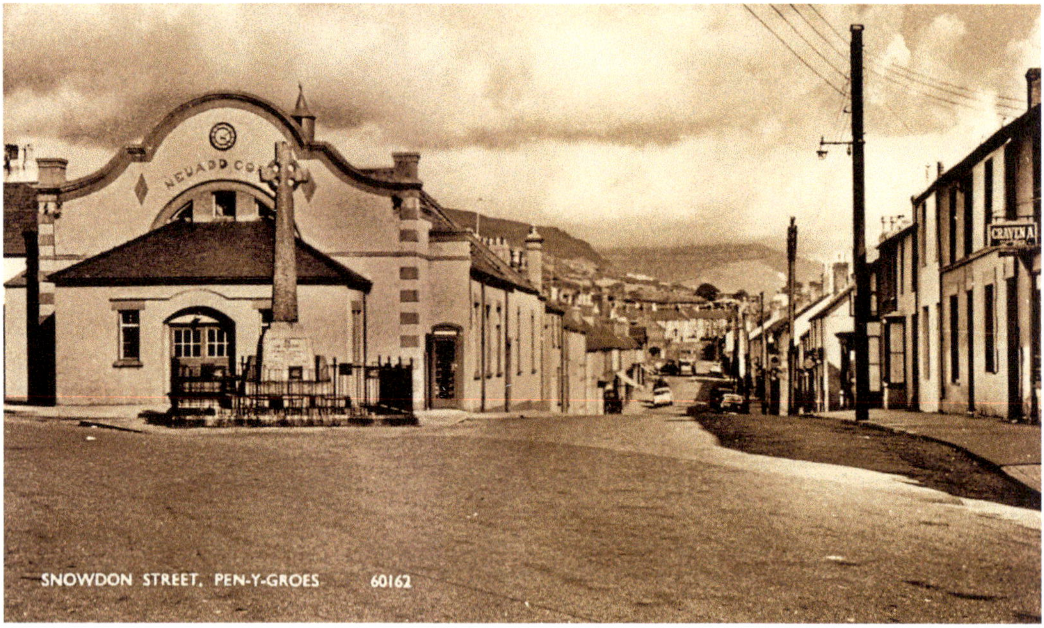

Snowdon Street, Penygroes, *c.* 1960

Penygroes is located in the former slate quarrying area of Dyffryn Nantlle, although most of the quarries are now closed down. The cycle path, Lon Eifion, passes near the village. It follows the route of the former Caernarfonshire Railway, which ran from Caernarfon to Afon Wen and closed in 1964. The edge of Lord Newborough's former estate, at Glynllifon, lies close to Penygroes and the village is the valley's main shopping and administrative centre. Eighty-eight per cent of its population are Welsh-speaking.

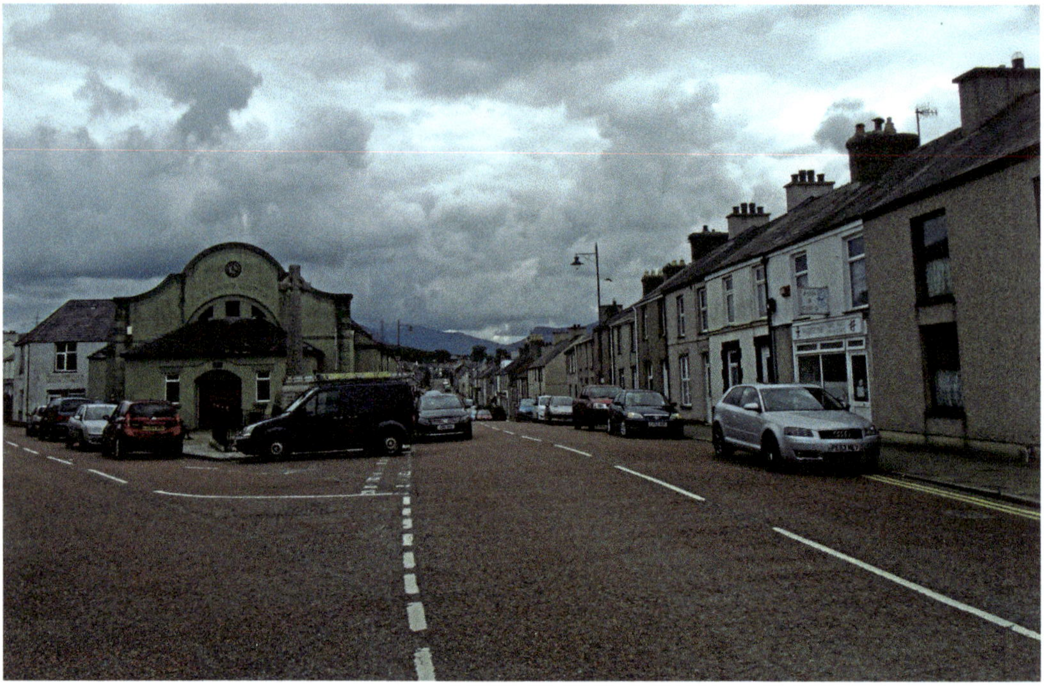

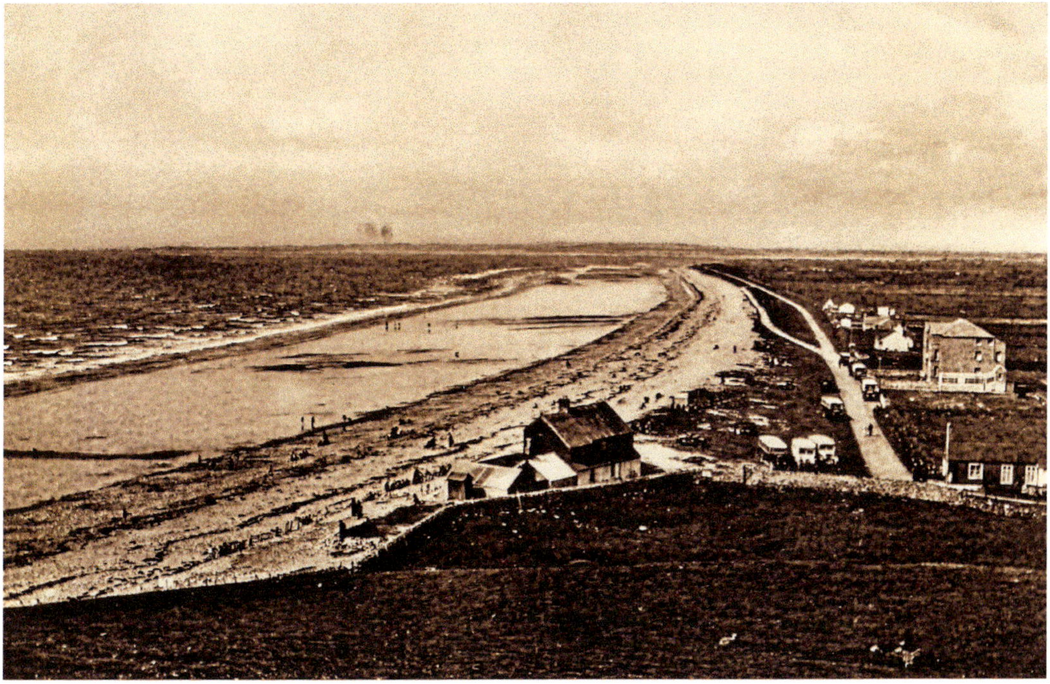

Dinas Dinlle, from the Cliffs (top), 1928, and from the Beach (below), 1989
Dinas Dinlle is a 'Site of Special Scientific Interest', with natural habitats, archaeological sites and historic connections. The cliff above the beach is known as Boncan Dinas and is occupied by an Iron Age hill fort, Dinas Dinlle. It was reoccupied by the Romans in the second or third century, and it is possible that a Roman lighthouse stood here. Small depressions in the ground are thought to be the site of Iron Age huts, the mound being the remains of a barrow.

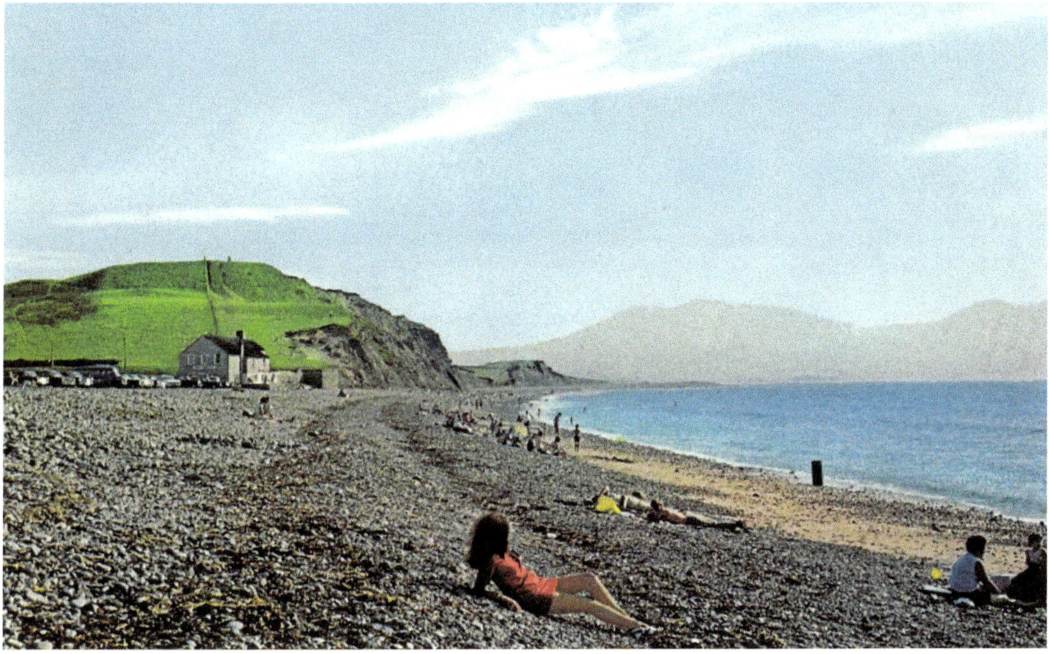

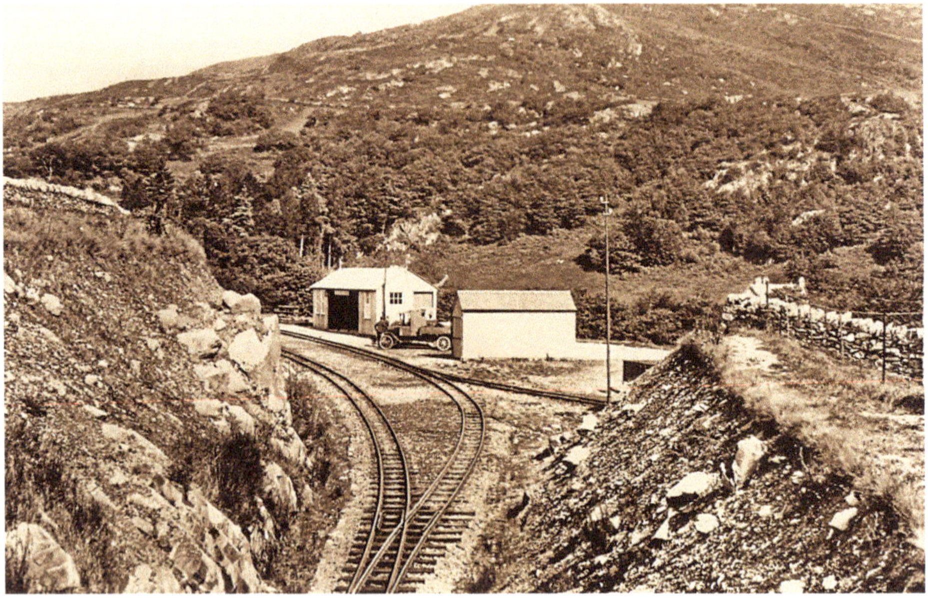

Beddgelert Station, Welsh Highland Railway, *c.* 1925

The original station operated from 1922 to 1936 and had a passing loop and three sidings. In 1922 the line ran from Dinas to Porthmadog, with the location being used as a 'border' station and trains reversing here in both directions. Work to rebuild the station began in December 2006 but completion was delayed for financial reasons. The new station was officially opened on 7 April 2009 by Lord Elis-Thomas. It is one of the busiest locations on the Welsh Highland Railway.

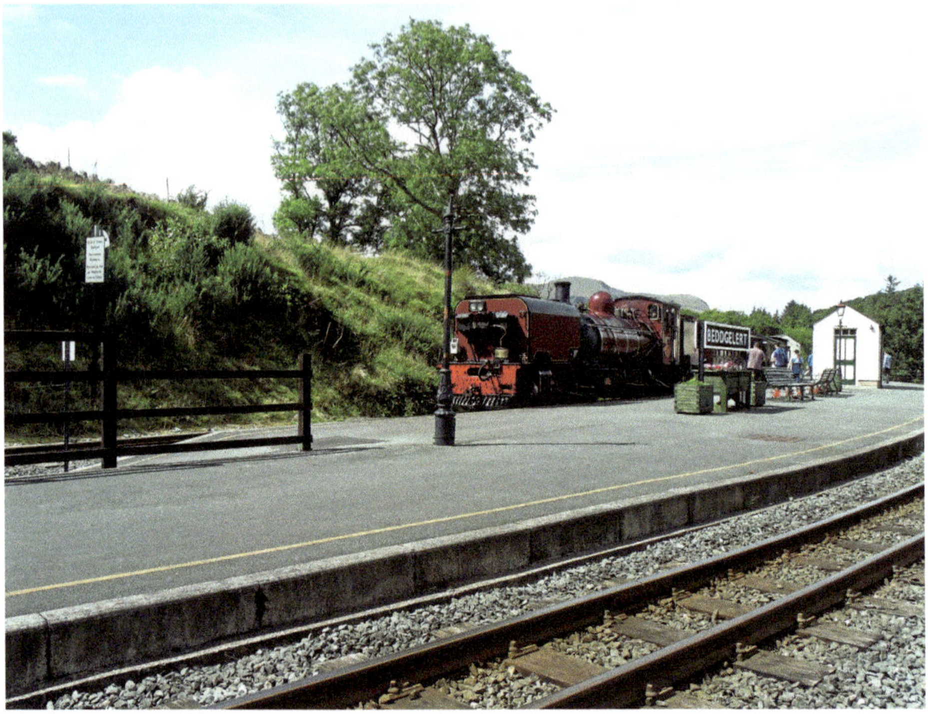

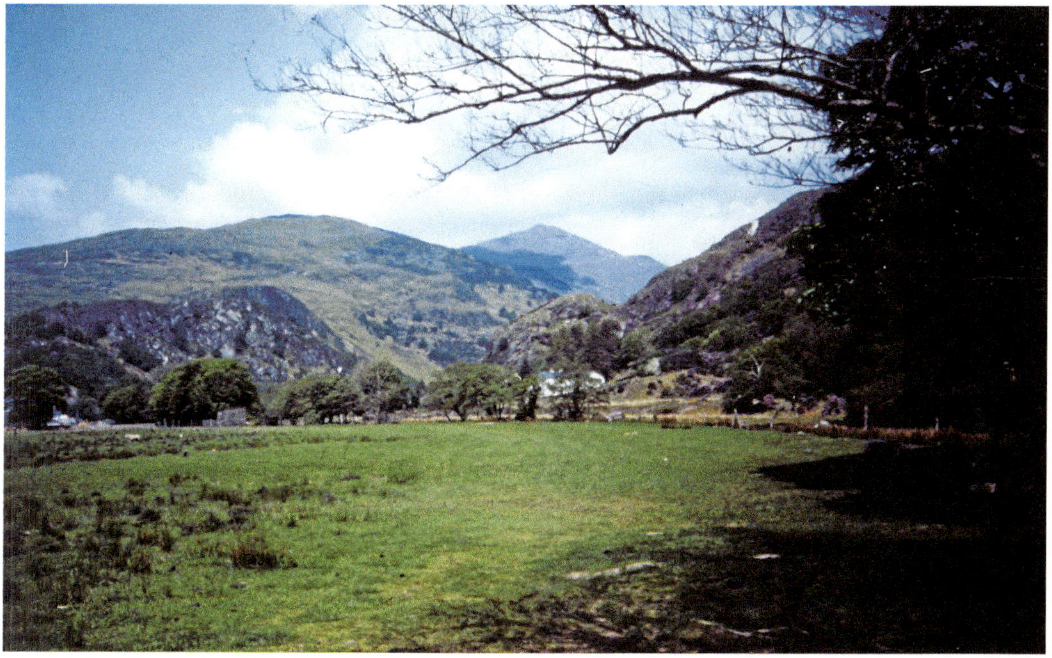

Aberglaslyn Pass, Looking Towards Snowdon and Beddgelert, 1989

The Welsh Highland Railway is the United Kingdom's largest heritage railway and runs for 40 kilometres (25 miles) in a southerly direction, from Caernarfon and terminating at Porthmadog. It passes the foot of Snowdon and the village of Beddgelert, and then makes its way through the magnificent scenery of the Aberglaslyn Pass and on to Porthmadog, where the new £1.25 million Porthmadog Harbour station opened in 2014. Construction of the Welsh Highland Railway started in the Aberglaslyn Pass in 1905.

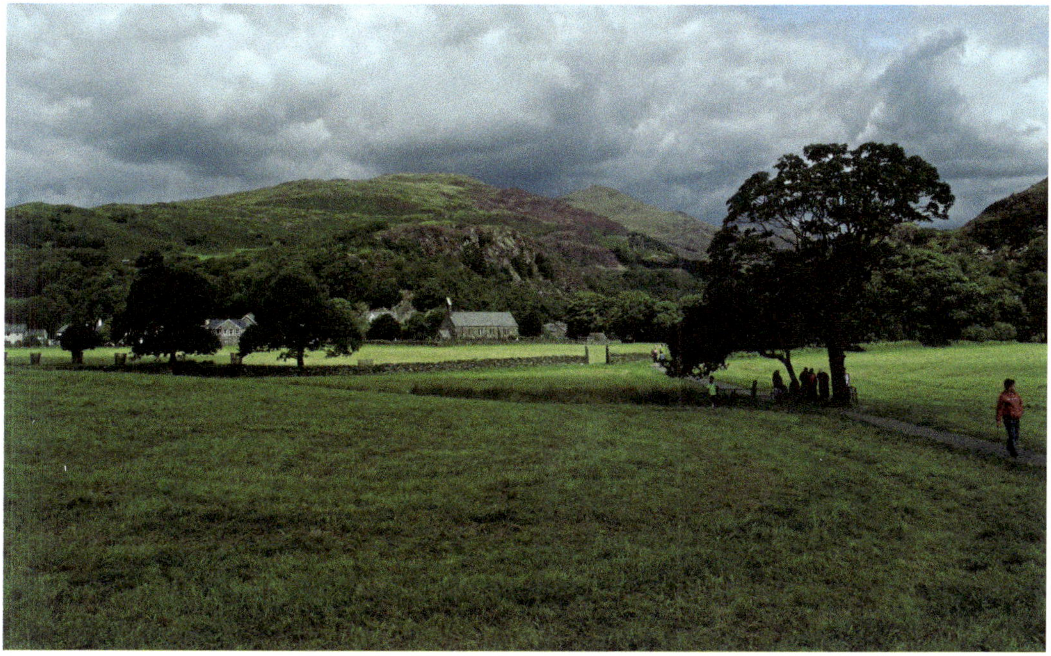

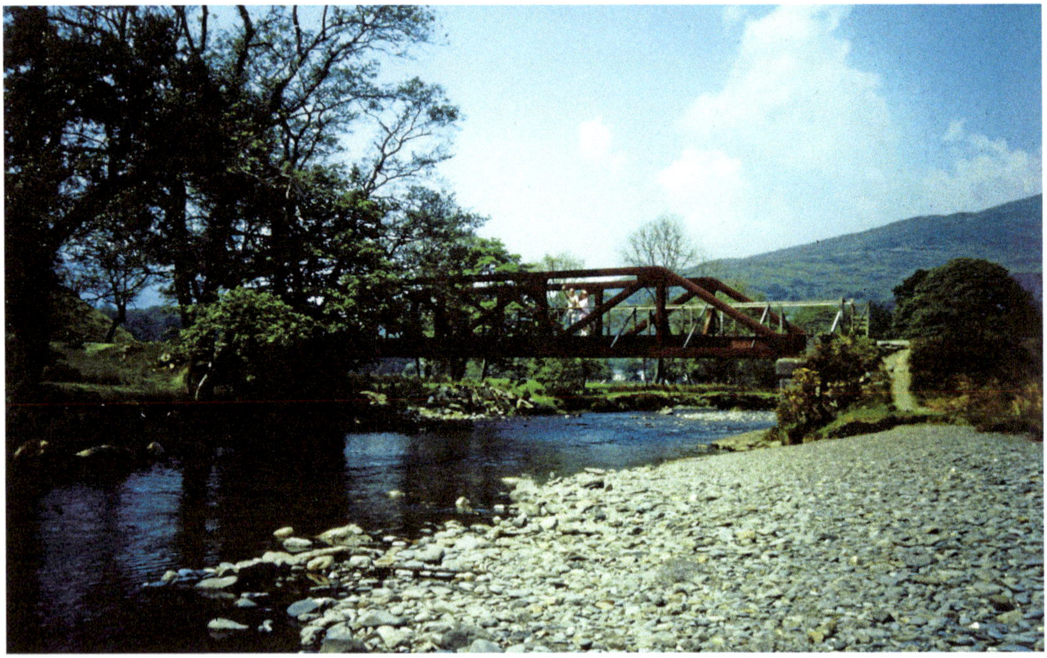

Pont Bryn-y-Felin, Welsh Highland Railway, 1989

In March 2006 a replacement girder bridge was installed to substitute the one removed in 1999. It was largely identical to the original bridge, which had not been maintained since 1936. It was weak through corrosion as a result, and had never been painted, or had holes drilled in its subframe to aid drainage, as had been suggested by the railway inspector in the 1920s. Because of these factors it was in an advanced state of disrepair when removed.

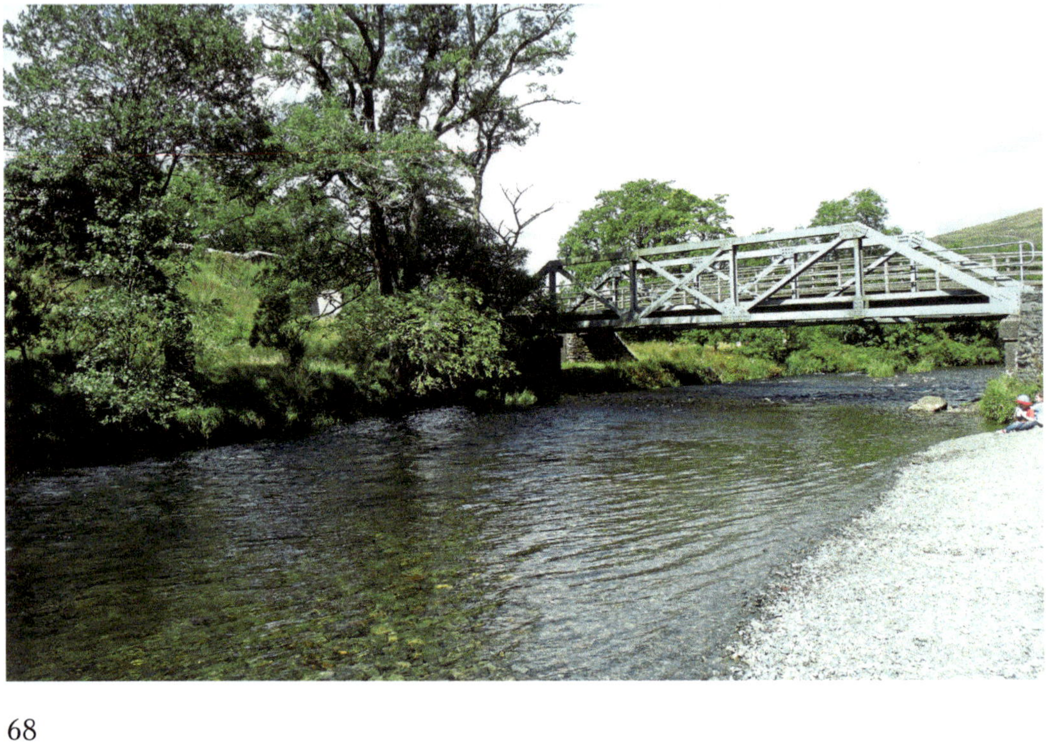

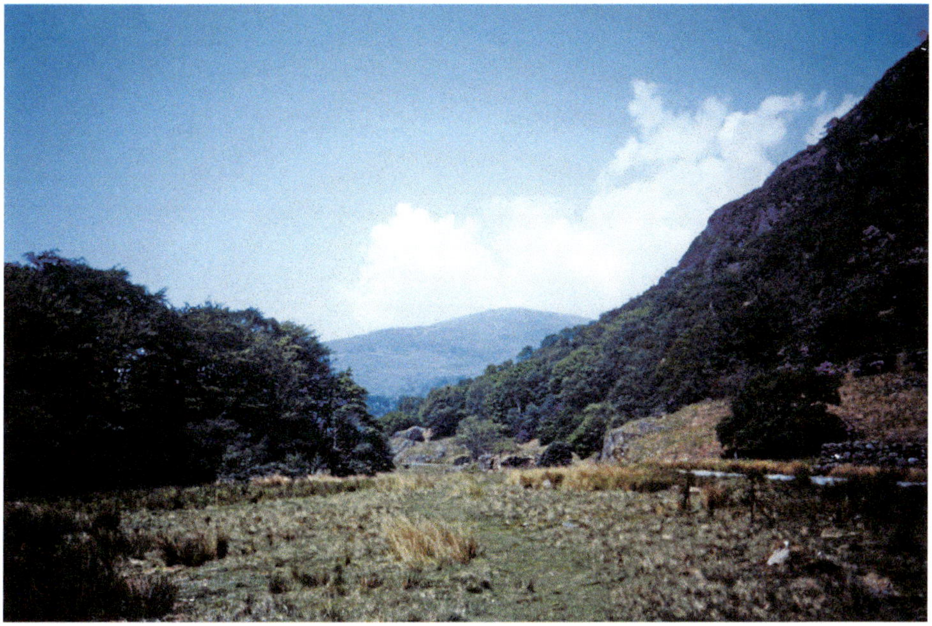

Trackbed of the Welsh Highland Railway, Looking Towards Snowdon, Aberglaslyn Pass, 1989, and Afon Glaslyn and Snowdon, 2017

After the Welsh Highland Railway's closure in 1937 the rails were requisitioned and removed for War Department use in 1941. The trackbed remained the property of the receiver of the company, with an iron girder bridge left to span the Afon Glaslyn. The course of the trackbed and three tunnels through the Aberglaslyn Pass became a popular route for walkers over the decades, until in 1995–96 the Ffestiniog Railway sought ownership for their scheme to rebuild the Welsh Highland Railway.

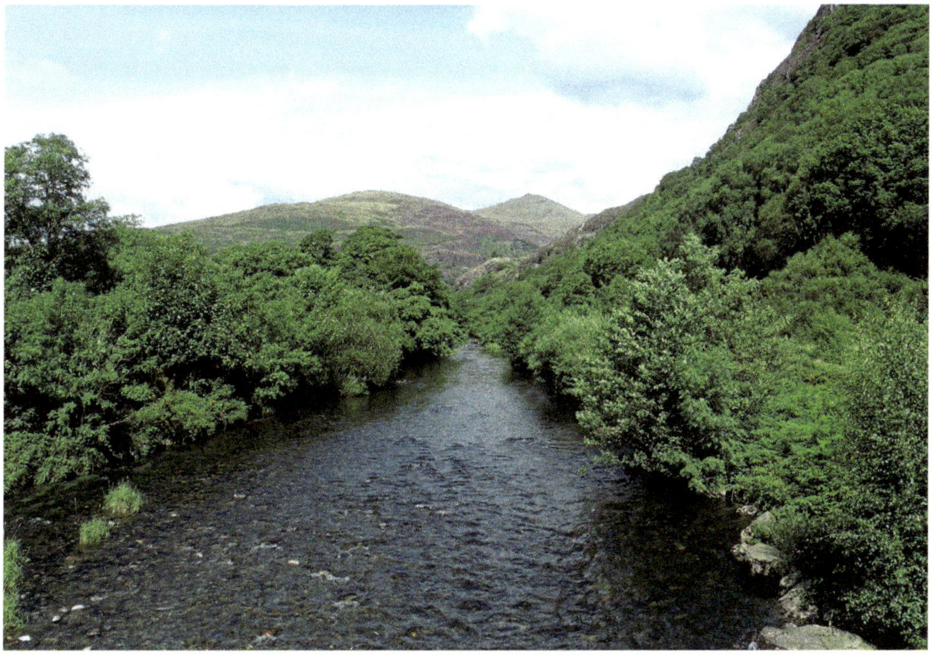

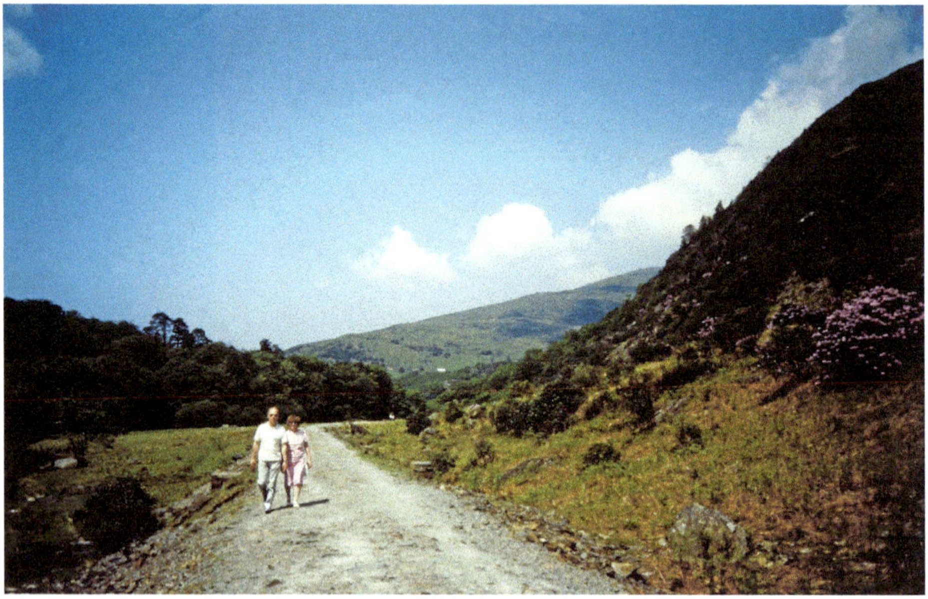

Trackbed of the Welsh Highland Railway, Looking Towards Snowdon (right), Pont Bryn-y-Felin (centre) and Caernarfon (left), Aberglaslyn Pass, 1989

A temporary Caernarfon railway station in St Helen's Road is the northern terminus of the narrow gauge Rheilffordd Eryri, or Welsh Highland Railway (inset). Work began on a permanent station for the town in February 2017. The new station is expected to open to passengers in spring 2018. The original station was opened on 11 October 1997, opposite the former locomotive works of De Winton & Co. and beneath the retaining walls of Segontium Terrace. It can be reached from St Helen's Road by a pedestrian footbridge.

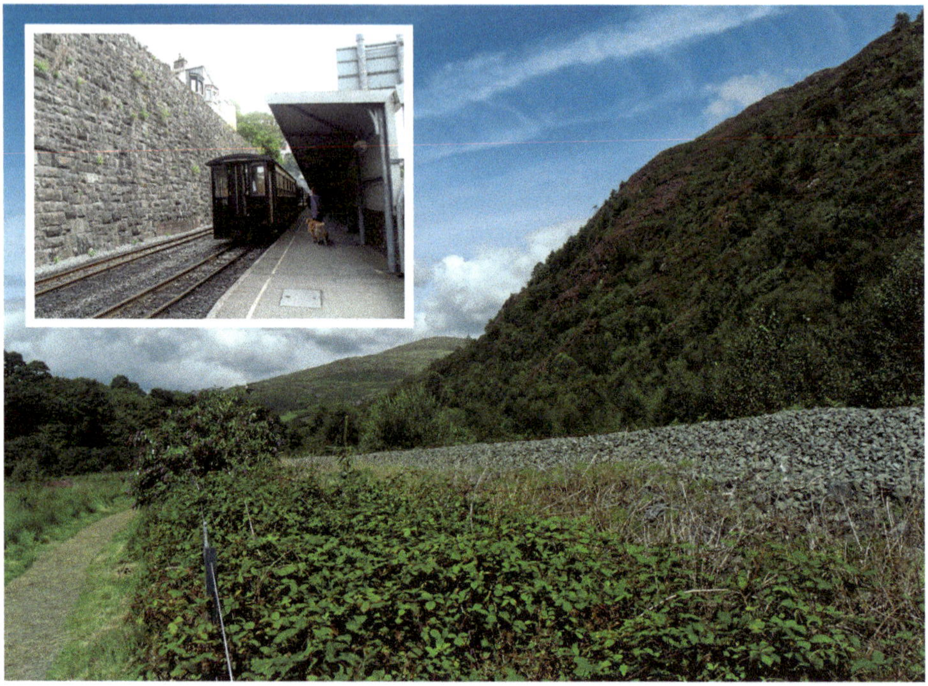

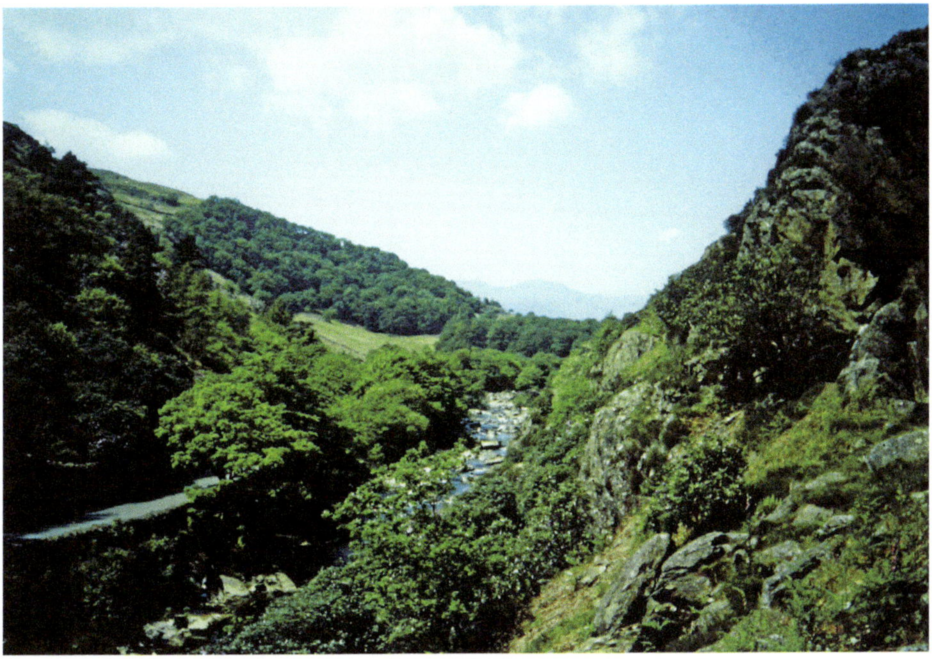

Aberglaslyn Pass, Looking Towards the Snowdon Range, from the Welsh Highland Railway (above), 1989, and Towards Pont Aberglaslyn (below), 2017
***Inset*: The Snowdon Range, 2017**

In 1900 permission was given to extend the railway to Beddgelert, with construction activities beginning in 1905–06 south of Snowdon and heading towards the village. However, construction of the railway's infrastructure came to a halt when the building company's money ran out. This meant that tunnels in the Aberglaslyn Pass and other earthworks were abandoned until 1914, when the unfinished railway was completed. The Welsh Highland Railway company came into existence in 1922, with the complete line opening for traffic in 1923.

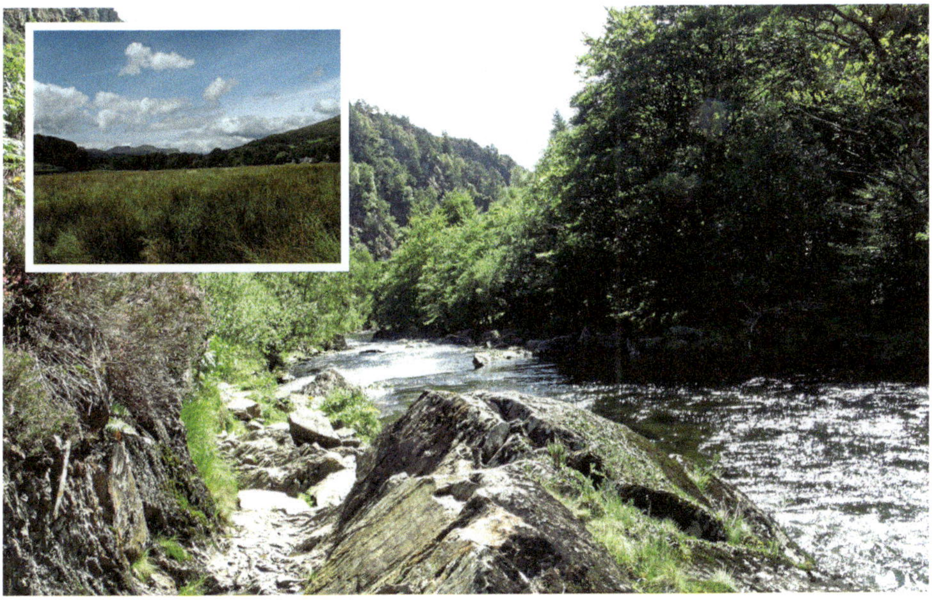

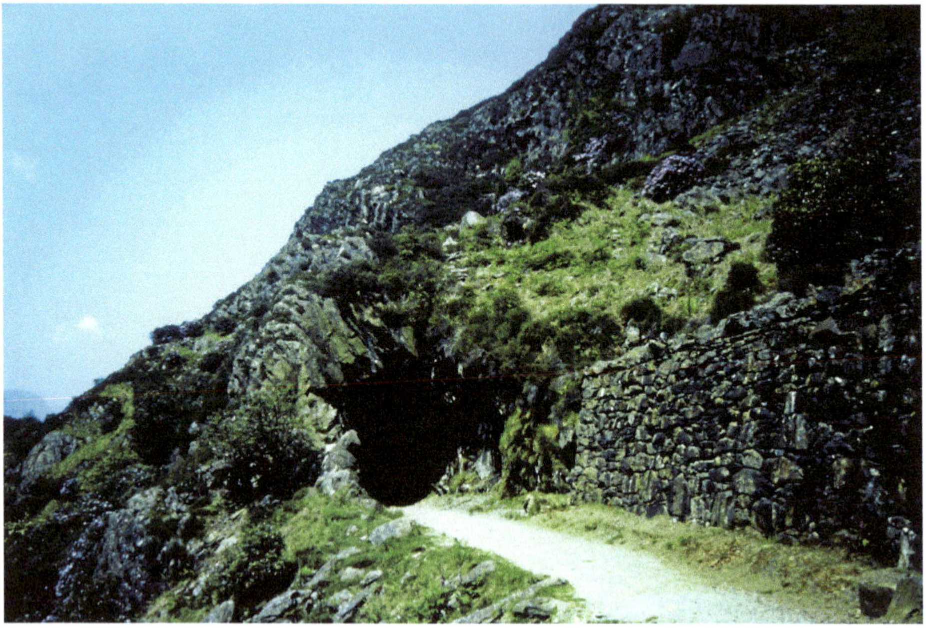

Tunnel on the Course of the Welsh Highland Railway (from the same location as the previous photograph), 1989, and (below) Steam Locomotive Heading Towards Beddgelert, 2017

The Welsh Highland Railway received funding, by way of loans, from the Ministry of Transport and local authorities. This, in effect, doomed the railway to failure because it could never earn enough to pay back the interest on the loans. These financial difficulties lead to the eventual closure of the line, with a steady decline in traffic from its opening year of 1923. There were no profits, and after the winter of 1923/24 the passenger service became seasonal only.

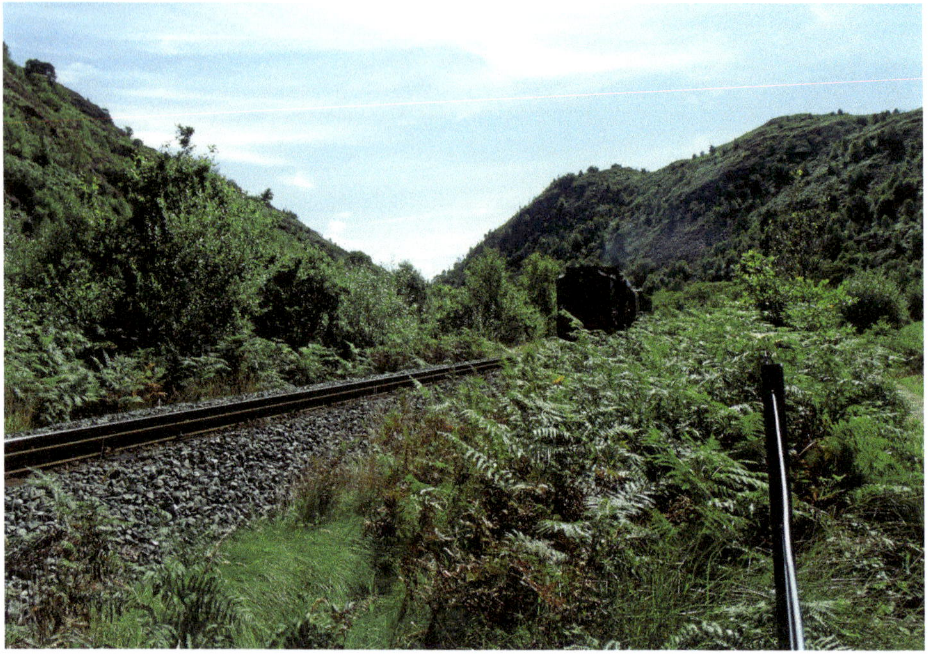

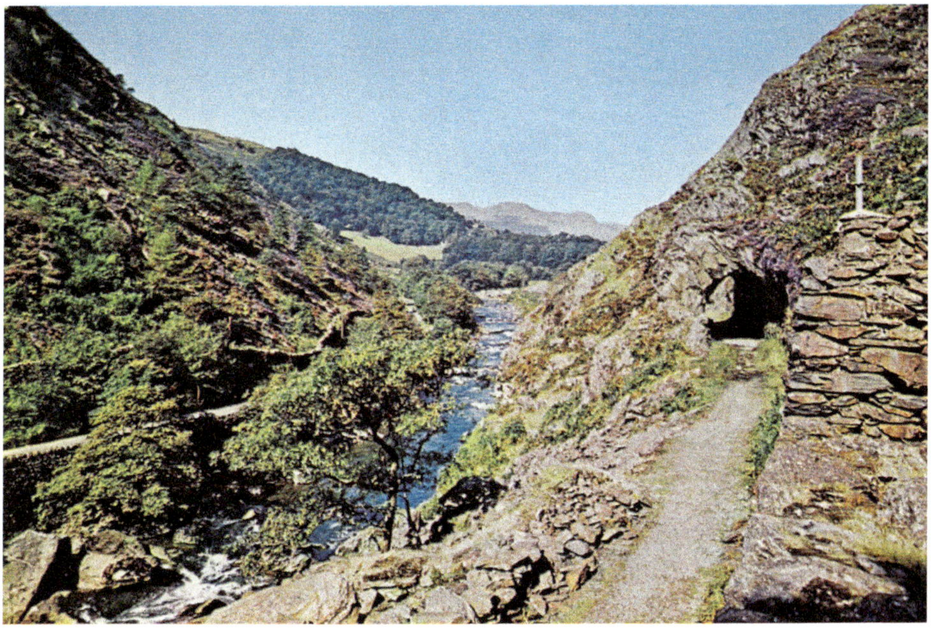

Aberglaslyn Pass, Trackbed and Tunnel of the Welsh Highland Railway, Looking Towards the Snowdon Range (above) and Pont Aberglaslyn (below), 1989

The A498 Beddgelert to Porthmadog road, via Pont Aberglaslyn, is shown on both photographs, with the Afon Glaslyn running through the Aberglaslyn Pass towards Y Cob at Porthmadog. In autumn 2000 the Welsh Highland Railway closed the trackbed to walkers, as a precursor to rebuilding the railway, which had already undergone some remedial work in order to make it safe. In the meantime the Fisherman's Path was rebuilt in order to provide an alternative route for walkers next to the Afon Glaslyn.

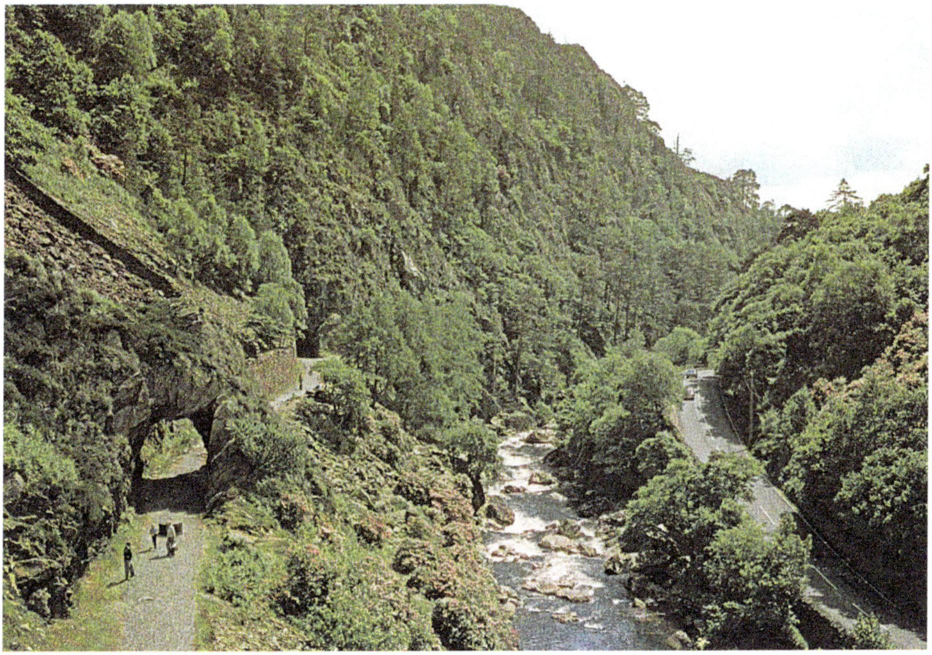

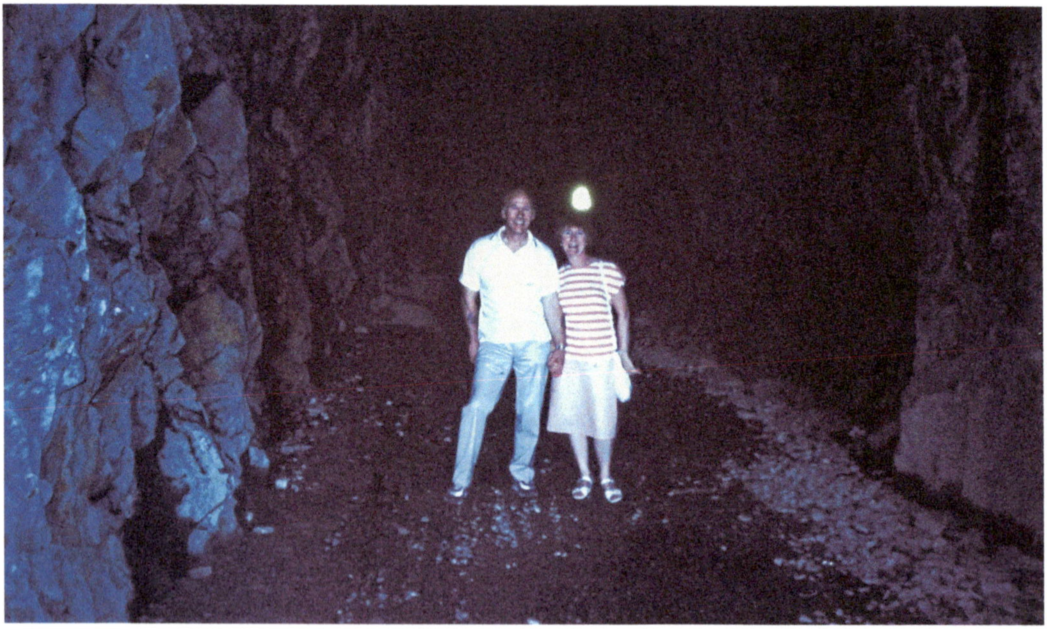

Inside the Next Tunnel on the Course of the Welsh Highland Railway, 1989, and Steam Locomotive Heading Towards Beddgelert, 2017

The Welsh Highland Railway was put into receivership in 1927. Reasons for its decline included a deterioration in the slate industry, tourists' preference for charabancs rather than rail tours, and local people using motor buses rather than train transport. The line continued, with a steady degeneration in the quality of service, until the last passenger train ran on 5 September 1936. All traffic was formally suspended on the Welsh Highland Railway from 1 June 1937. Some parts, like Rhyd Ddu station, were sold off.

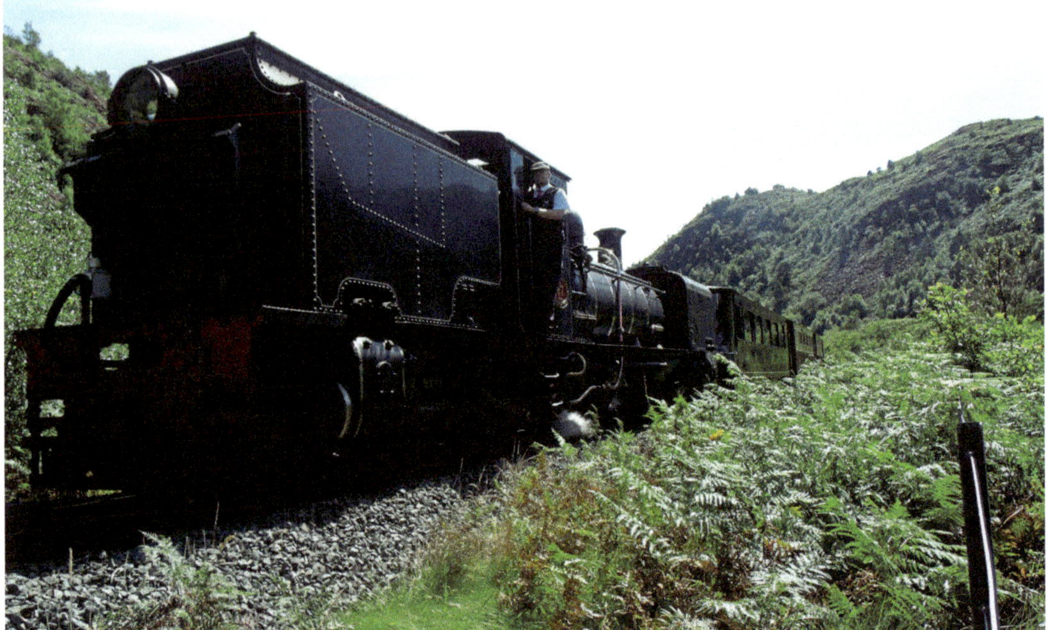

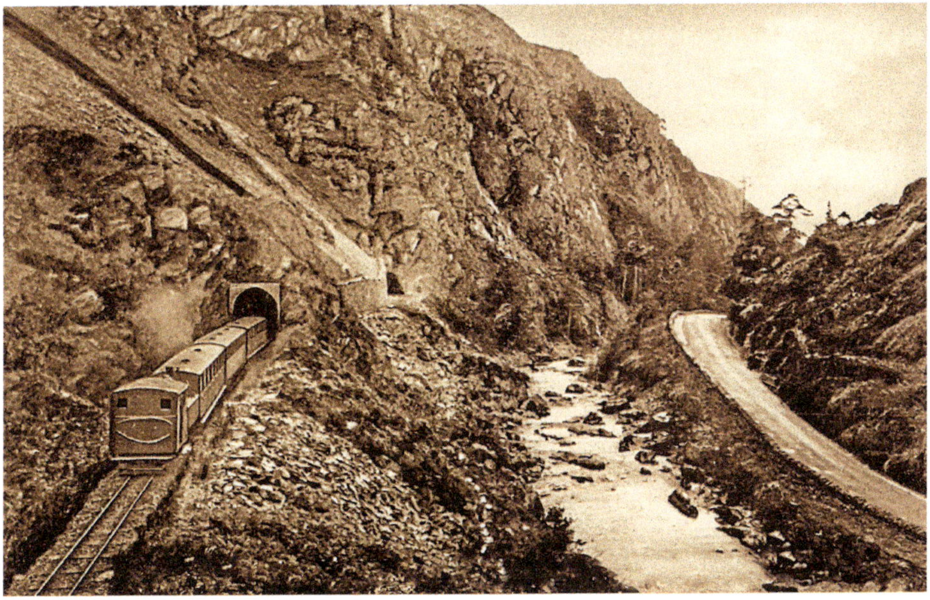

Welsh Highland Railway, Aberglaslyn Pass (*c.* 1925) and Towards Beddgelert (below), 2017
As can be seen from this panorama of around 1925, the views from this section of the Welsh Highland Railway are extremely impressive. It is not surprising that the public continued to unofficially use the trackbed and tunnels as a footpath until construction work on the railway made it too dangerous to do so. It offered better views for walkers than those from the Fisherman's Path, and the novelty of walking through tunnels was also an attraction, as was the direct route to Nantmor.

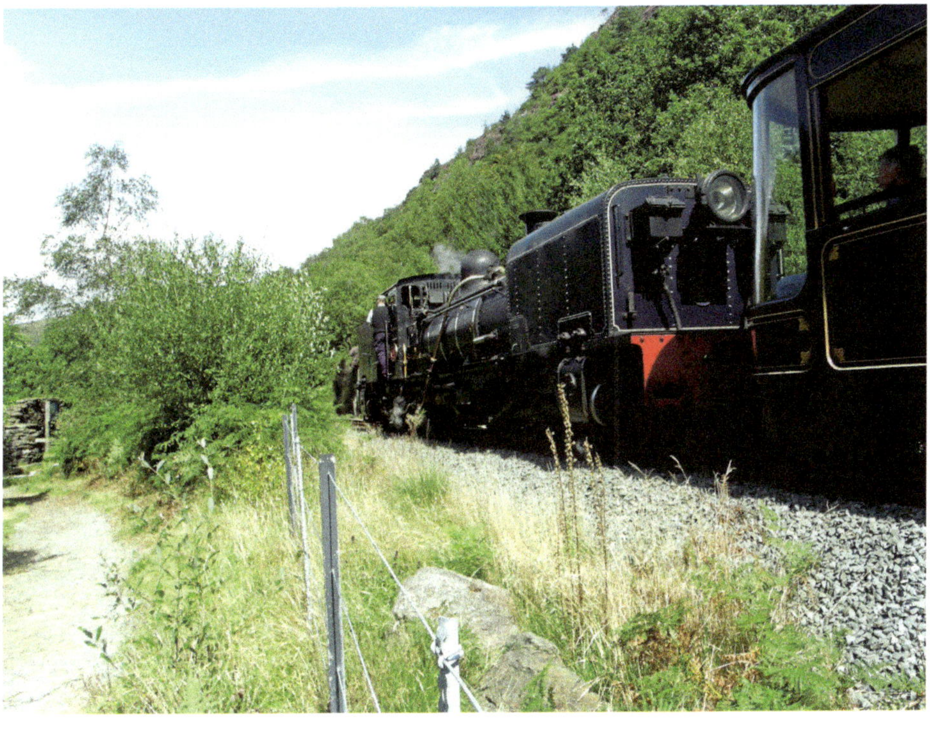

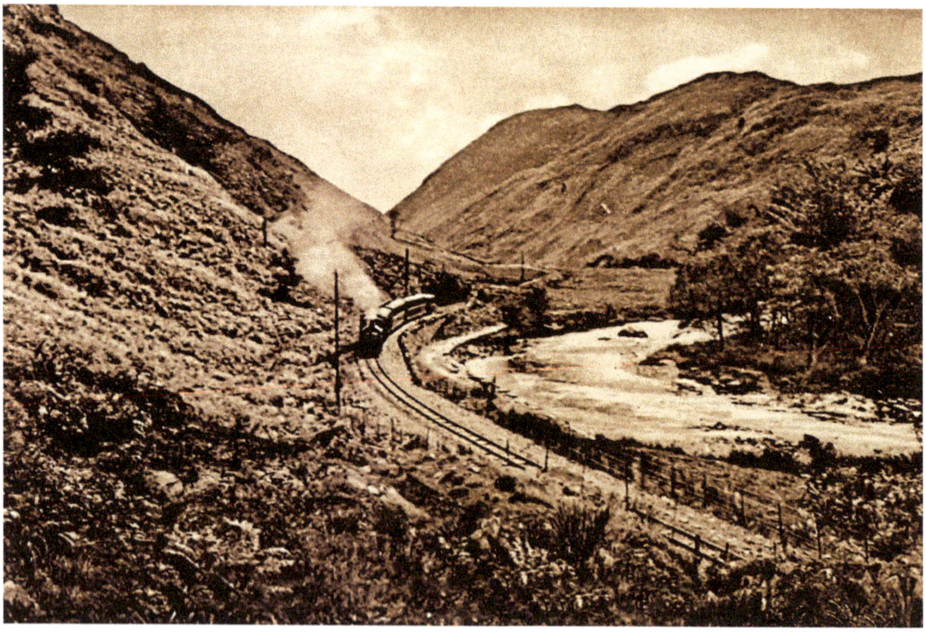

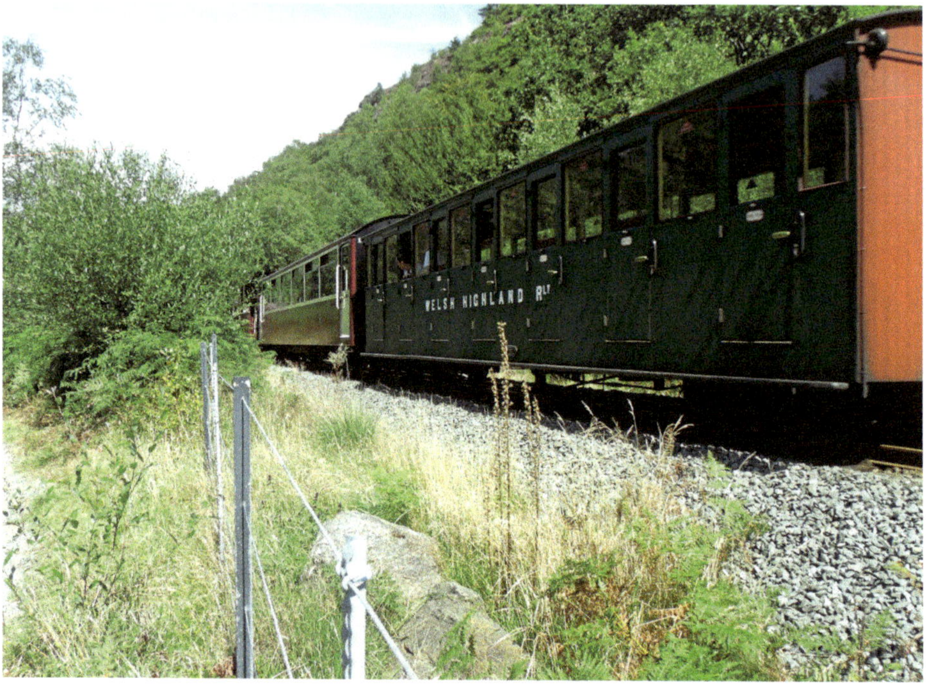

Welsh Highland Railway, Aberglaslyn Pass (*c.* 1925) and Heading Towards Beddgelert, 2017
Another magnificent panorama through the Aberglaslyn Pass, before the Welsh Highland Railway closed in 1937. The pass is clearly defined by the steep slopes of the surrounding mountains and the Afon Glaslyn. The new infrastructure was not to reach this point again until August 2007, with the relaying of track across Pont Bryn-y-Felin. By mid-October, track-laying had already passed beyond the railway tunnels and the stretch of rock-cuttings and embankments near Nantmor.

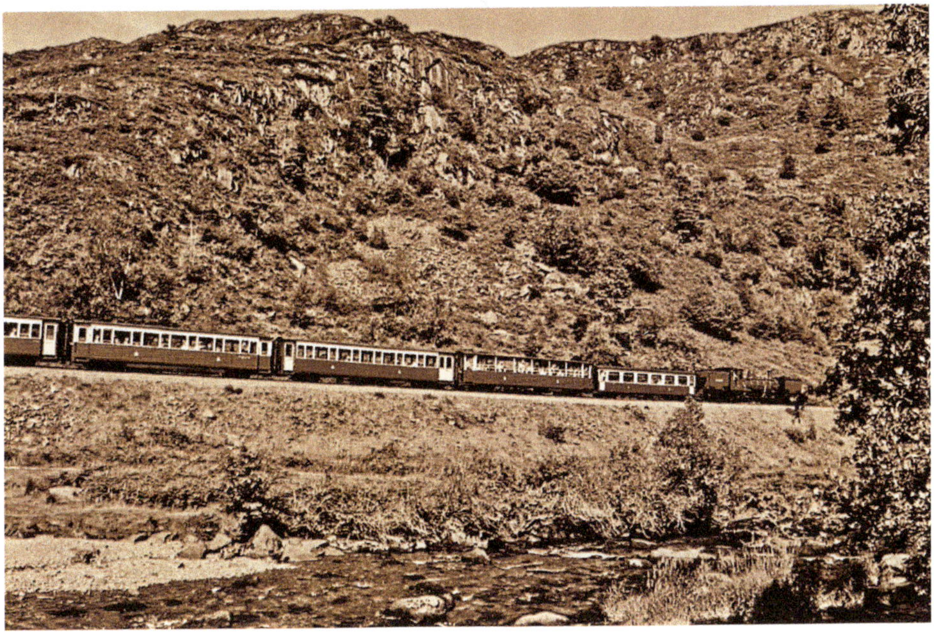

The Afon Glaslyn and Welsh Highland Railway (Beyer-Garratt) Heading Towards Porthmadog, Aberglaslyn Pass, 2010

Just below Pont Aberglaslyn lies Llyn Glas, the former site of a harbour used to transport copper ore from Cwm Bychan. The copper sulphate washed down from the surrounding hills gives the Afon Glaslyn, a turquoise hue. Until the early nineteenth century the Afon was navigable for small boats at high tide as far as Pont Aberglaslyn, just 1.6 kilometres (1 mile) south of Beddgelert. In 1812 the construction of the embankment across the Traeth Mawr (Large Beach) estuary, known as Y Cob, allowed landowners to reclaim much land.

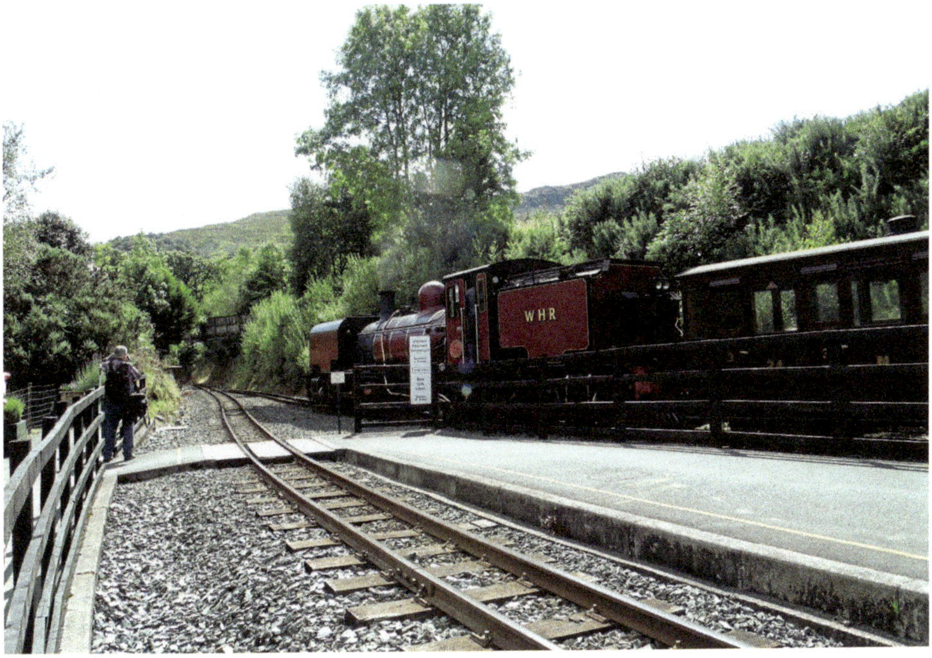

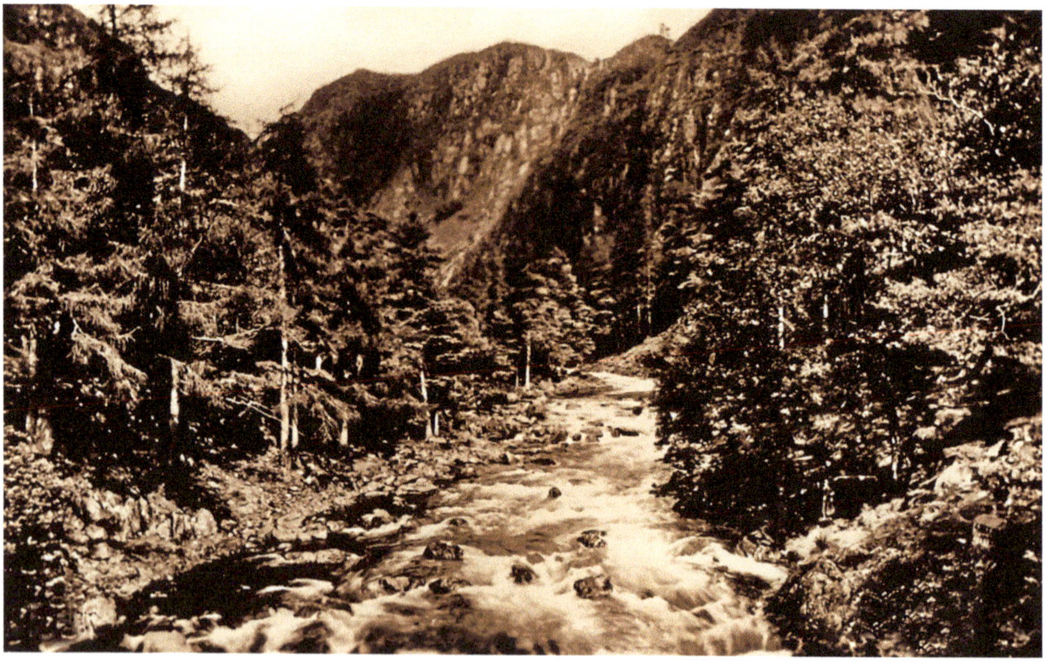

Aberglaslyn Pass from Pont Aberglaslyn, *c.* 1930

The Aberglaslyn Pass is a narrow gorge, south of Beddgelert, in the Snowdonia National Park. It is intersected by the Afon Glaslyn, flowing from Mount Snowdon to the Bay of Cardigan. The Aberglaslyn Pass has many footpaths running alongside the river, giving extensive views. Before building Y Cob at Porthmadog in the early nineteenth century, the tide reached up to Pont Aberglaslyn, providing important access to the north coast and avoiding the need to sail around the Llyn Peninsula.

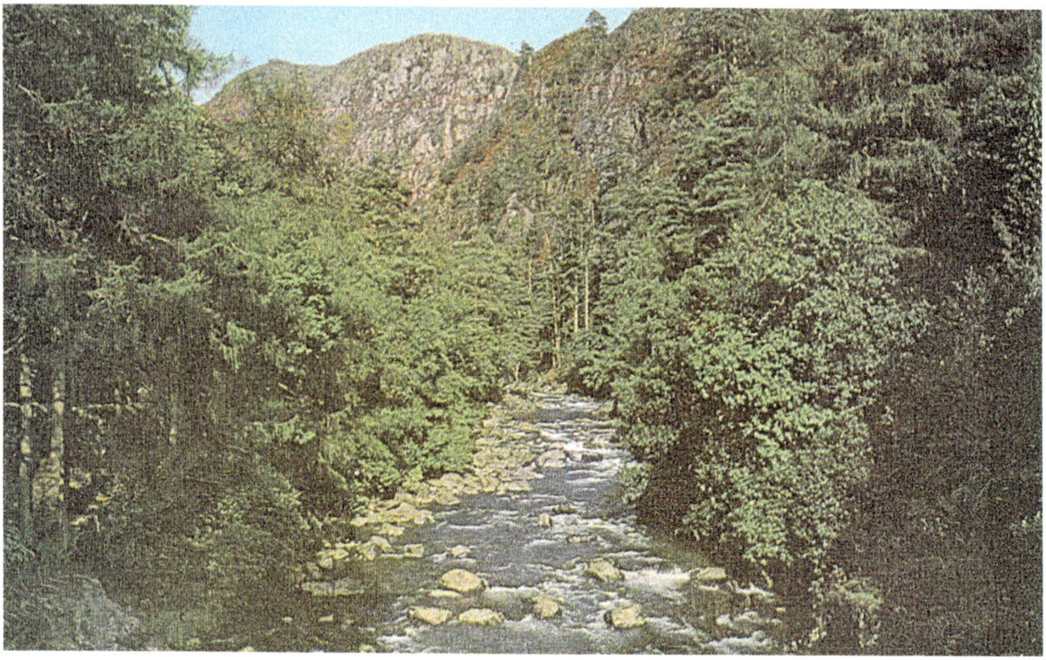

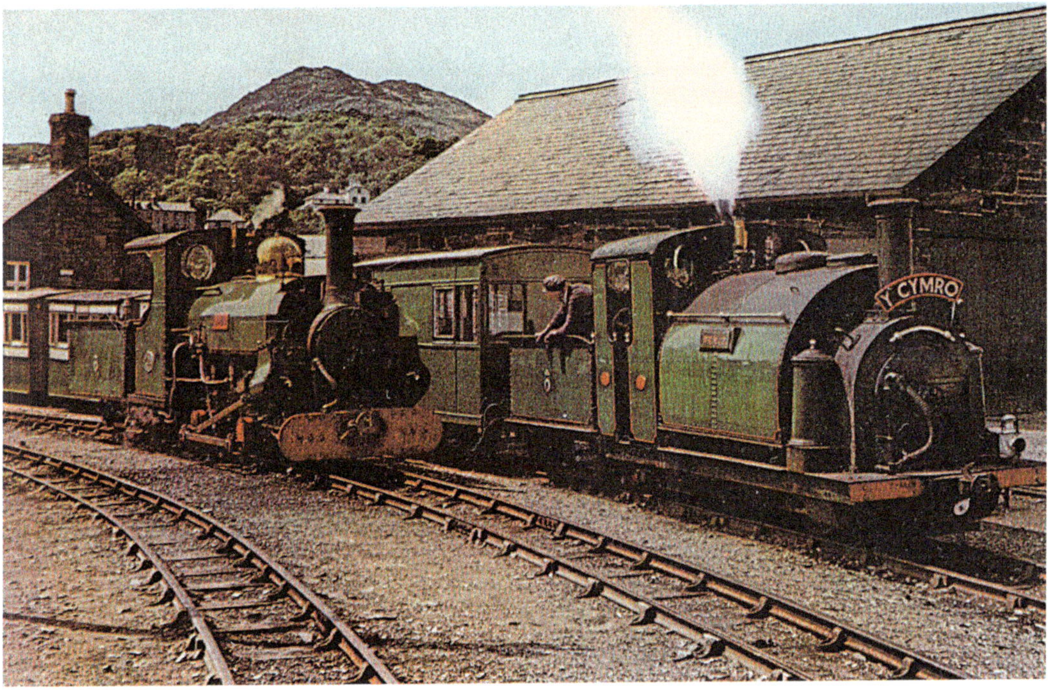

Blaneau Ffestiniog Railway and Y Cob, Porthmadog, c. 1975

Y Cob at Porthmadog is a 1.4 kilometre (0.8 mile)-long causeway crossing Traeth Mawr and the Afon Glaslyn estuary, now used by the Welsh Highland Railway. The original embankment was constructed by William Maddocks (1773–1826) from 1808 to 1811, easing travel between Mid- and North Wales. It was breached in 1812 and repaired, strengthened and reopened in 1814. The Ffestiniog Railway later used it to transport slate from nearby quarries to the newly created port at Porthmadog (Porth Madoc), thus guaranteeing its prosperity.

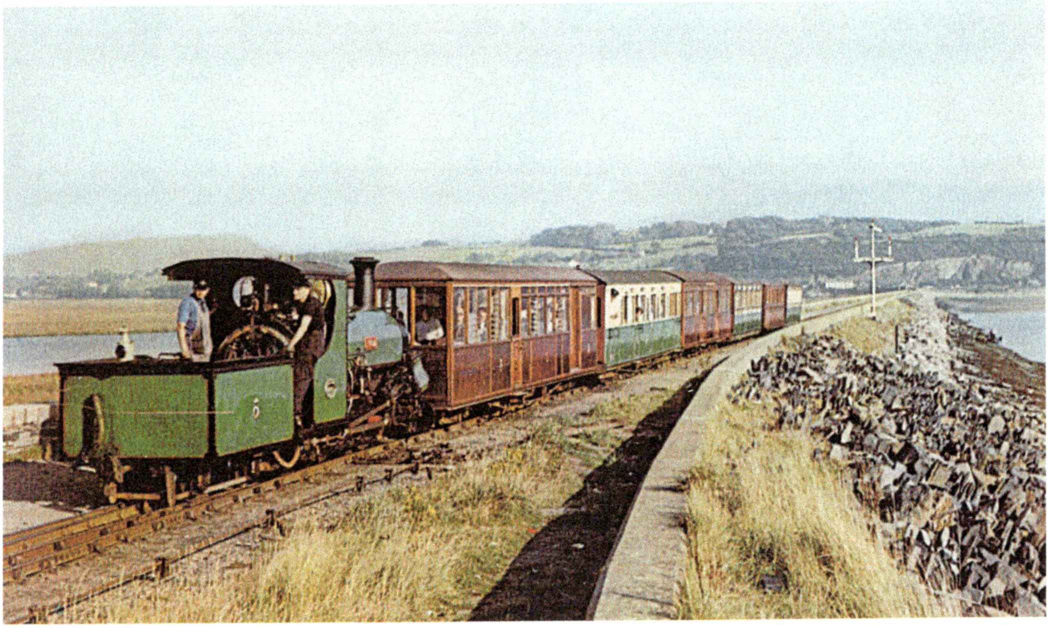

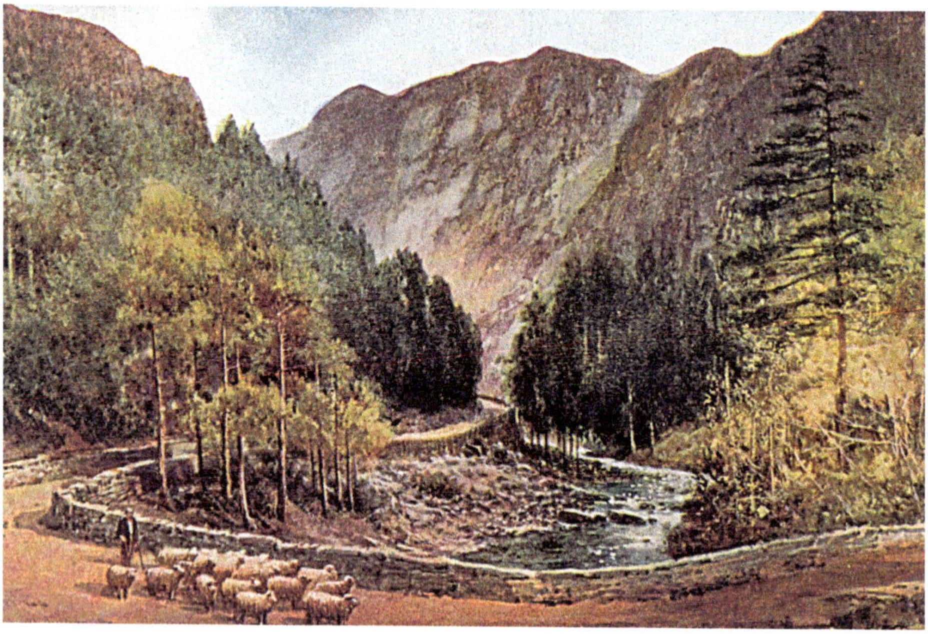

Sheep Being Driven Through the Aberglaslyn Pass (c. 1900) and Sheep Shearing Season near Beddgelert (below), 1991

Sheep farming remains vitally important to the rural economy of Wales. There are approximately 10 million sheep in Wales, with sheep farming accounting for eighty per cent of agricultural production in the country in 2011 alone. Breeds favoured by modern wool producers include the Badger Face Welsh Mountain, the Balwen Welsh Mountain, and the Black Welsh Mountain. The photograph, taken in August 1991, shows newly sheared sheep being driven off the mountain and onto fresh pastures, where they will eventually lamb around January.

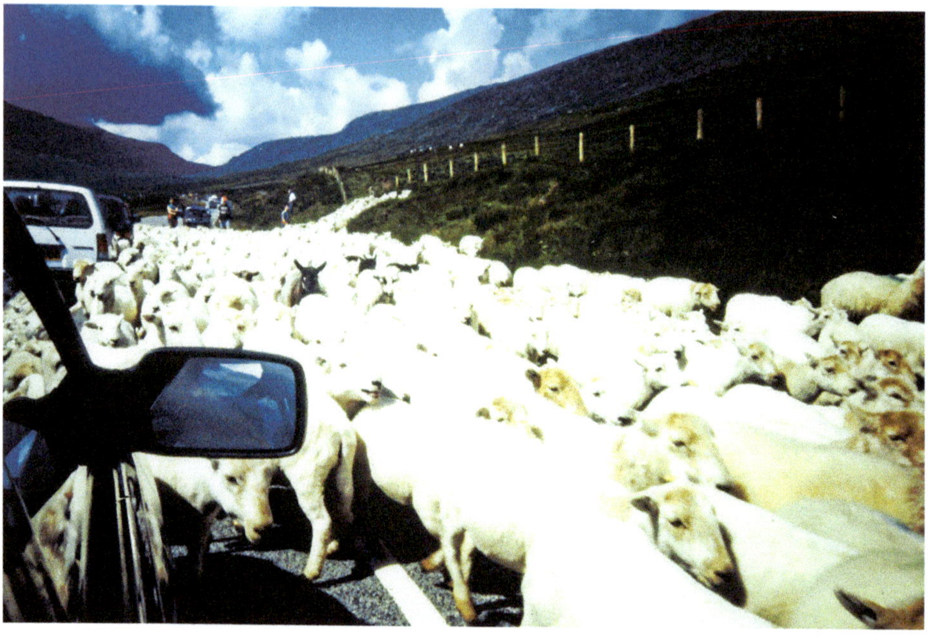

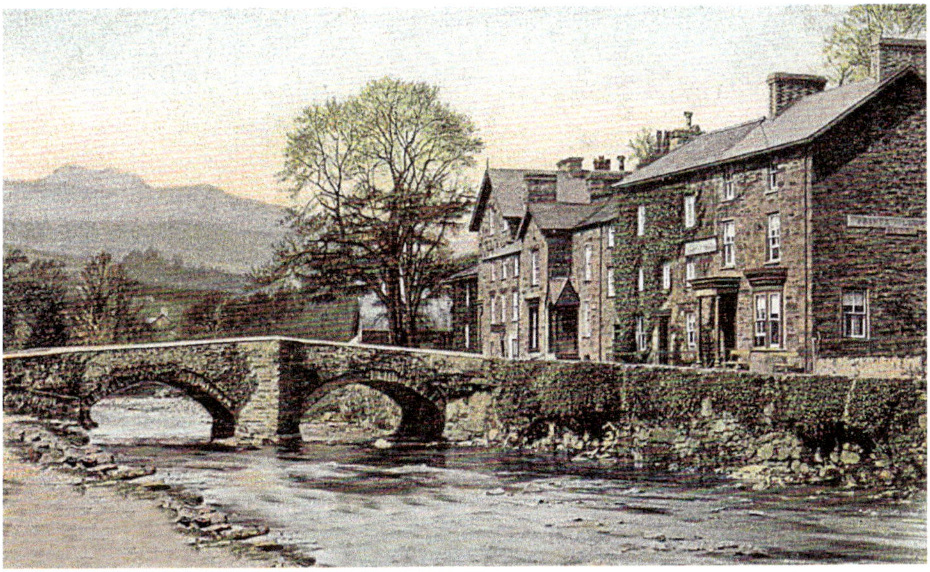

The Bridge, Beddgelert, *c.* 1900

The village is situated at the confluence of the Afon Glaslyn and Afon Colwyn, on the edge of the Snowdon massif, with Moel Hebog to the west. Just above the confluence of the rivers, in the centre of the village, is the old stone bridge, complete with two arches. It carries the A498 to Porthmadog and is too narrow at this point to allow two vehicles to pass. Alfred Bestall wrote and illustrated his *Rupert the Bear* stories while resident in Beddgelert.

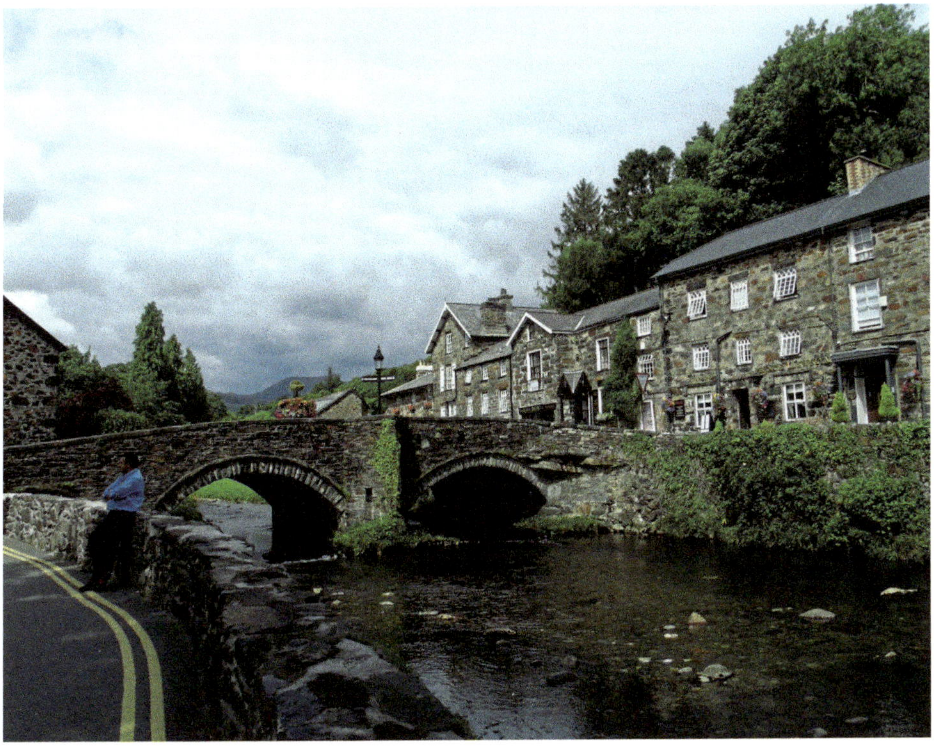

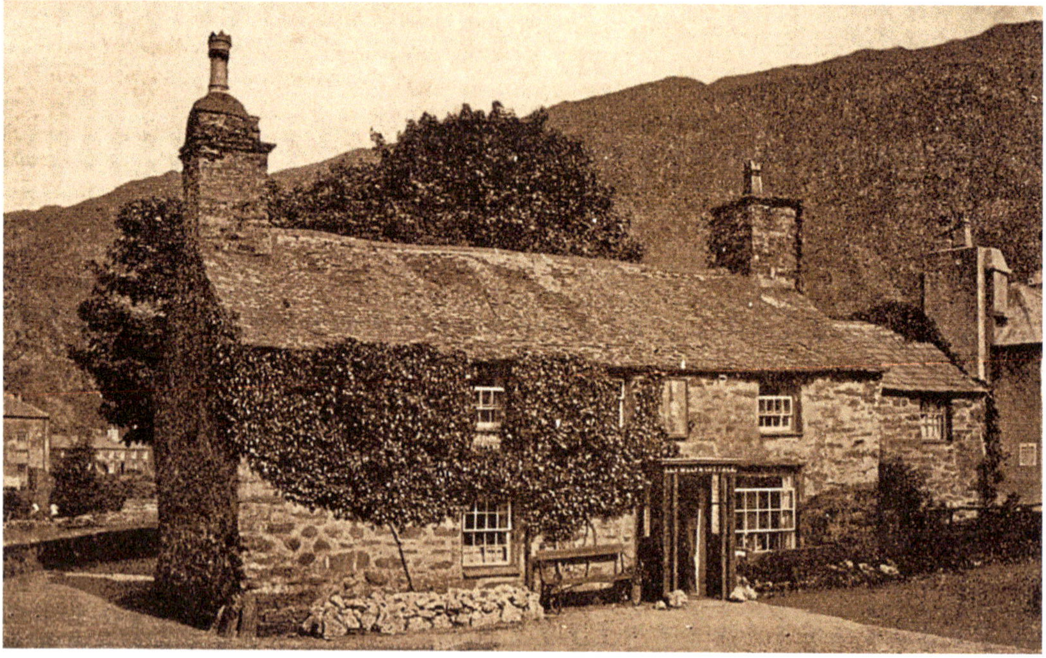

Llywelyn Cottage (Bwthyn Llywelyn), Beddgelert, *c.* 1910

The National Trust owns this seventeenth-century cottage, which has an exhibition about the area's history and wildlife. Beddgelert has a population of 455 (according to the 2011 census). The legend of Gelert's Grave dates from the eighteenth century and was an attempt to lure more tourists to the area. The village is actually named after Gelert, a sixth-century saint. Gelert's 'tomb' stands in a meadow below Cerrig Llan. Snowdon dominates the skyline, a few miles to the north.

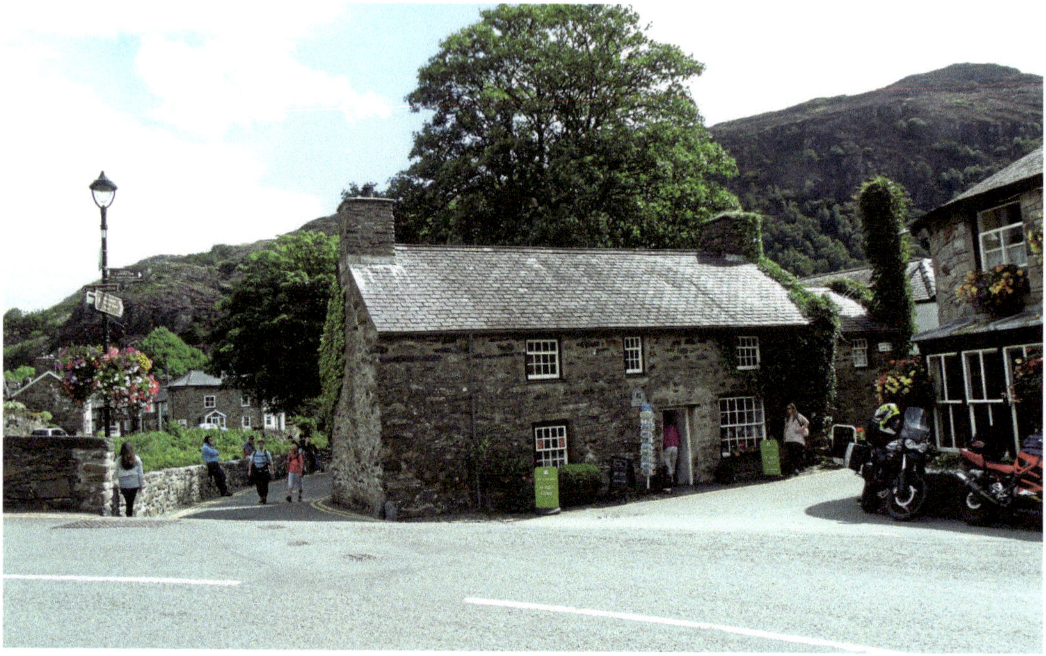

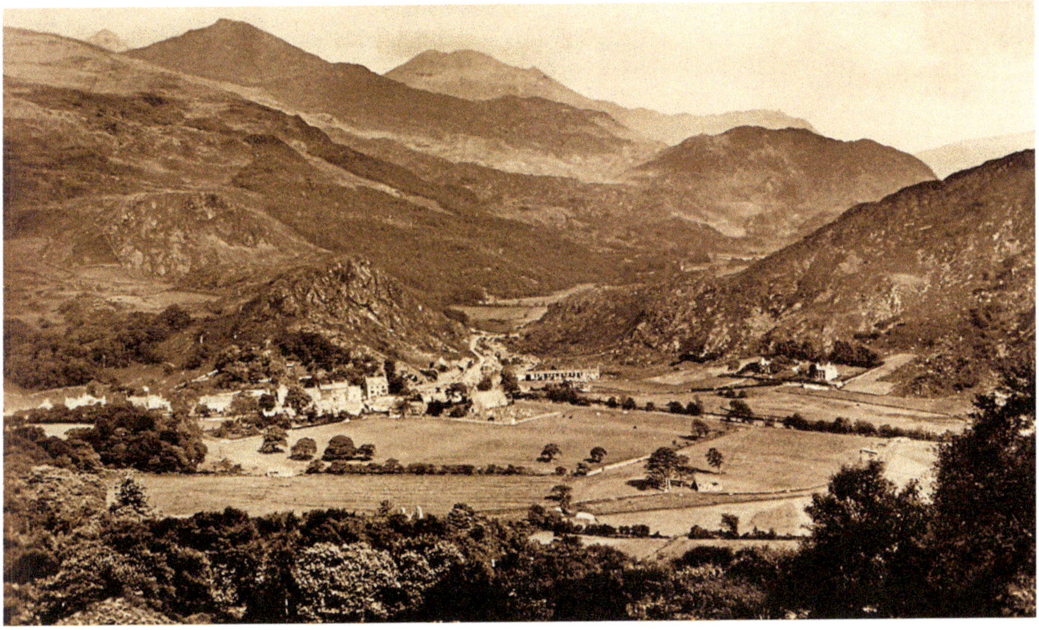

Beddgelert Village, *c.* 1910

Beddgelert was once a busy port; before the construction of Y Cob at Porthmadog the river was tidal and ships could reach Pont Aberglaslyn. The village can also claim to be the site of two Welsh myths – the vanishing mountain and the castle of Dinas Emrys, said to be where Merlin gave his first prophecy and possible site of the Holy Grail. Yr Wyddfa (Snowdon) is the 'great tomb', where a giant killed by King Arthur is believed to be buried at the summit.

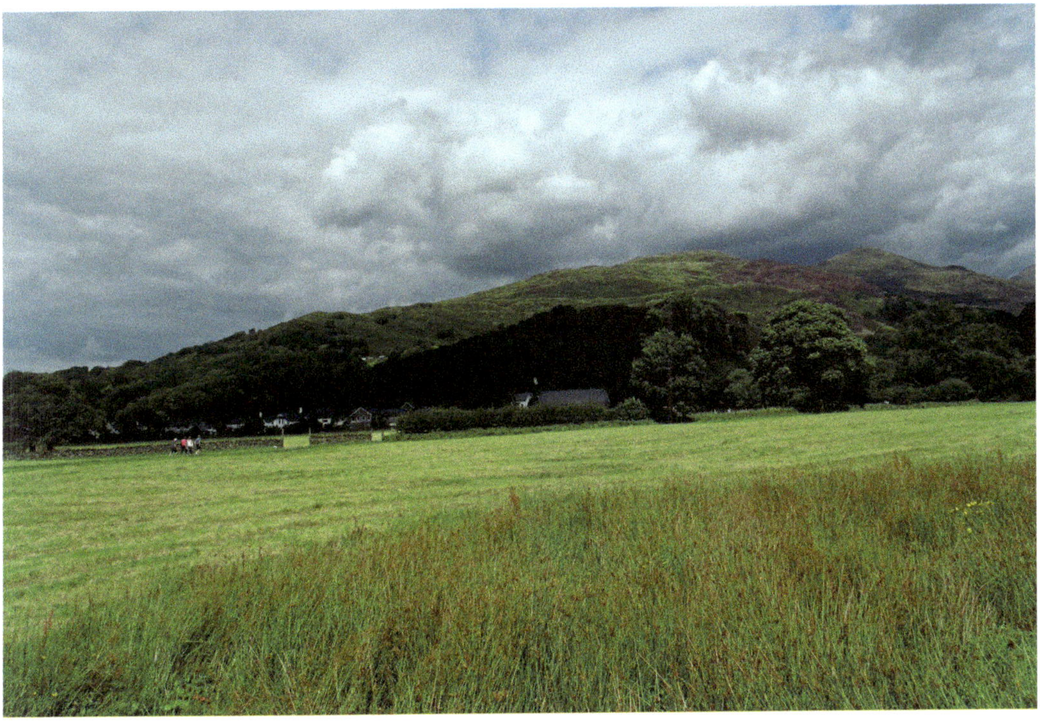

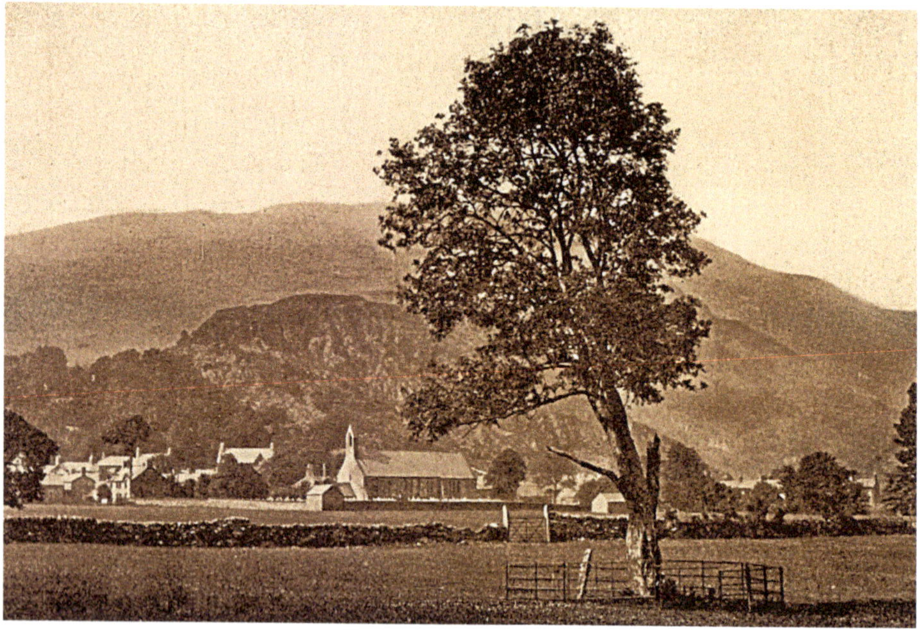

Gelert's Grave and St Mary's Parish Church, Beddgelert, *c.* 1910

This Grade II listed building is located at one of the oldest Christian communities (Celtic Clas) in Wales, established in the sixth century. In the thirteenth century it was the site of an Augustinian Priory. Following fire-damage the church was repaired and restored in the fifteenth century; and after the sixteenth-century Dissolution of the Monasteries, the Priory reverted to a parish church. There are medieval remnants, including transept arches and some stonework around the lancet windows, with Victorian and twentieth-century modifications.

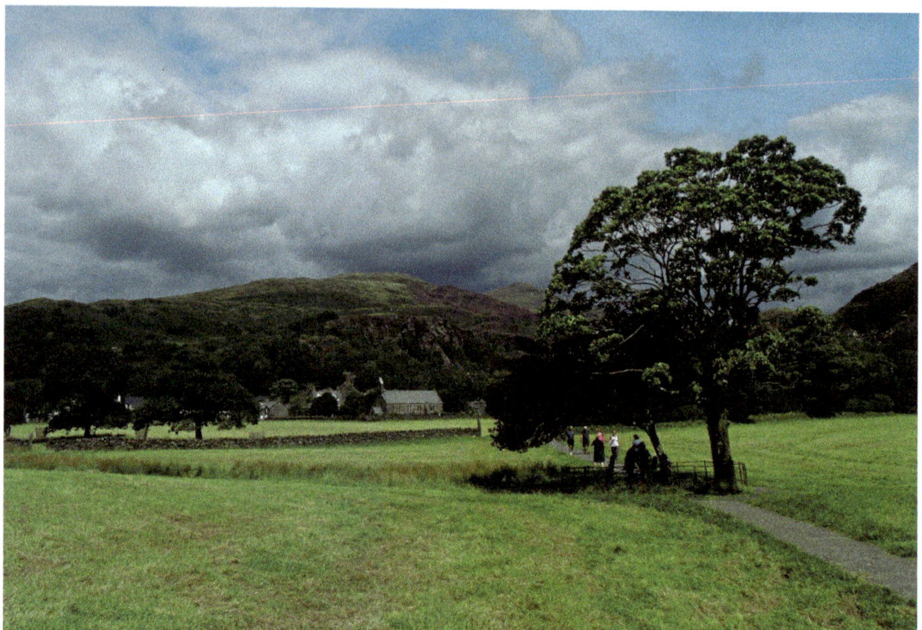

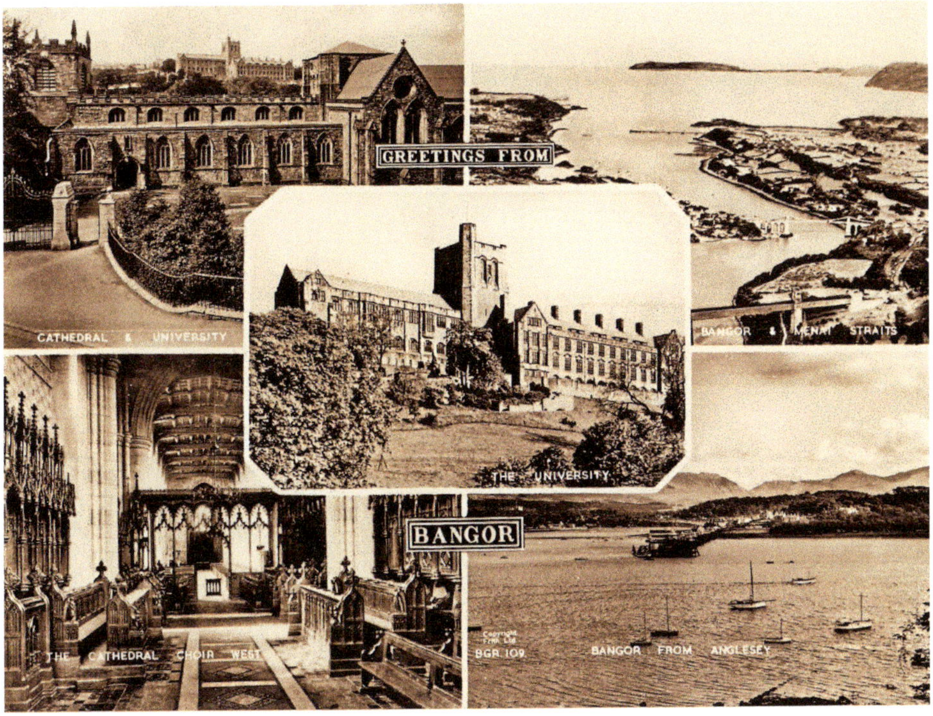

Bangor Cathedral, Cathedral Close (above and below left), *c.* 1950

In around AD 530, Deiniol, a noble Welshman, was given land by Maelgwn, King of Gwynedd, which he enclosed with a fence known as 'bangor'. Deiniol then built a church inside the enclosure, surrounded by huts in which his followers lived. Acting as missionaries, they increased the number of inhabitants, encouraging them to worship in the church. A Celtic monastery (Clas) was established because of this. In around AD 546 Deiniol was consecrated as Bishop, reputedly by St David, and the church became a cathedral. Deiniol died in around AD 572.

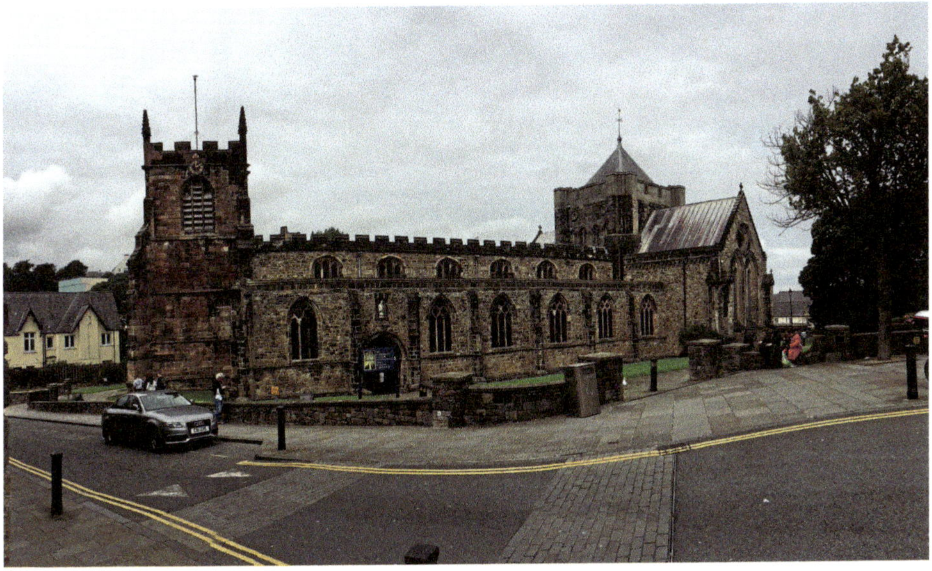

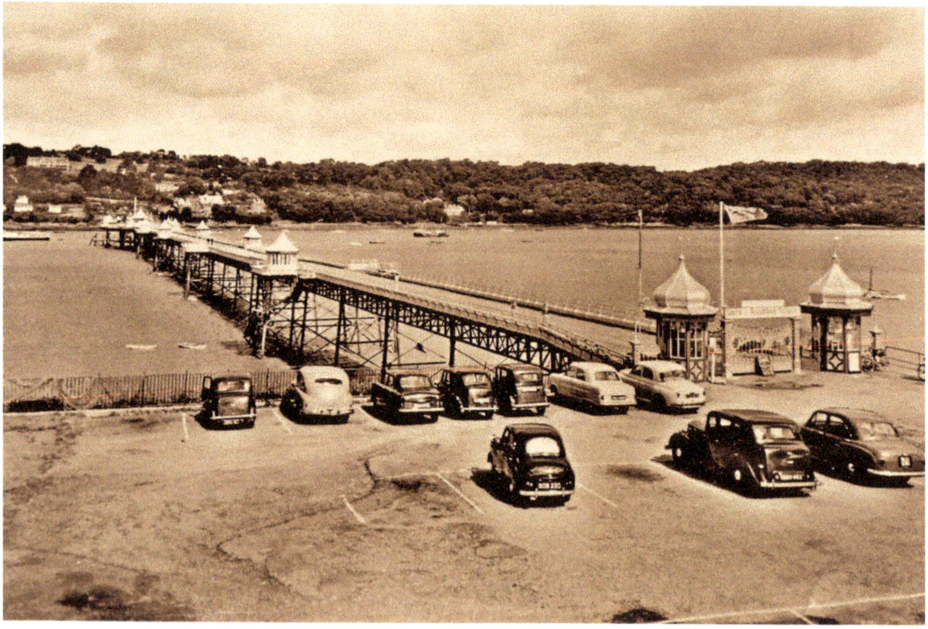

Garth Pier, Ffordd Garth, Bangor, *c.* 1950

Garth Pier is a Grade II listed structure and is currently 460 metres (1,500 feet) long, making it the second longest pier in Wales and the ninth longest in the British Isles. It was designed by J. J. Webster of Westminster, London. Originally 470 metres (1,550 feet) long, the pier has cast-iron columns, with a metal structure of steel throughout, including the handrails. It opened on 14 May 1896, the opening ceremony being performed by George Douglas-Pennant, Second Baron Penrhyn.

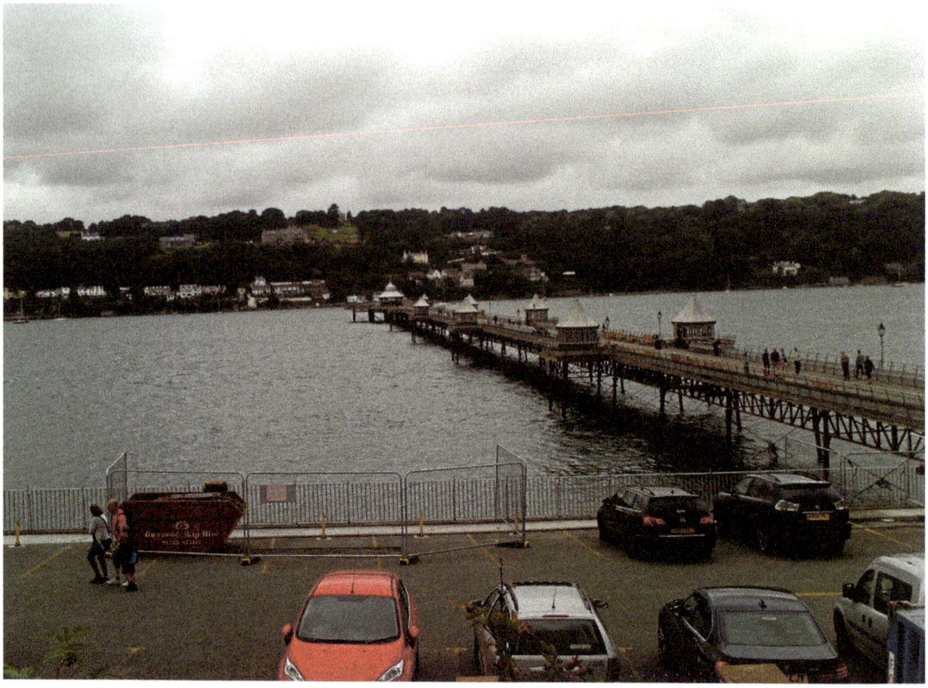

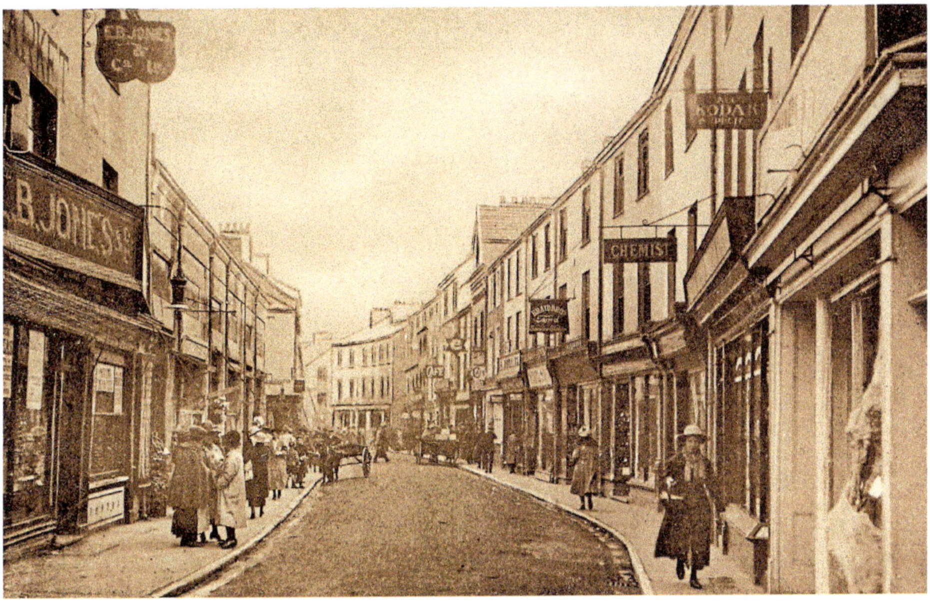

Stryd Fawr (High Street), Bangor, *c.* 1910
Today traffic has restricted access to the shopping centre. The city centre has two modern shopping centres (Menai and Deiniol) and was redeveloped in the 2000s. There is a range of larger stores and smaller independently owned shops, a cinema and a theatre. Bangor is one of the smallest cities in the United Kingdom, but it is also a city with a strong cultural identity, where Welsh is the chosen language of the vast majority (despite the official figures).

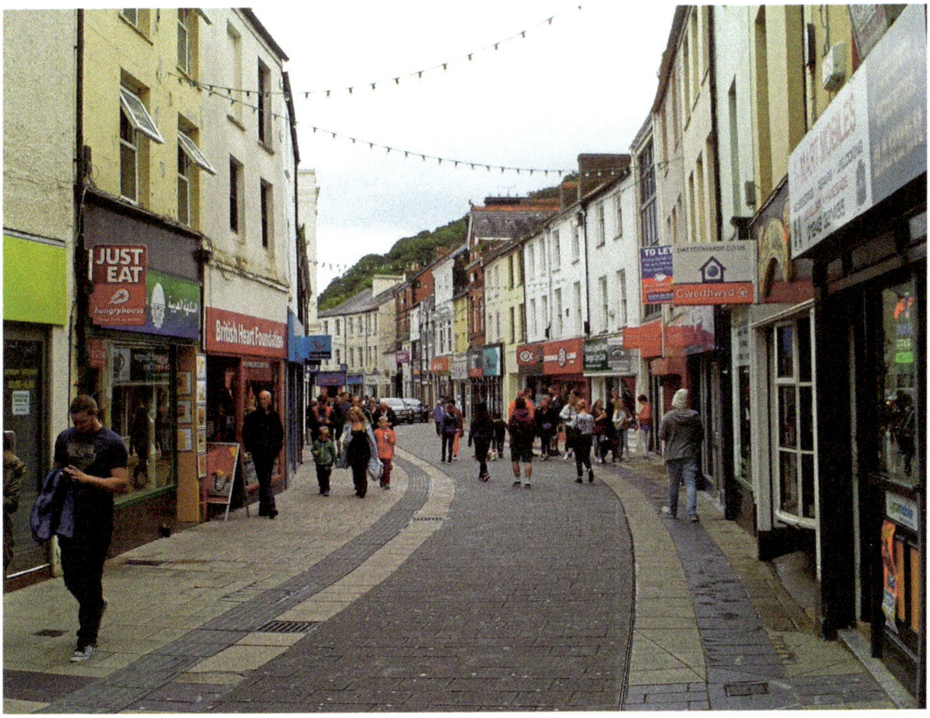

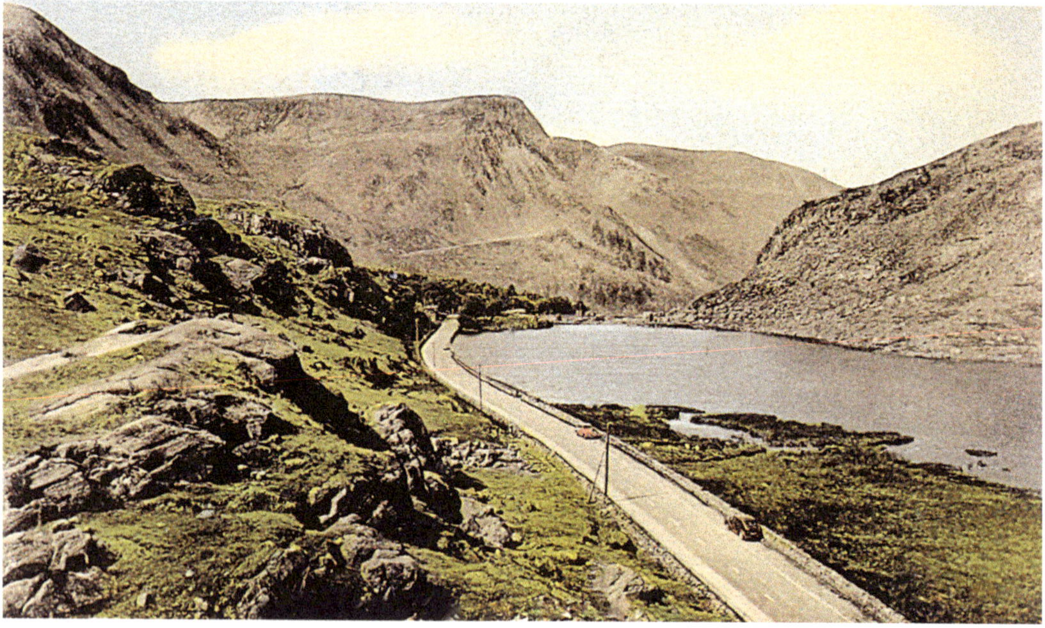

Nant Ffrancon Pass, *c.* 1930

The Nant Ffrancon Pass is a steep-sided glacial valley, typically U-shaped. The Pass drops into Bethesda between the Glyderau and the Carneddau mountains. The valley starts in Cwm Idwal, carrying water from Llyn y Cwn, through Twll Du and Llyn Idwal, to join the Ogwen Valley below the Rhaeadr Ogwen (Ogwen Falls) on Afon Ogwen. Nant Ffrancon is possibly the least agriculturally developed glacial valley in Gwynedd. Monuments from the Neolithic and Bronze Ages, as well as evidence of Iron Age hill forts and medieval settlements, have been found here.

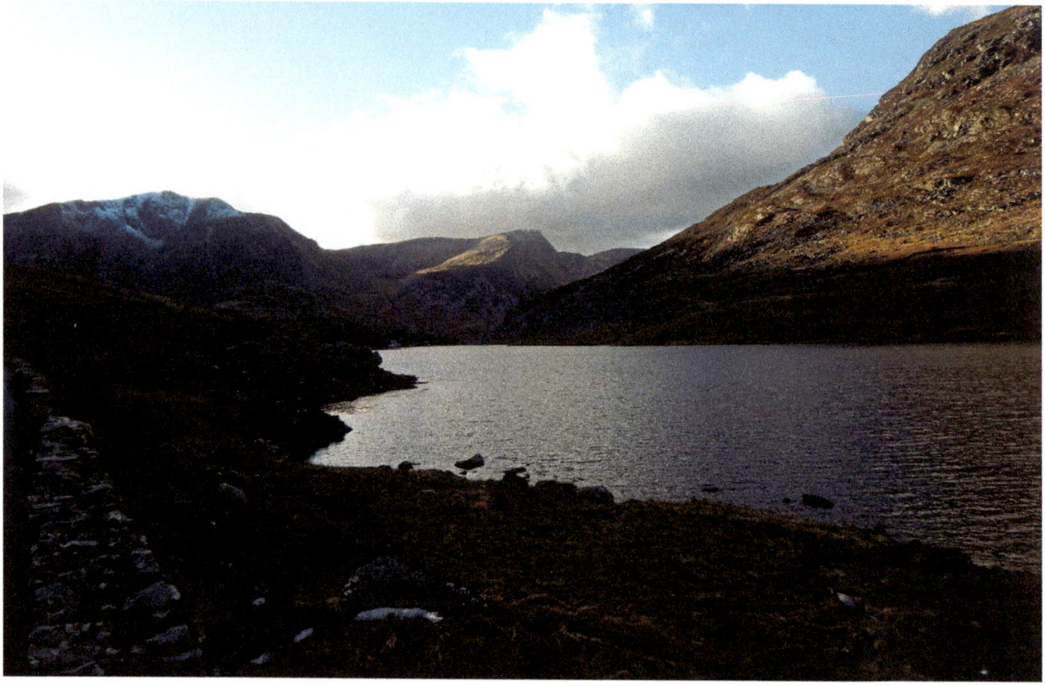

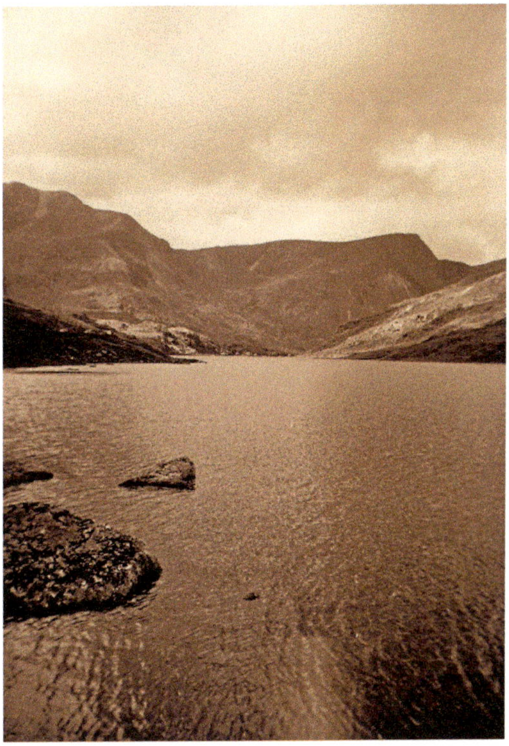

Llyn Ogwen (Lake Ogwen), Nant Ffrancon Head, 1961

The Nant Ffrancon Pass runs between Bethesda and Llyn Ogwen, which borders onto Gwynedd and Conwy. The summit is 312 metres (1,024 feet) at Pont Wern-gof, about a third of a mile beyond the eastern end of Llyn Ogwen. From here the road descends to Capel Curig and Betws-y-Coed. The A5 Holyhead to London trunk road was constructed by Thomas Telford between 1810 and 1826. The original road through Nant Ffrancon was constructed by Lord Penrhyn in the late eighteenth century.

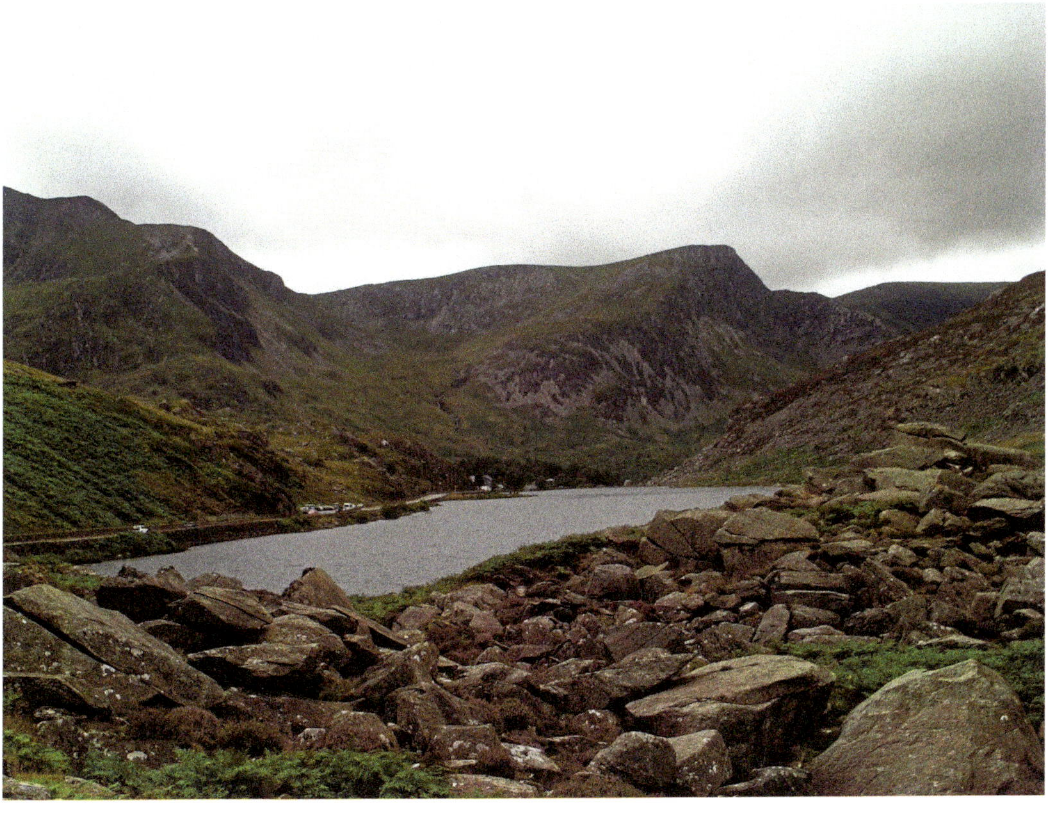

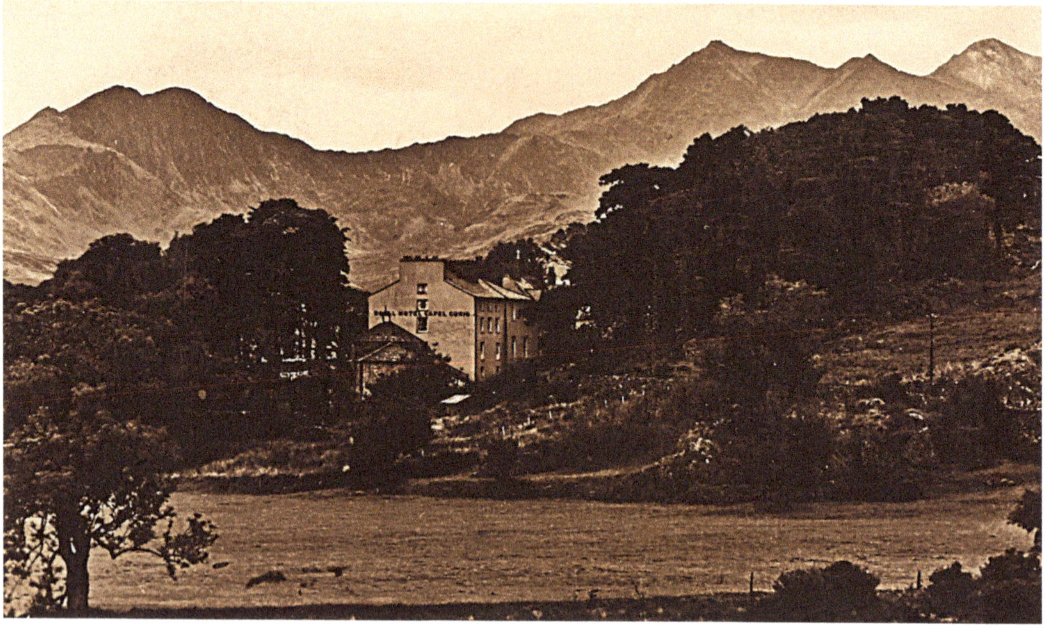

Yr Wyddfa (Snowdon) from Ffordd Bangor, Capel Curig, 1931

Snowdon (Yr Wyddfa) is the highest mountain in Wales, at 1,085 metres (3,560 feet) above sea level. It is located in the Snowdonia National Park (Parc Cenedlaethol Eryri), Gwynedd. It was formed of volcanic rocks in the Ordovician period, with the massif extensively affected by glaciation, creating the pyramidal peak of Snowdon and the aretes of Crib Goch and Y Lliwedd. It is popular with climbers and walkers, and the summit can be reached by a number of well-known paths.

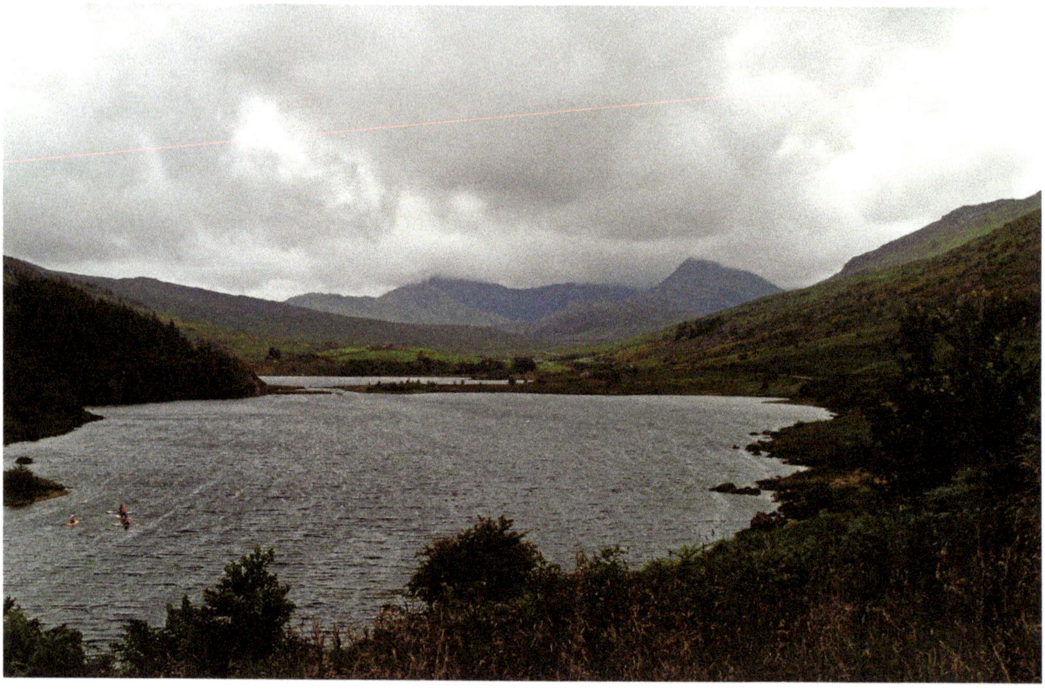

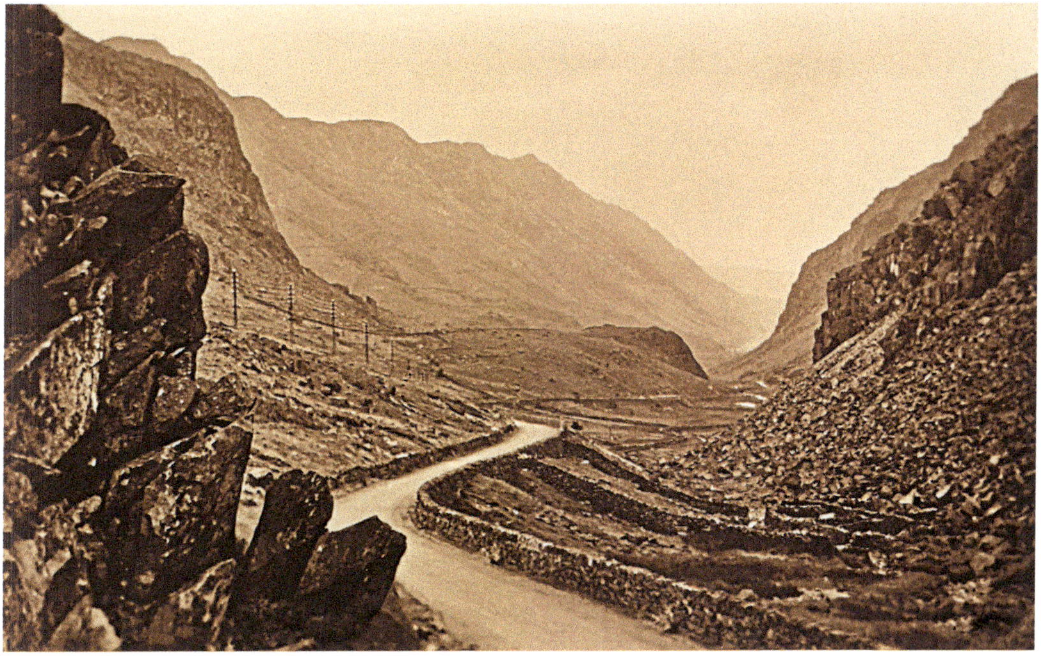

Llanberis Pass, *c.* 1920

The Pass runs for just over 8 kilometres (5 miles) from Llanberis to Pen-y-Pass, providing some picturesque mountain views. The twin lakes of Llyn Padarn and Llyn Peris cut through the mountain ranges of Yr Wyddfa and Glyderau, which form the Pass. At Pen-y-Pass, the highest point in the gorge, stands a Youth Hostel converted from an old coaching inn, the Gorphwysfa Hotel. At the village of Nant Peris is the ancient fourteenth-century Church of St Peris, with the twelfth-century Dolbadarn Castle nearby.

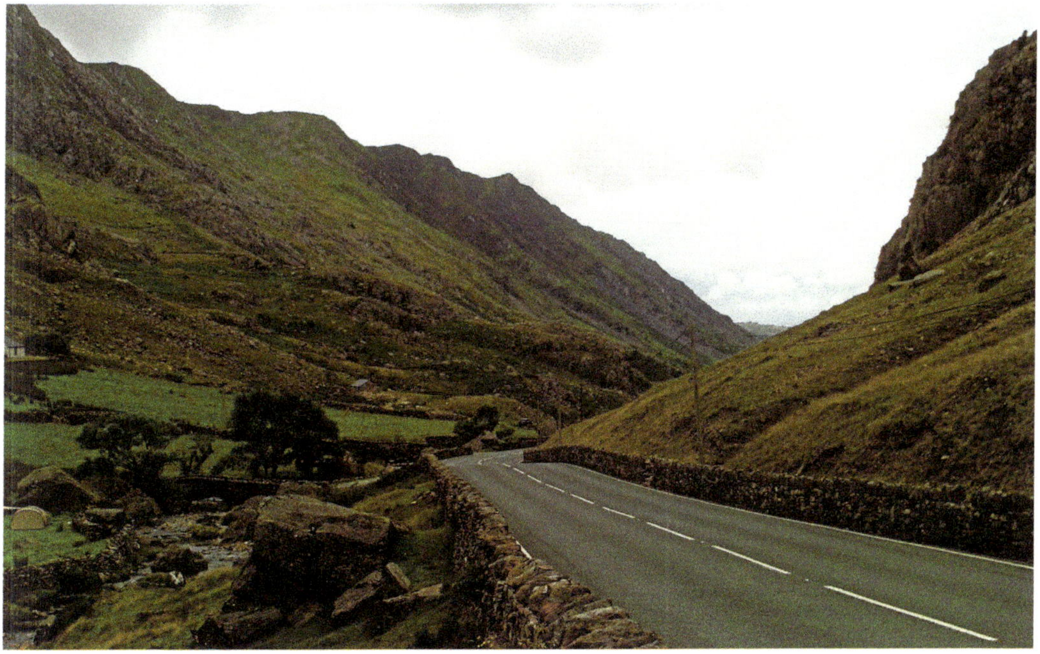

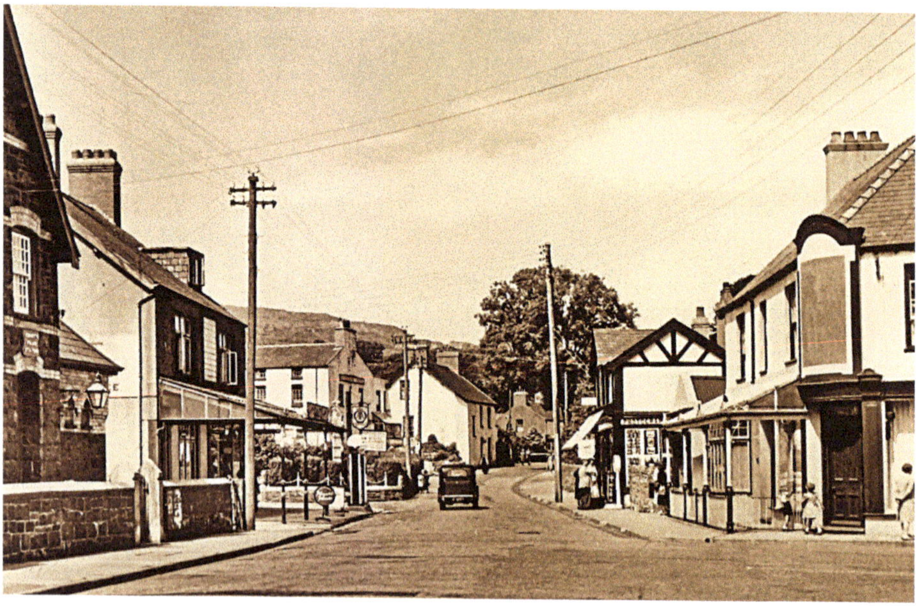

Stryd Fawr (High Street), Llanberis, *c.* 1950

Thousands of walkers and climbers visit the village every year as a centre for exploring the nearby Snowdon massif. The Welsh Slate Museum is situated in the former workshops of the Dinorwig Quarry, showing much of the original machinery and equipment. Nearby Dolbadarn Castle was built by Llywelyn the Great in the thirteenth century; it was an important military symbol, with a fine example of a Welsh round tower. It was taken by Edward I in 1284 and raw materials from it were used for Caernarfon Castle.

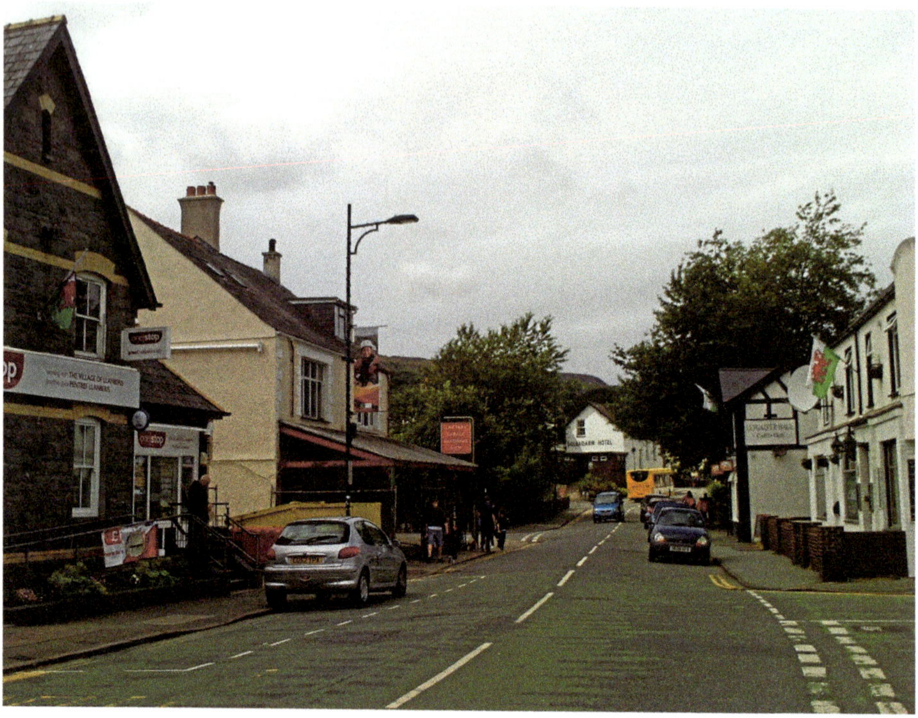

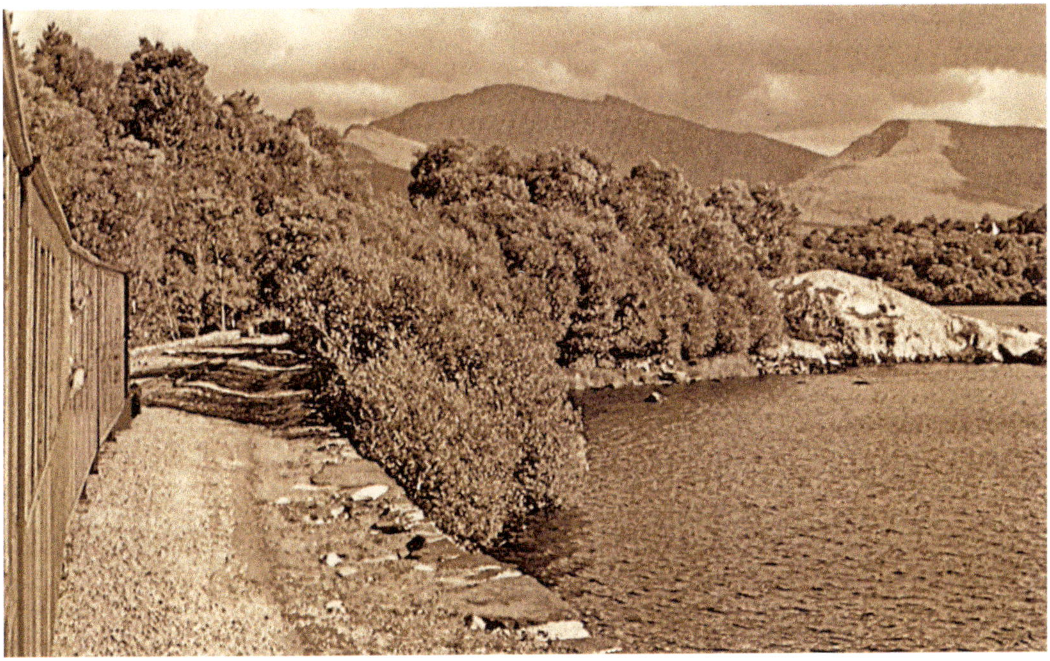

Llyn Padarn and Yr Wyddfa (Snowdon) from Llanberis Lake Railway, *c.* 1971
***Inset*: Dolbadarn**

Llyn Padarn and Llyn Peris cut through the mountain ranges of Yr Wyddfa and Glyderau, which forms Llanberis Pass. Llyn Peris is a glacial lake, flanked on one side by the old slate quarry of Dinorwig and about 1.8 kilometres (1.1 miles) long. It forms part of the lower reservoir of Dinorwig Power Station. The Llyn takes its name from St Peris, an early Christian saint, who settled here. The village of Llanberis sits between these lakes, with the railway, opened in 1971, 4 kilometres (2.5 miles) long.

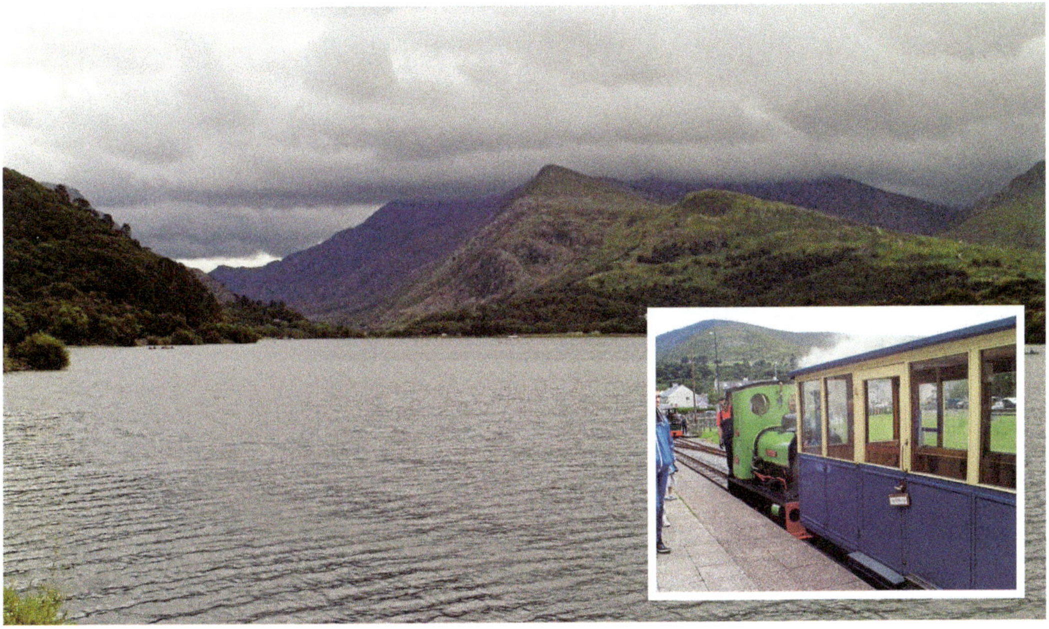

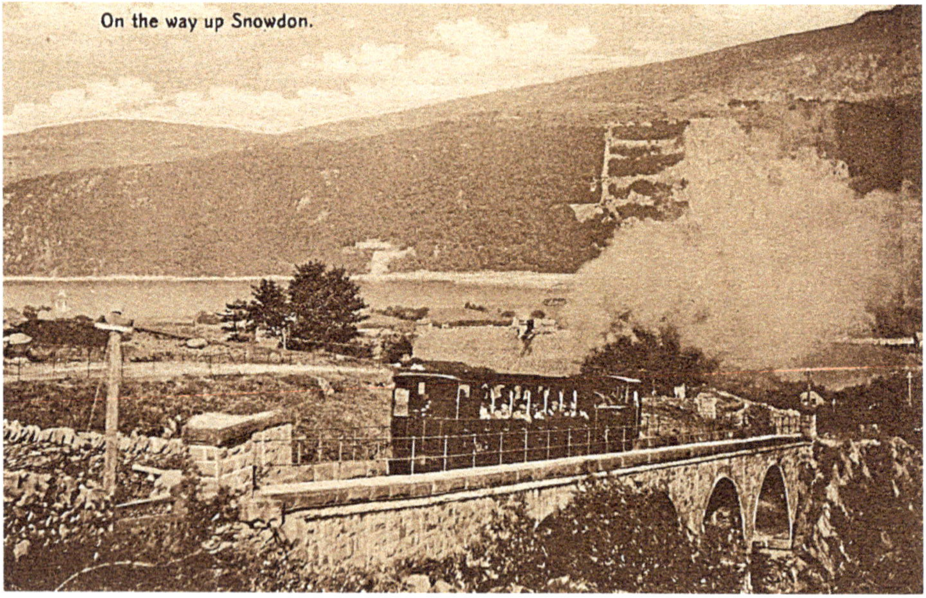

Ascent of Yr Wyddfa (Snowdon), *c.* 1910

The Rheilffordd Yr Wyddfa (Snowdon Mountain Railway) is a narrow gauge rack and pinion mountain railway, opened in 1896, which carries passengers the 7.6 kilometres (4.7 miles) from Llanberis to the summit station. The summit also houses a café, built in 2006, to replace the one built around 1930. The railway usually operates to the summit station from Whitsun to October, and is dependent on the weather and customer demand. It carries more than 130,000 passengers annually, by either steam or diesel locomotives.

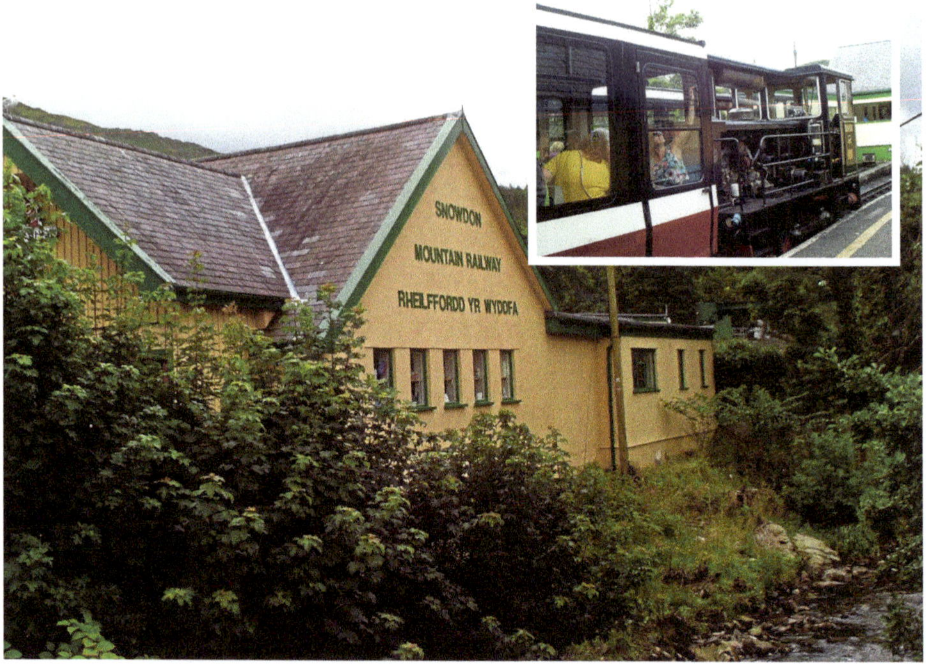

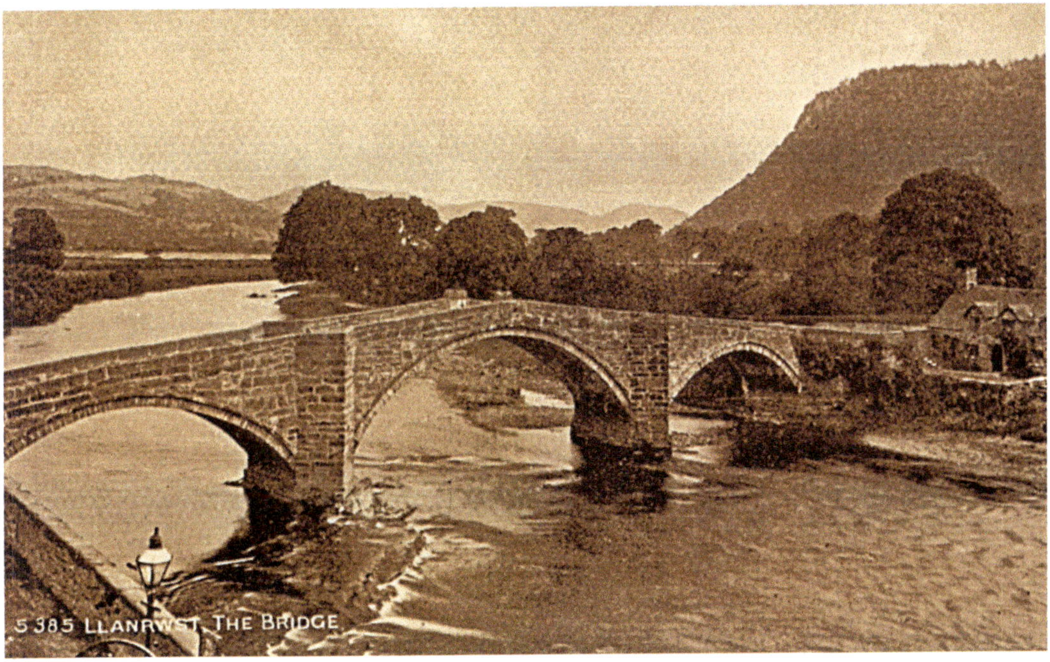

Pont Fawr, Llanrwst, *c.* 1910

Although in Conwy it is a gateway to the National Park, Snowdonia starts about three quarters of a mile away, on the other side of the Afon Conwy. Llanrwst is a market and tourist town. The parish church of St Grwst holds the stone coffin of Llywelyn the Great. Pont Fawr, a narrow, three-arched stone bridge said to have been designed by Inigo Jones, was built in 1636 by Sir Richard Wynn, of Gwydir Castle. It connects Llanrwst to nearby Trefriw.

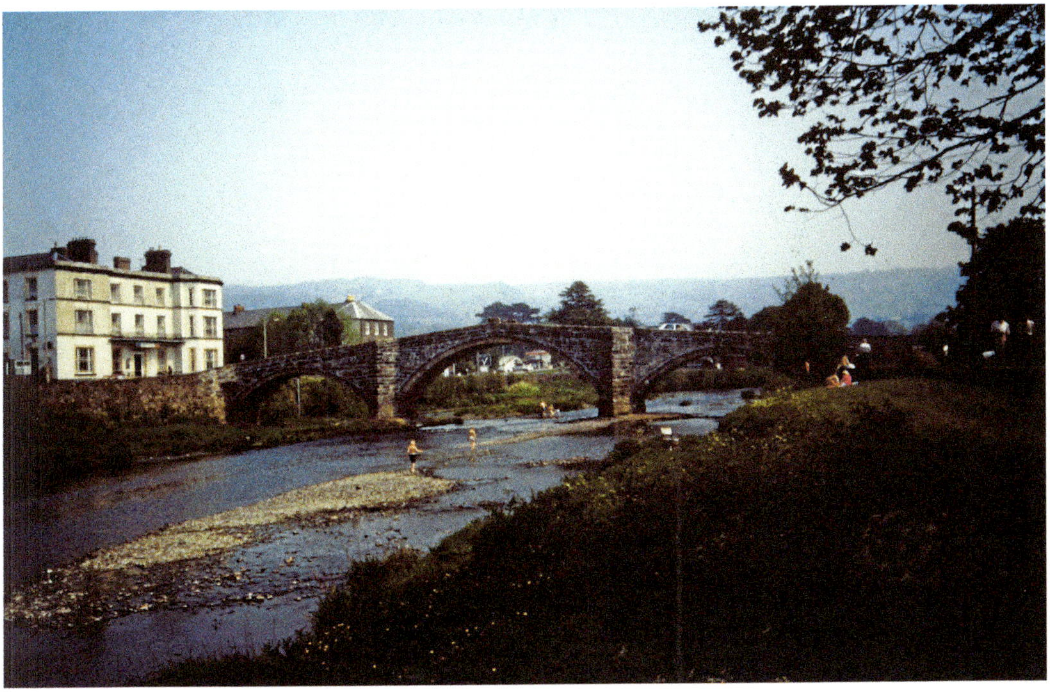

About the Author

Steven Dickens lives in the Flixton area of Manchester, although his Welsh family roots originate from the city of Bangor and the village of Bethesda, in Gwynedd. He has an academic background in modern history, and is a retired charge nurse and college lecturer who has written and published several journal and magazine articles on genealogy and local history. He is also the author of several *Through Time* volumes, including *Bangor & Around Through Time*. Steven is married to Sarah, and they have three sons and three daughters.

Acknowledgements

Caernarfon – (https://en.wikipedia.org) Caernarfon Castle Official Website & Segontium Roman Fort – (http://cadw.gov.wales) Caernarfon Record Office, Gwynedd Archive Service, Gwynedd Council, Caernarfon, LL55 1SH; Castle Square, Caernarfon – (dcfw.org/castle-square-caernarfon/) Old Ordnance Survey Maps, Bangor 1913 (Caernarvonshire Sheet 6.12. Alan Godfrey Maps. December 2001), Old Ordnance Survey Maps, Caernarfon 1913 (Caernarvonshire Sheet 15.04. Alan Godfrey Maps. April 2000), The History of Caernarfon – (http://information-britain.co.uk), The Welsh Highland Railway Project – (www.whrsoc.org.uk).

Thanks to my parents, John and Barbara Dickens, whose collection of photographs I have used in this publication.